Marina Cantacuzino is an autho[r] journalist who has written for m[any] including the *Guardian*, *Dail[y Tel]* response to the invasion of Iraq, [and started a pro]ject collecting stories of people who had lived through trauma and injustice, and yet sought forgiveness rather than revenge. As a result, Cantacuzino founded The Forgiveness Project.

Praise for *Forgiveness*

'There have been few more appropriate and vital moments for this fascinating book to emerge than now ... The complexity of the practice of forgiveness, its meanings, its measure as a force for change are all here – and most of all, its power to prevent the repetition of the worst in our human behaviour and the possibility of finding freedom from hatred' **Emma Thompson**

'A wise and generous investigation of one of life's most difficult but necessary experiences' **Richard Holloway**

'This important book will speak to anyone who has ever suffered harm, or caused harm to others; which is all of us. The work is unflinching in its honesty and emphasis on forgiveness as a process that cannot be imposed; but it is also immensely hopeful' **Gwen Adshead**

'This reassuring and uplifting book testifies to the truth of forgiveness ... Both provocative and full of hope' **Jon Snow**

'A profoundly moving and important book'
Professor Anthony Costello

'It is absolutely remarkable how Marina Cantacuzino navigates the vast and complex terrain of forgiveness with such sensitivity, honesty and insight. I cannot think of a more relevant subject for these challenging times' **Angela Findlay**

'In this highly readable book Marina explores how individuals achieve forgiveness and how it can break the cycle of hate, revenge and retaliation, and how it can transform the lives of both the perpetrator and the victim or their loved ones' **Professor Simon Baron-Cohen**

'*Forgiveness* is a profoundly thought-provoking and beautifully written book. A wonderful, heart-breaking, elevating read' **Bea Setton**

FORGIVENESS

AN EXPLORATION

MARINA CANTACUZINO

**SIMON &
SCHUSTER**

London · New York · Sydney · Toronto · New Delhi

First published in Great Britain by Simon & Schuster UK Ltd, 2022
This edition published in Great Britain by Simon & Schuster UK Ltd, 2023

Copyright © Marina Cantacuzino, 2022

The right of Marina Cantacuzino to be identified as the author
of this work has been asserted in accordance with
the Copyright, Designs and Patents Act, 1988.

1 3 5 7 9 10 8 6 4 2

Simon & Schuster UK Ltd
1st Floor
222 Gray's Inn Road
London WC1X 8HB

www.simonandschuster.co.uk
www.simonandschuster.com.au
www.simonandschuster.co.in

Simon & Schuster Australia, Sydney
Simon & Schuster India, New Delhi

The author and publishers have made all reasonable efforts
to contact copyright-holders for permission, and apologise
for any omissions or errors in the form of credits given.
Corrections may be made to future printings.

A CIP catalogue record for this book
is available from the British Library

Paperback ISBN: 978-1-3985-1366-2
eBook ISBN: 978-1-3985-1365-5

Typeset in Bembo by M Rules
Manufactured in the United States of America

Contents

PROLOGUE

'Stories are the secret reservoir of values:
change the stories individuals and nations live
by and tell themselves, and you change the
individuals and nations.'

BEN OKRI

Wilma Derksen knows exactly what it means to be the public face of forgiveness, having been both lauded and vilified for forgiving her daughter's killer. Labelled by the media as the voice of mercy, she has spent the last thirty-six years of her life facing the relentless forces of public scrutiny, coming to terms with a tragedy that has both defined and consumed her.

For many it makes no sense at all as to why Wilma and her husband Cliff decided to forgive the man who took their daughter's life; and in particular why they made this decision just hours after the body of thirteen-year-old Candace was found on a bitterly cold January day in 1985, bound and frozen in a shed in Winnipeg, Canada.

The hunt for Candace Derksen, who disappeared on her way

home from school, stretched over seven weeks, and so to locals her killing has always felt both intimate and personal. When I met the Derksens, nearly thirty years later during a visit to Canada in 2013, the story was still imprinted on many people's psyches, not least because the man who had been convicted of the crime six years earlier was now appealing his prison sentence. I was invited to share a meal around the Derksens' kitchen table with a couple of their oldest friends, who, like them, were both practising Mennonites. Over dinner, the conversation ambled between Winnipeg's unseasonably cold weather that October, my research for a Winston Churchill Memorial Fellowship, which was the reason I was in Canada, and Wilma's latest publication as a prolific author and journalist.

Afterwards, Wilma took me into their front room, and here, among her books and family photographs, she proceeded to explain exactly why the couple had chosen to forgive their daughter's killer.

'It was a very easy decision to make,' said Wilma. She explained how on the day Candace's body was discovered friends and neighbours had brought food and gifts to the house, something which for a few hours provided consolation for the parents and their two other children, putting a layer of loving protection between the family and that dreadful discovery. A little later, shortly after most of their friends had left, there was a knock on the door and a stranger stood there, dressed in black. He had read about the tragedy in the newspaper, and he wanted to help. He told them he was also the parent of a murdered child and was here to warn them of this alien and frightening world they were about to enter. Then he proceeded to list everything he had lost since his daughter's death. He told them he had lost his health, his relationships, his concentration and his ability to work. He had even lost all memory of the child he held so precious because now the story of the murder was lodged so deep in his brain that it left little room for anything else.

The stranger's appearance at their door was an unspoken invitation to an exclusive club of parents bereaved and broken through murder. But Wilma and Cliff were determined not to join. Finding themselves almost comforting the man, they politely listened and then showed him to the door. 'His arrival in our home was a kind of reckoning,' said Wilma, 'because having just been through the immense pain of losing our daughter, it now seemed we might lose everything else as well.'

This was how forgiveness became a lifeline for the Derksens – a conscious decision born out of a dread of what 'unforgiveness' might bring. Having been presented with the bleakest of futures, the couple went to bed that night and made a solemn vow. They promised themselves that they would respond very differently, by instead trying to forgive the person who had wreaked havoc in their lives, even though, at this point, they didn't know who the perpetrator was.

As Mennonites, you might presume their faith had called them to forgive, but I have met plenty of Mennonites, Quakers and Christians of every denomination for whom forgiveness would never be an option under such circumstances. No, this was an instinctive choice made by two bereft parents on the night their missing child had been found murdered. As they looked out at the desolate landscape ahead, they decided that forgiveness was the only possible route to release them from a lifetime of suffering. Pain is always the greatest motivator to forgive.

In the coming months and years, forgiving their daughter's killer proved an invaluable way of navigating the endless snares and complications of traumatic loss. But it has never been easy. 'Little did I know that the word forgiveness would haunt me for the next thirty-seven years – prod me, guide me, heal me, label me, enlighten me, imprison me, free me and, in the end, define me,' says Wilma, who has faced every kind of criticism imaginable for choosing to forgive her daughter's killer. 'From the beginning

I was right out there in public – confessing to everyone the desire of my heart. But when I joined Family Survivors of Homicide, I was quite forcibly told to forget about using the word "forgiveness" because all they could see were the dangers of forgiving. In some ways that was good for me because, as a Mennonite, it made me lose the religious lingo and forced me to be more authentic. Forgiveness is a hard word; it demands a lot of you and is so often misunderstood. At times it was incredibly tough. People said we couldn't have loved Candace because we forgave.'

When I've listened to other people's stories of traumatic loss, I'm aware that the pain doesn't ever end. You may learn to manage it, but things will happen along the way to push you down into the pit. And when that happens, you have to steer your way out all over again. And the obstacles will vary; some people have had their pain thrown right back in their face by an offender who refuses to show remorse; some have been ostracised by loved ones who find forgiveness in such circumstances inexplicable and even insulting; and some have had to wrestle with interminable unanswered questions for crimes that remain unsolved. The Derksens were indeed repeatedly frustrated and disappointed by a legal system that over the years promised resolution and then took it away.

It wasn't until 2007 that the police finally arrested someone for Candace's murder. Mark Edward Grant, who had a long criminal record, was charged with first-degree murder based on a DNA match. The murder trial began twenty-six years to the day after Candace's body was found and the jury swiftly found the defendant guilty of second-degree murder. The Derksens' relief was palpable; they could breathe again knowing what had happened to their daughter and that a dangerous man had been taken off the streets. Even though they had forgiven many years earlier, there had been no human being to bestow their forgiveness upon. It had been an abstract notion, what Wilma describes as a 'lifestyle choice', a way of finding peace in a maelstrom of uncertainty. Now they could look the perpetrator in the eye and know exactly who had murdered their daughter and who it was they had chosen to forgive.

What followed must have been another kind of torture for the Derksens. Just after I left Winnipeg in October 2013, the Manitoba Court of Appeal overturned Grant's conviction because it was shown that the trial judge had made an error in not allowing the defence to present evidence that pointed to another possible killer. This ruling was then appealed, but the Supreme Court of Canada upheld the Appeal Court's decision. In 2017 a retrial of Grant took place one day shy of the thirty-second anniversary of Candace's body being found. This time, the jury found Grant not guilty, accepting the defence's argument that DNA evidence in the prosecution's case was 'fundamentally flawed'. Grant was subsequently released, meaning that the case of Candace Derksen's murder remains unsolved.

You might expect the Derksens' forgiveness to have been severely tested by all this, but it never really has been. Perhaps this is because the couple forgave so early on – long before they knew the possible identity of their daughter's killer. Nor has the fact that this crime remains unresolved ever crushed them. In fact, quite the reverse; doubt and uncertainty seem to have acted as a cushion. With Grant's acquittal, Wilma later told me she had felt a surge of freedom, as if a huge weight that she didn't even know she had been carrying was lifted from her shoulders. And it kept lifting, she said, as she began to imagine a life where she would no longer continually have to answer for a convicted criminal. 'Maybe this is a new kind of justice ... poetic justice,' she pondered.

Of the many stories I have heard over the years, Wilma's remains one of the most enduring to me, perhaps because of her unwavering commitment to forgive despite meeting so many barriers. For Wilma, forgiveness remains something fresh and ongoing; an ever-present position of the mind which takes on many different forms at different times. Even though on some days she may not be able to muster the strength to forgive, nevertheless it has been a constant intention; as she says, a 'North Star' to follow, 'a mantra' to comfort and assuage.

Through my work with The Forgiveness Project, I have met many hurt and traumatised people who have found healing through their resolve to forgive. But I have also met others who, while turning their back on hatred and vengeance, have not necessarily found recovery through forgiveness. In fact, whether someone chooses to forgive or not isn't really the issue. What is important is that hurt people are able to find peace with things they cannot change and are able to recognise that if hate is left unchecked, it may eventually corrode.

When I started collecting forgiveness stories in 2003 as a personal journalistic project, one of the first people I interviewed was Alistair Little – a former UVF (Ulster Volunteer Force) paramilitary from Northern Ireland. Alistair made it very clear to me that he didn't want to be part of any initiative that would present forgiveness in a way that might make those who had been harmed feel obliged to forgive, because he said this would place an even greater burden on victims. He told me, just minutes after we'd first met at a community centre in Belfast, 'I've met people who haven't been able to forgive, but who haven't allowed the event to paralyse them. It just means that as human beings they've been hurt beyond repair. Who are we to say they should forgive?'

Alistair could never forgive himself for taking another man's life in a deliberate act of sectarian violence. His story was not an unusual one for a boy growing up in the 1970s on the embattled streets of Belfast. In order to avenge the murder of a friend's father by Republicans, he joined the UVF at the age of fourteen. 'When I was seventeen, I walked into the home of a man I didn't know and shot him dead. I had asked to do it,' he told me. While serving a prison sentence in the Belfast prisons of Long Kesh and H-Blocks, he finally came to a place of believing that what he had done was wrong. It was here that he started thinking about the suffering of his enemy.

It was a slow and painful process. 'There was huge cost in terms of loneliness and isolation,' he said. 'But I came to realise that people who use violence – myself included – see things only from one angle. They don't see that if you use violence yourself, you encourage revenge and hatred in others. You end up with a never-ending circle of violence.'

After his release from prison at the age of thirty, Alistair's life became increasingly focused on building bridges between adversaries and preventing further conflict within sectarian settings. After Northern Ireland's imperfect peace was delivered by the Good Friday Agreement, he became tireless in these endeavours, travelling the world to support people in creating their own peace-building processes. Often edgy and always candid, Alistair invariably fascinated those I introduced him to. His honesty was disarming and his remorse for having killed a man evident for all to see. In addition, his uneasy relationship with forgiveness (in part because he never felt he deserved it) helped me clarify my own thinking around this most amorphous of subjects.

Meeting Alistair was a defining moment for me. I knew then that the stories I was collecting had to illustrate every aspect of this complex subject and map the myriad ways that forgiveness might manifest as a radical alternative to hammering away at hate. I knew also that my focus must be on exploring the contours of forgiveness rather than attempting to encourage, persuade or convince people to forgive. The last thing I wanted to do was parade the act of forgiving as a panacea for all ills, as something people *must* do in order to heal, or as the only way to rid themselves of their demons. This realisation has grown within me over the many years of working in this field because I strongly believe that proselytising, no matter what you believe in, is dangerous, for the simple reason that when a light becomes glaringly bright it ceases to illuminate and instead just blinds you.

I wasn't even completely sure at the point of first meeting Alistair Little why forgiveness interested me or what I might end up doing with the stories I was collecting and curating. The project at this stage was just a very personal response that had grown out of my anger at the Bush/Blair 2003 invasion of Iraq. It was my attempt as a journalist to create some kind of counternarrative to the bellicose language of payback and tit-for-tat that was grabbing all the headlines. I had become convinced that bombing civilians would only intensify resentment and that the more you slam down hard on people the more they will regroup and re-emerge in a stronger and more resistant way.

I was interested in forgiveness as a response to being hurt because gentle people have always attracted me more than resolute ones, vulnerability more than strength. I have also always believed there are very few truly malevolent people in the world. As a journalist I wanted to create a portfolio of stories that displayed personal healing journeys from victims and survivors who could express their power as much as their pain. I wanted the voices of individuals to be heard, and their experiences of healing through trauma to be witnessed close up. And I wanted to place these stories alongside those from perpetrators of crime and violence who had transformed their aggression into a force for peace. Most importantly, I wanted these stories to be accessible to a wide range of people by revealing the gritty, messy, risky but authentic narratives of forgiveness.

In the end, thanks to practical and financial support from two women – Dame Anita Roddick, the social activist and founder of The Body Shop, and Jilly Forster, founder and chief executive of Forster Communications – Alistair Little's story became part of *The F Word* exhibition, which launched at the Oxo Gallery on London's South Bank in January 2004. Alistair's large portrait with his 800-word testimony printed alongside it hung next to the stories of Patrick Magee, the former IRA activist also known as the Brighton bomber, and Jo Berry, the daughter of one of the five people killed by Magee when his bomb exploded at the Grand Hotel, Brighton, during the 1984 Conservative Party Conference. On opposite walls hung many more similar restorative narratives from across the globe. The idea was to show that these individuals, who had discovered peaceful solutions to conflict and who had humanised rather than demonised their enemy, might be unusual, but they were not exceptional. Many of those whose portraits hung on the gallery wall came in person to the launch of *The F Word* exhibition and afterwards all of them reported that their time spent together had created a wonderfully healing and restorative space.

The exhibition was a success beyond my wildest imagination, drawing widespread media attention and attracting thousands of visitors. In the aftermath of the bitter Iraq War, these narratives of hope seemed to tap into a deep public need to find humanity in a world full of hate. And so, a few months later, to satisfy the multiple requests I was receiving from people wanting to use the stories as a tool for peacebuilding, I founded The Forgiveness Project charity as a means of taking the work further. The Forgiveness Project remains today an organisation that works with people of lived experience with the aim of understanding how we heal, restore and rehumanise. It specifically supports both victims/survivors and former perpetrators to explore how lives can be rebuilt following hurt and trauma. Over the years it's become clear that these 'restorative narratives' have the power to transform lives; not only by supporting individuals to deal with issues in their own lives, but also by helping to build a climate of tolerance, hope and empathy.

I was determined right from the start that The Forgiveness Project should be a place of enquiry rather than persuasion, an offering and never a prescription. This book is my attempt to distill some of my thinking and learning about forgiveness. It includes the personal stories of others because they have experienced what it means to forgive or be forgiven in ways that I haven't, and because they have had insights that are both helpful and enlightening. Everything I have gleaned about this complex subject comes through the experience of those I have talked to, stories collected from the 'edges of human endurance'.[1] This book is very much an exploration intended to raise as many questions as it might provide answers.

I am not an academic, or a philosopher, or a psychologist, or a theologian. I am a writer and facilitator of other people's stories and, having thought long and hard about the meaning, values and limits of forgiveness, am eager to share them and all that I have learnt.

'Storytelling is the bridge by which we transform that which is private and individual into that which is public,' wrote German-born political theorist Hannah Arendt in 1958. I certainly believe that these stories collected and shared by The Forgiveness Project are not simply subjective first-person testimonies but go beyond the realm of the individual, forming part of the collective memory of communities, helping to reshape how others view the world.

Many books have been dedicated to analysing the meaning of forgiveness. Not all scholars agree on a definition and individuals who have forgiven or been forgiven express it in a myriad of different ways. I called the exhibition *The F Word* precisely to reflect the fact that forgiveness is a word that no one can agree on. The academic Dr Fred Luskin[2] became so overwhelmed with all the convoluted, unsatisfactory definitions of forgiveness being bandied around that I heard him once say he had instead now opted for the single word of 'freedom'.

I prefer to let stories illustrate the meaning, but if I'm pressed for a definition of forgiveness, I sometimes quote Luskin – only

I tend to go a little further. For me, forgiveness means making peace with things or with people you cannot change. It is therefore about reconciling with psychological pain and relinquishing the burden of hatred and the desire for revenge. But it is more than just an act of acceptance and letting go, because it requires an additional radical ingredient which stretches our humanity – and that is a degree, perhaps just the faintest hint, of compassion or empathy for the person who has hurt you. This is the really hard part, because when you think of Wilma and Cliff's story, it is probably beyond most people's capabilities to imagine how this couple found compassion for the person who could do such savage things to their daughter.

Just as I was mulling over this idea, I heard Mina Smallman, the mother of two murdered daughters, talking about forgiveness on the BBC's *Today* programme. It was New Year's Day, 2022, and she had been chosen as the programme's guest editor that morning. For a moment, Smallman's words challenged my belief that forgiveness requires some compassion or empathy for the person who has hurt you. Talking about how she had come to forgive her daughters' killer, she said, 'It's not that you feel compassion for them. It's that you don't carry that anger and frustration within you. You can walk on without having to look at that person.'

Here was Smallman clearly stating that forgiveness does not include compassion. And yet, in that same interview, she also talked about the gratitude she had for her Christian faith, as it had helped her to 'forgive this young man'. There it was in that tiny phrase. She didn't call him a monster; she didn't call him evil. She called him a young man, by which we can deduce that she saw him as a human being, just like herself. That's what I mean by a hint of compassion.

1

A MESSY BUSINESS

'The whole area of forgiveness is like a huge
spectrum ... at one end you have a fracas in
the playground, and at the other end you've
got mass slaughter and yet you've got this one
word that is supposed to fit everything.'[1]

JULIE NICHOLSON

Probably my favourite description of forgiveness is attributed to the
American author Mark Twain, who supposedly said, 'Forgiveness
is the fragrance that the violet sheds on the heel that has crushed
it.' I like this because it shows forgiveness to be messy, that it grows
out of damage, but that it is also potentially a healing balm. Some
advocates of forgiveness don't see this complexity, promoting
instead forgiveness as a tidy, almost foolproof remedy with which
to heal both individual and societal wounds. This is the kind
of positioning that can understandably give people the wrong
impression.

The pull to forgive is flexible and changeable; not a one-
size-fits-all, nor a single magnanimous gesture in response to an

isolated offence, but rather part of a continuum of human engagement in healing our own brokenness. Forgiving is something that
one day may come easily and the next day evade you altogether. It
is fluid and forever changing, just like the definitions endeavouring
to describe it. From all the stories that I've collected, forgiveness
can be distilled into an energy that can both transform and dis-
turb, soothe and upset. It has the power to alleviate pain, but it
can provoke it too. It can bring meaning to sorrow, but also it can
confuse. It's a place of contradiction as well as clarity.

Anger and justification come from believing we are right,
staking our positions and creating competing narratives. Trust is
built when we accept that we don't know everything and where
our motivation is no longer to 'win' at all costs. I see a profound
connection between forgiveness and 'not knowing', in the sense
of embracing ambiguity and uncertainty.

'Forgiveness is not about forgiving the act but forgiving the
imperfections which are inherent in all of us,' declared Samantha
Lawler as we were preparing for an event held at a civic centre in
Minneapolis as part of a forgiveness symposium. It was the first
time I'd met Samantha and I had just spent the afternoon hearing
about how her father had strangled her mother at the family home
at Fort Lauderdale in Florida when Samantha was eighteen.

For the next thirteen years her life became an intoxicated blur,
muted by a potent mix of grief and anger – grief that she'd lost
her mother and anger that her father had destroyed the family. She
vowed never to see him again. 'People would tell me it was good to
cry,' she told me, 'so sometimes I would spend a whole afternoon
crying – but as the years passed it made no difference to the level
of grief and hopelessness I felt.' It was only when Samantha joined
a three-day personal development workshop with the Landmark
Forum that her heart began to open and, for the first time, she felt a
powerful connection with all those who had suffered. At the end of
the course, determined to reconcile with the people in her life she

had lost touch with, she decided to contact the facility where her father was incarcerated to arrange a visit. To her astonishment, she was told that the prison had been trying to get hold of her because her father was in a critical condition and dying.

And so, in October 2012, she set out from New York to Florida to visit him. 'I was only given ten minutes with my father,' she said. 'He was unrecognisable, a shell of his former self. He'd had multiple strokes and his muscles had atrophied. He also had AIDS. He was breathing from a tube, couldn't talk and was handcuffed to the bed.' However, for the entire ten minutes Samantha's father held her gaze until she felt both calmed and overwhelmed. Now at last she had a clear image of what judgement looked like. 'Suddenly I realised he was doing what I'd always wanted – suffering terribly. But in that moment I got to see how his suffering in no way relieved my suffering. Not only was our prolonged suffering ineffective, but rather it was actively working against the potential for my healing. The shock and the appalling state he was in wiped the slate clean. I told him over and over how much I loved him and that I forgave him. And I apologised for waiting so long to come to see him and to tell him this. I realised later that during those ten minutes there were no feelings of hate or guilt, or right and wrong. There was just a deep connection. No conversation was necessary, no apology. For ten minutes I got my dad back and when I left, I felt this incredible weight drop away.'

'Forgiveness is not about forgiving the act but forgiving the imperfections which are inherent in all of us.' I've always appreciated Samantha's framing of forgiveness as something which is larger than the damage done and which makes us in part responsible for all of humanity's transgressions, for the simple reason that we are all human. It has also helped me to understand how it is that people are able to forgive things which most of us would consider unforgivable. I now understand that when people forgive appalling acts of barbarism and viciousness, it is not the offence they are

forgiving but humanity itself for failing and for being fallible. They empathise not because they tolerate the harm done but because they can somehow find compassion for people with twisted minds hell-bent on cruelty – the kind of people Shakespeare described as 'ruined pieces of nature'.[2] They are able to stand in soiled shoes imagining something of what it is like to be possessed of a callous heart, consumed by aberrant compulsions.

When you hear in the news about the latest appalling act of cruelty, labels like 'animal' or 'evil' or 'monster' may well feel entirely appropriate for the perpetrator. At times of moral revulsion, it is almost impossible to imagine such people as candidates for forgiveness. But the fact is that some rare people do choose to forgive the kind of person society calls a 'monster', not to excuse that person but in order to free themselves. Or the forgiver perhaps sees evil as an expression of childhood trauma, understanding that a child's moral growth can be thrown off course by violence and deprivation, storing up problems for society that explode when these children become angry adults. Or the forgiver may see evil as an expression of a person becoming brutalised or brainwashed, resulting in a limited capacity for empathy and an inability to distinguish right from wrong. Empathy is simply a muscle – if not exercised it ceases to have function or power.

In *The Devil You Know*, Gwen Adshead tells of her experience working as a psychiatrist at Broadmoor high-security psychiatric hospital in England. In the introduction she challenges the reader to enter a world where 'good and evil, ideas of right and wrong, as well as identities like victim and perpetrator, are not set in stone and can coexist.' Discovering this intimate interconnection between good and evil is the only way I can make sense of forgiveness for acts that are so unbearable they stain the very essence of humanity. The author and Holocaust survivor Primo Levi discovered it when he remarked of his Auschwitz concentration camp guards: 'These were not monsters. I didn't see a single monster in my time in the camp. Instead, I saw people like you and I who were acting in that way because there was Fascism, Nazism in Germany. Should some form of Fascism or Nazism return, there would be people, like us, who would act in the same way, everywhere.'[3]

The same sentiments are reflected by Aleksandr Solzhenitsyn in *The Gulag Archipelago 1918–1956*, in which the Nobel prize-winning Russian dissident gives a striking explanation of why we prefer not to take responsibility for humanity's most heinous crimes: 'If only there were evil people somewhere insidiously committing evil deeds, and it were necessary only to separate them from the rest of us and destroy them. But the line dividing good and evil cuts through the heart of every human being. And who is willing to destroy a piece of his own heart?'[4]

I have often been told that the concept of forgiving and forgetting has no place in any serious discourse about forgiveness, most specifically when talking of the worst crimes and offences. And yet, if forgiveness is about releasing hatred and reconciling with pain, then inevitably it must mean divesting of some painful memories, which in turn indicates fewer intrusive thoughts[5] and less stress and anxiety. I remember one mother whose adult daughter had been murdered telling me that after many years she had come to embrace forgiveness as her 'eleventh-hour lifeline', but she also told me that sometimes she would feel guilty because while forgiving had given her back her life, it also meant she no longer thought about her daughter every minute of the day. This happens when the dynamic that has entangled two parties in any relationship no longer has the same emotional charge. As poet and philosopher David Whyte writes: 'It is that wounded, branded, unforgetting part of us that eventually makes forgiveness an act of compassion rather than one of simple forgetting.'

For actress Sharon Stone, forgiveness has also been a sharp issue, and something she has explored as a result of childhood sexual abuse and the years of silence that followed. 'I believe in "forgive and remember" not "forgive and forget",' she told *Saga Magazine* in an interview in 2021. 'Forgiveness is for your own benefit. But when you forgive people who are dangerous, you have to put them in a cage in your mind and never go back to it.' In her memoir *The Beauty of Living Twice,* Stone documents how she rebuilt her life following a massive brain bleed at the age of forty-three and revisits her childhood as one of four siblings growing up in a small Pennsylvanian town with a mother who she didn't believe loved her and a grandfather who abused her. She describes herself as an incest survivor and even though her grandfather died when she was fourteen, it was many years before she confronted her mother about the abuse. Dorothy Stone hadn't known and was bitterly sorry. However, the disclosure created a precious bond between mother and daughter and in the *Saga* interview Stone says of her mother: 'If I hadn't finally stopped keeping this horrible secret, I would never have known her. Never have understood her and certainly never have had the opportunity for her to mother me now that I've entered my sixties and my mother is in her mid-eighties.'

For Stone, breaking the silence meant remembering and confronting her psychological pain, which in turn opened up the possibility of forgiveness and resolution. Desmond Tutu captures the essence of what is happening here in his words: 'Forgiveness does not mean condoning what has been done. It means taking what has happened seriously and not minimising it; drawing out the sting in the memory that threatens to poison our entire existence.'[6] This is redemptive memory of the kind that South African author Pumla Gobodo-Madikizela speaks of when she addresses the impact of the atrocities caused by the apartheid regime that stripped Black people of their dignity in particularly shocking and systematic ways: 'If memory is kept alive in order to cultivate old hatreds and resentments, it is likely to culminate in vengeance, and in a repetition of violence. But if memory is kept alive in order to

transcend hateful emotions, then remembering can be healing.'
Forgiveness, insists Gobodo-Madikizela, is not to overlook the
deed but to rise above it.

Sometimes forgiveness appears through gritted teeth, forced
and expedient. There is an example of this in Steve McQueen's
masterful three-part documentary series *Uprising*,[7] which sheds
essential light on the story of the New Cross house fire which
killed thirteen young Black people in south London in 1981. The
film is an important contribution both to the reality of racism in
London in the 1980s as well as to the community's enduring pain
of having lived through decades without justice. Towards the end
of the documentary, a mother whose son perished in the fire talks
of how she has had to come to terms with two inquests failing to
hold anyone responsible. 'I know that Andrew's not going to come
back,' she says, 'and I will probably go to my grave and I will not
know ... who started the fire.' And then she says, almost inaudibly,
'I will have to leave them at the foot of the cross.'

The interviewer's voice is heard off screen asking her to explain
what she means. 'I forgive them and forget them,' she shrugs. It
is unclear whether this forgiveness comes as a promise made to
her god or because she knows that without it she may succumb to
overwhelming grief, but whatever it is you know that this mother
who lost so much has been comforted by having somewhere to
place and transform her agony. Her ache to forget does not refer
to the memory of her dead son, but to the imprint of faceless perpetrators branded on her heart.

Although 'forgive and forget' feels offensive when applied to
deep wounds caused by harm that cannot simply be erased, the
phrase has always made perfect sense to me when in the context of
minor but pervasive and niggling grievances; those familiar resentments that show up throughout our lives, where, for instance, you
might remember that you had a fight with a friend several years
ago but you can't remember what the fight was all about because

you've moved on and the friendship has remained unscathed. If you were to hold on to that episode and continue to remember every last detail all these years later, it would probably mean that you hadn't forgiven.

Many years ago, long before I had thought to focus all my work on exploring ideas of forgiveness, a journalist colleague showed me a letter he had written to his uncle in which he had tried to bring resolution to an inheritance dispute that had run on for years. My colleague had finally agreed to give in to his uncle's demands so as to move on with his life. I read the letter, which he had spent a long time writing and which meticulously went over the sequence of events, listing exactly who had done what and when. It was balanced and without bile, ending with a wish to maintain a good relationship with his uncle. However, the very last line, written almost like a casual sign-off, struck a very different tone. It read: 'And I want you to know that I forgive you.'

My colleague clearly thought he was being both conciliatory and magnanimous, but offering forgiveness, especially to someone who clearly believed they were in the right, would, I felt, do no good. Shortly after that he went to live in America and I didn't see him for a few years, but when we did meet again, over a meal in a London restaurant, I asked him how things had worked out with his uncle. I wasn't surprised to hear that his uncle had not replied to his letter, and that they had barely seen each other since. Much of our evening together was then spent talking about the hurt he still felt due to the way he'd been treated by his blood relative.

I refer to this instance as an example where, in order to experience the efficacy of forgiveness, a measure of forgetting is required to move beyond the hurt. My colleague thought he had forgiven – certainly he wanted to – but in actual fact he had not. And I knew he hadn't because he hadn't forgotten. In a situation like this you can't really forgive and continue to boil away with active resentment because relinquishing resentment is part of a forgiveness process. I'm not saying my colleague should have totally wiped the memory from his mind, just that, in order for him to have truly forgiven, I think he wouldn't have still been nursing the grudge. It's the same when people say about some fairly minor transgression, 'I'll forgive but I'll never forget.' The act of forgiving may be a grand gesture of absolution, but the promise never to forget feels more like a threat.

In 2000, when clinical psychologist Peter Houghton was diagnosed with a terminal heart condition, he wasn't expected to live until pioneering surgery provided him with an artificial heart and gained him seven extra years of life. For much of his working life he had counselled dying patients at London's Middlesex Hospital, so now in his recovery he started to map his own journey back from the threshold of death for a book that was published the following year called *On Death, Dying and Not Dying*.[8] In it he says something interesting about forgiving and forgetting. Recalling that he had often advised dying people to make amends and, where necessary, apologise, he now attempted to do the same thing himself. But he was surprised when most of the people he tried to apologise to couldn't remember the things he was apologising for. Others felt there was nothing to forgive and never had been. Houghton concludes, therefore, that these things he had done 'were no longer alive to them as they were to me.' Initially he was confused, realising that he had been living with regret for actions which had harmed him more than those he had – or believed he had – harmed. The people in his life he had reached out to had clearly been able to forgive and forget more easily than him. 'It gave me a new perspective,' he writes. 'For the first time I felt able to accept myself, my life and not to worry about the darkness in it.'

There are so many assumptions made about forgiveness that it's sometimes difficult to find a footing on such unstable ground. It interests me that some people assume The Forgiveness Project must be a religious organisation because of the strong association between forgiveness and Christianity. I have also encountered a yawning lack of interest from critics of forgiveness who presume the subject to be weak, dreary, or irrelevant. And very occasionally I've been greeted with disapproval, irritation and outright anger when talking on the topic. The mother of an abducted child once rebuked me at a conference when she heard I was from The Forgiveness Project. I don't blame her, as I may have done the same in her position if I assumed someone was about to tell me that I *should* forgive the person who'd taken my child. On another occasion a therapist in a book club that a friend belonged to refused to even open my first book, which was a collection of stories from The Forgiveness Project, remarking crossly that she would never read a book that suggested hurt people should forgive their tormentors because, she said, this would only inflict further damage on her clients.

I understand that the word 'forgiveness' triggers religious associations, which is why therapists may feel uncomfortable using it, but this particular psychotherapist misunderstood my intention. I've never wanted to create a world where everyone seeks to forgive the pain they've endured. All I've ever wanted to do is to offer up forgiveness as a suggestion, an invitation if you like, as a way of breaking the cycle of suffering when nothing else works, and if only for the sole purpose that there are people out there who have been deeply wounded who tell me it has helped. It won't of course always help, not for all people, nor in all circumstances, but it may be worth considering as a creative alternative to the corrosive power of bitterness. I try to discourage the commonly held notion that to forgive means to condone or look the other way and I have never promoted forgiveness as an imperative, but rather pointed out the dangers of sanitising or simplifying what it means to forgive because I know that so often it is an arduous and exhausting task, risky and unpredictable.

A few years ago, I had a bruising encounter on Skype with an American social media specialist who operates in the world of love and forgiveness and who wanted to connect with the work of The Forgiveness Project. Before long the conversation took a bizarre turn. After signposting me to some motivational quotes she had recently posted on Twitter, she said I should replace the photo on my personal Twitter account with a more smiley one if I wanted to attract more followers. She also pointed out that because some of my tweets were political, anyone interested in 'love and forgiveness' would not be interested in me, as I came across as an 'angry, unforgiving person'. By now I was looking fairly downcast, easing myself out of the frame of the screen. 'Just look at your body language,' she chastised. 'You can't come across like that if you want to go viral and promote love and forgiveness.' The encounter showed me again what I knew already – that the world of love and forgiveness can be a pretty unforgiving place. But it also made me even more determined to position conversations around forgiveness in ways that might attract those who would otherwise dismiss it as soft, syrupy or irrelevant.

Although I have encountered some people who are weary or distrustful of forgiveness, I've met many more who think of it as the key to alleviating suffering, who talk about it in terms of a rare mystery medicine and who complain that it is rarely contemplated and little understood. Sometimes these fans come from unexpected quarters – for example the TV news producer who spoke to me as if he'd just discovered something incredibly precious and was determined to get many more forgiveness stories on air. Interest in *The F Word* exhibition has come from surprising places too. A fire station in Seattle once used some of the stories for their diversity training; and a doctor at a Southampton hospital shared these same stories with his medical students to help them become 'better doctors' and because it was his firm conviction that a cornerstone of the barriers and bridges to understanding diversity was forgiveness.

Positive encouragement has also come from countless individuals across the world who, over the years, have written to me describing their own healing paths. Many have told me that staying bound to the pain of the past no longer serves them and for this reason they have started instead to move into the uneven territory of forgiveness. Even for these proponents of forgiveness there exist two distinct camps. On one side there are the unilateral forgivers for whom forgiveness is an act of self-healing and requires nothing from the wrongdoer. Here forgiveness is entirely in the gift of the one who has been harmed. On the other side are the bilateral, conditional forgivers who believe forgiveness is a contractual relationship between the wronged and the wrongdoer to be earned and deserved through apology or reparation. Here forgiveness is only offered with an invitation to repent. For some people forgiveness just isn't possible without a relationship – as one friend put it to me, 'Forgiveness requires some kind of mutuality because in that moment everything can melt.'

Father Michael Lapsley, who was severely injured in a bomb attack, is someone who holds firm to this position. In April 1990, at the height of the apartheid repression,* Fr Michael, a priest and member of the African National Congress (ANC), was living in exile in Zimbabwe when he was sent a letter bomb through the post. He lost both his hands, one eye and had his eardrums shattered. The lethal explosive device had been placed between the pages of a religious magazine and sent by senior officials of South Africa's security forces. Their aim: to eliminate this outspoken priest who was a prominent supporter of South Africa's liberation struggle. While the regime failed to take out their target, they must surely have assumed that Fr Michael's influence would now

---

* Apartheid ('apartness' in the Afrikaans language) was a system of legislation that upheld segregationist policies against non-white citizens of South Africa for nearly half a century.

at least be permanently diminished as he lay in agonising pain in a Harare hospital.

When, many years earlier, as a newly ordained priest, Fr Michael told friends that his religious mission was to understand what it meant to be human, he could never have imagined how this would show up in his life. Now, nearly twenty years after his sense of mission had in 1973 brought him from his home in New Zealand to serve the poor and the marginalised in South Africa, he faced a frightening and uncertain future, knowing he would have to accept help from carers for the rest of his life. However, buoyed by his faith in God and with the love and prayers from friends all over the world, it was in Harare's Parirenyatwa Hospital that Fr Michael's story of survival became acknowledged, reverenced and given moral content as his road to physical and mental healing began.

After months of receiving expert physical and psychological medical care, first in Zimbabwe and then in Australia, he returned to South Africa fragile but determined to find meaning in his suffering. By now, two functional metal hooks had been fitted as prosthetics to provide a level of independence that enabled him to eat, use a camera (a favourite hobby) and drive a car. Reminded every minute of the day of his extreme physical limitations, he suddenly found himself belonging to a minority outsider group. It was not a group he could ever have wished to join and yet it was here among the sick and disabled that he discovered a new sense of belonging. Brokenness, incompleteness and imperfection were key to forging the ministry of his second life as his recovery centred on developing a deliberate mindset of survival, that of victor over victim. I once heard him give a sermon at Westminster Abbey in London in which he referred to one of South Africa's greatest leaders, Chief Albert Luthuli, who had always maintained that those who think of themselves as victims eventually become the victimisers of others. Similarly, Fr Michael had come to the conclusion that 'People give themselves permission to do terrible things to others because of what was done to them.'

In his memoir *Redeeming the Past: My Journey from Freedom Fighter to Healer*, he describes how he came to understand that while his lifelong pursuit of equity and justice may nearly have destroyed him, there were unquestionably profound rewards to be found too: 'I am immeasurably richer for the journey I've traveled, and so my life is not full of regrets. Of course part of me says, "If only I had realized it was a bomb and not opened it," but God has enabled me to make my bombing redemptive. Some people who have had horrible things happen to them are, to be sure, survivors, but they remain prisoners of a moment in their past. I think there is another step that requires moving away from being an object of history – someone to whom something terrible has been done – to becoming a subject of history once more. This means becoming someone who once again participates in shaping and creating the world. Therefore, I began to realize that if I were consumed by hatred, bitterness, and a desire for revenge, I would be a victim forever.'

Fr Michael has always maintained that while he does not hold on to hate, nor does he forgive those responsible for sending him the letter bomb. He told me for *The F Word Podcast*:

Often when I tell my story I say I am not filled with hatred, bitterness, self-pity or the desire for revenge and then people say to me, 'Oh, you are a wonderful example of forgiveness'. And I say 'but actually I didn't mention the word forgiveness'. Even as we talk today, I don't know who sent the bomb. I don't know who made it. I don't know what the chain of command is. So, for me in a way forgiveness is not yet on the table. Now, I do speculate in my mind the possibility of somebody knocking at my door and saying, 'I am the one who sent you that bomb, will you forgive me?' Of course, I don't actually know how I would respond but I speculate that I might say to that person,

'Well, excuse me sir, do you still make letter bombs?' and he says, 'No, no, actually I work just around the corner from you at the Red Cross Children's Hospital, will you forgive me?' And, my answer is, 'Yes, of course, of course I forgive you.' And then perhaps we would sit and drink tea and I say, 'Well, sir, I have forgiven you but I still have no hands. I will always need somebody to assist me for the rest of my life. Of course, you will help pay for that person – not as a condition of forgiveness but as part of reparation and restitution.'

When I started to collect forgiveness stories in early 2003, I kept hearing about a forgiveness conference that had taken place a few years earlier at the spiritual community of Findhorn in Scotland where Fr Michael Lapsley had been invited to speak. According to one or two people present, some members of the audience had taken issue with his position on *conditional* forgiveness, questioning whether insisting on accountability before forgiveness might be hardening his heart. Their underlying puzzlement was perhaps arising from the question: *how is it possible that a man of God cannot forgive?* Fr Michael has always been very clear that he has become both a better person and a better priest since the bombing, but he points out that even though his 'humanness and limitedness' may demonstrate how compassion and gentleness are stronger than evil and hatred, still this is not forgiveness. During his Westminster Abbey sermon, he used the term *bicycle theology* – questioning the notion that if someone were to steal your bicycle, would you just shrug it off and tell them 'I forgive you'? No, he insisted, first you'd want your bicycle returned; only then can you offer forgiveness. A couple of years later, when I questioned Fr Michael further about this, he said, 'Often we reduce forgiveness to saying sorry, but we don't commit ourselves to reparation and restitution, which are also key elements of the journey of forgiveness.'

Those who do not go along with Fr Michael's theory of bicycle theology claim that if your peace of mind depends on an apology and remorse (which you may never get if the offender is dead, incapable or unknown), you are then simply placing the power in the wrong hands and will always be inextricably linked to the source of your pain.

In the summer of 2020, just after the end of the first Covid-19 lockdown, sisters Nicole Smallman and Bibaa Henry were found fatally stabbed in a park not far from where I live in north-west London. To hear about this horrendously sadistic random attack was distressing enough, but what added to the public's sense of outrage was the police's deeply flawed response. Not only were they dreadfully slow to search for these two Black women, but after their bodies were eventually found by Nicole's boyfriend, two Metropolitan Police officers were discovered to have taken selfies at the crime scene and shared the photos with others. The mother of the murdered women is Mina Smallman, who eighteen months later would be a guest editor on the BBC's *Today* programme. Smallman is a retired priest and was the Church of England's first female archdeacon from a Black or minority ethnic background. When I first read about her, I wondered how on earth she would bear this terrible loss and doubted whether forgiveness would ever be part of her lexicon.

During the months that followed, Smallman barely spoke to the press, but a year later, after nineteen-year-old Danyal Hussein was found guilty of her daughters' murders, she started to speak out publicly, questioning whether the delay in finding her daughters' bodies was because they were two missing Black women. When she was asked why the case had not received the same level of outrage as the kidnap and murder nine months later of a young white woman from south London, Smallman told BBC News: 'Other people have more kudos in this world than people of colour.'[9]

The interview revealed Smallman to be an impressively resilient woman, occupying the dual roles of mother and activist, fighting to change a racially biased police service in honour of her daughters' lives. When asked whether she could forgive, she said quickly and unequivocally, 'I have! I already have. I've surprised myself, actually. When we hold hatred for someone it's not only them who are held captive, it's you, because your thoughts become consumed by revenge and what you'd like to do to them. I refuse to give him that power. He is a nonentity to me ... He has no power in our lives.' This kind of forgiving has nothing to do with reconciliation. Quite the reverse. This is forgiving as a way of severing all ties: forgiving as a form of erasure.

For this reason, Desmond Tutu has described forgiving 'as the best form of self-interest', and it is why Marian Partington – whose sister was murdered by serial killers Fred and Rosemary West – explains that she has forgiven the unrepentant Rosemary West in order not to be corrupted by the brutality of what happened, and so that she might 'live a full life and not be stuck in a place of revenge'.

In her memoir *If You Sit Very Still*, Marian writes with remarkable eloquence and courage about healing and traumatic loss in relation to forgiving Rosemary West. She rarely talks about forgiving Fred West, who committed suicide in prison before his murder trial and in so doing removed himself from any final reckoning. I've had many long conversations with Marian about forgiveness and have always liked the way she describes it as finding a new relationship with pain, an act of liberation through feeling empathy for the suffering of the perpetrator. At Rosemary West's trial, as Marian heard about West's violent upbringing, she suddenly felt a flicker of compassion for 'the impoverishment of a soul who knew no other way to live than through terrible cruelty'. Marian has also often suggested that forgiveness should be thought of as a verb rather than a noun, something that can be practised and participated in because it is active, fluid and 'alive'.

A counterpoint to this framing of forgiving comes from

Reinekke Lengelle, a researcher, poet and professor of therapeutic writing, who ever since her husband's death has focused on teaching bereavement writing. She has much to say about forgiveness, and in a blog entitled 'To Forgive is Not a Verb' she explains: 'To forgive is technically a verb like "to swim" and "to jump" so we are hoodwinked by the concept. We believe we have to do something, which, of course, we don't know how to do. You can conjugate "to forgive", but it is not actionable.'[10]

I agree with Lengelle that it is almost impossible to teach the skills of forgiveness because unlike driving or swimming you can't just go out and learn how to 'do' it. But although I'm doubtful anyone can forgive just from joining a forgiveness class, I'm equally certain you will only succeed in embracing forgiveness, whether for yourself or for another, if you line yourself up for it – if, more than an intellectual pursuit, it becomes a heartfelt intention.

Lengelle claims that as long as we try to *do* forgiveness or *get* forgiveness, 'it's frustrating and adds insult to injury'. However, 'doing' and 'getting' forgiveness have two very different drivers. Yes, going out to get or ask for forgiveness can feel off balance. I once witnessed a victim empathy course in an American prison where the prisoners were writing letters to their victims asking for their forgiveness. The letters were an exercise in empathy and were not intended to be delivered to the recipient, but it struck me as the wrong emphasis. Should not the letter rather have been about saying sorry, taking responsibility and expressing a vow to make amends? As Alistair Little has said, asking for forgiveness just places yet another burden on the victim.

If it is selfish or missing the point to ask for forgiveness, what about 'doing' forgiveness? I've met many people who have been hurt badly by family feuds, friends disowning them, bosses bullying them, who years later – when the hurt still won't subside – wish they could 'do' forgiveness as a way out or a way through. The trouble is they have no idea how. I can offer no single or foolproof way, and there are multiple teachers of forgiveness out there presenting pathways to forgiveness, but nothing in my mind is as helpful or as illuminating as hearing the real stories of those who have considered and grappled with forgiveness, whether or not they have accepted it.

So often the arts serve best to express complicated narratives. There is much in Edward St Aubyn's Patrick Melrose novels that sheds meaning on what Professor Duncan Morrow, a politics lecturer in Northern Ireland, has called 'the impossible yet essential need for forgiveness'. In St Aubyn's semi-autobiographical fiction the central character, Patrick, wrestles over the course of five books with the impact of a traumatic childhood, through a drug-addicted adulthood, the wreckage of his once-wealthy family's fortunes and his own troubled experiences of parenthood. St Aubyn's biting prose conveys uncomfortable insights into Patrick's sexually abusive father while excavating wounds that never heal; the search for redemption is as much about the author as Patrick, who never seems to quite lay the ghosts to rest or quieten the demons. Nevertheless, the principal assumption is that in order to feel whole again, Patrick must move beyond the search for consolation in drugs, sex, alcohol, flattery and love. As St Aubyn himself has implied in several interviews, healing must come from seeing how things *are*, not how they were or how they could have been. A kind of 'ground zero of reality'[11] where only renunciation can set him free.

The Patrick Melrose novels explore what it looks like for a traumatised person to lean towards forgiveness. Initially Patrick toys between opting for forgiveness or revenge, realising that while neither will change the past, forgiveness is the less attractive because it represents a collaboration with one's persecutors. Later, exhausted by hatred, he concludes the only liberation is eventual indifference or detachment. Finally, a vision of wholeness is glimpsed by understanding the reality of forgiveness as something that is messy, inconsistent and full of contradictions. St Aubyn writes of Patrick: 'Only when he could hold in balance his hatred and his stunted love, looking on his father with neither pity nor terror but as another human being who had not handled his personality especially well; only when he could live with the ambivalence of never forgiving his father for his crimes but allowing himself to be touched by the unhappiness that had produced them as well as the unhappiness they had produced, could he be released, perhaps into a new life that would enable him to live instead of merely surviving. He might even enjoy himself.'[12]

I heard Brené Brown talking once about how it had taken her many years of studying forgiveness to understand it. She told of the moment it had all become clear. She had heard a story about a man and woman in a relationship where he had had an affair. Neither had wanted the marriage to end but both were stuck in an unhealthy dynamic where he couldn't let go of shame, and she couldn't let go of blame. As Brené Brown was contemplating this situation she realised that something must be killed off in this marriage for the couple to move on either alone or together in life. And then she said something very powerful: 'The reason why forgiveness is so hard is that in order for us to forgive, something has to die and we have to grieve something.'

You have to know what you have lost and mourn it in order for something new to be born. You have to realise it may never be the same again – but there is always the possibility that it could be more beautiful. Grief is therefore an inherent part of forgiveness. It may be that what has to die is our justified right for vengeance, our certainty that we are right, our assumption that we can keep the relationship we want, our expectation that people will always treat us as we want them to.

2

THE DARK SIDE

> 'Hope is the story of uncertainty, in coming to
> terms with the risk involved of not knowing
> what comes next.'[1]
>
> REBECCA SOLNIT

'To hell with the foolish idea of forgiveness!' One of those who
has questioned the paradigm of forgiveness is the British journalist and former politician Matthew Parris, who argued in a 2015
article for *The Times* that forgiveness is weak, shallow and stupid,[2]
and that those who choose to forgive have been duped in some
way. The article was prompted by a court case in Germany when,
at the age of ninety-four, former SS guard Oskar Gröning, also
known as the 'Bookkeeper of Auschwitz', received a four-year
prison sentence after being found guilty of being an accessory to
the murder of 300,000 people, seventy years after the event. The
article focused on what Leon Schwarzbaum, an Auschwitz survivor, had said when asked if he could forgive Gröning: 'No. I lost
thirty members of my family in Auschwitz.' Parris's definition of
forgiveness is by his own admission unsophisticated, having learnt

it from a schoolteacher who instilled in him at an early age that forgiveness was a Christian concept that meant washing clean or being washed clean. Perhaps it's no wonder Parris has little truck with this promise of impossible piety since his teacher told him that when you 'really forgave it was like waking up in the morning and realising it had all been a bad dream.'

This is not my understanding of forgiveness. Waking up in the morning and realising your suffering has all been a bad dream feels more akin to a practice known as 'radical forgiveness'. This quick-fix, entirely unconditional form of forgiving, created and practised by the late Colin Tipping, has indeed at its core the promise to wipe the slate clean. 'Unlike conventional forgiveness, which is difficult and takes forever,' I heard Tipping once declare as he conducted a forgiveness ceremony at Les Journées du Pardon conference in France in 2012, 'radical forgiveness is easy and fast-acting. The tools simply dissolve the pain and leave you feeling peaceful and happy.' In his book *Radical Forgiveness*, he goes even further, claiming, 'If radical forgiveness can't forgive Hitler, it can forgive nobody. Like unconditional love, it's all or nothing.'[3]

In the *Times* article Parris concludes that 'there can be no doubt those able to persuade themselves they have forgiven, and been forgiven, find the experience liberating,' but he clearly believes such forgiveness is not so much a true response as a hoped-for remedy. It is certainly true that some people, perhaps driven by faith or instructed by counsellors, might persuade themselves they have forgiven, but for most of those whose stories I've collected, curated and shared, forgiveness isn't something you can simply convince yourself of.

Leading yoga teachers Joel Kramer and Diana Alstead[4] explain exactly why some people are so opposed to the idea of forgiveness, and particularly the type of forgiveness that demands nothing from the wrongdoer: 'To forgive without requiring the other to change is not only self-destructive but ensures a dysfunctional relationship will remain so by continually rewarding mistreatment.'

There's a dark side to everything, and I've always been interested in the darker side of forgiveness, by which I mean those times when forgiveness is pushed on you, when it's felt to be insincere or when it can actually make matters worse. Some proponents of forgiveness prefer not to explore this dark underbelly, but I find it revealing. For a start, it's important to recognise the existence of pseudo forgiveness. If you reach forgiveness through justification or coercion, or because you feel obliged in some way, that's pseudo forgiveness or even fake forgiveness. Imagine sports celebrities asking for forgiveness after they've been found cheating, or bank executives pleading for pity following the collapse of the banking sector – in this context forgiveness feels like a shame-faced pathetic gesture, or the last gasp of the condemned. Some people use forgiveness as a way of assuaging guilt. An example might be the letter Luciana Gimenez Morad claims to have once sent to Jerry Hall after her eight-month affair with Mick Jagger had come to an end, asking for Hall's forgiveness. Morad, who had also had a child with Jagger, said she never received a reply, so it's probably fair to presume Hall considered the apology either too little too late, or a crass attempt at reputation repair. The possibility that this might have been a genuine step towards repentance or an attempt to build bridges between two mothers whose children shared the same father is somewhat overshadowed by the fact that Morad chose to share the story of her unanswered forgiveness letter with the media.

Forgiveness can also seem an outrage when it comes to far more brutal crimes. Take the case of Richard Wilson, whose sister was murdered along with twenty of her fellow bus passengers in Burundi by Hutu rebels. Richard has frequently spoken about the limitations of forgiveness when governments use it to avoid accountability.[5] He also frames forgiveness as 'a moral absolutism combined with wishful thinking, which seems both dangerous and demeaning.'[6] Desmond Tutu and others, he claims, promote

forgiveness and reconciliation as the only truly viable alternatives
to revenge, retribution and reprisal. 'But what of those like me,'
he asks, 'who had neither a wish for revenge nor any intention of
reconciling with an unrepentant murderer?' As the co-founder of
Stop Funding Hate, Richard is certainly not a person consumed
by a desire for revenge; his gripe is simply one shared by philosopher and author Professor Charles Griswold, that when a profound
moral concept like forgiveness is too loosely defined, then the
danger is that it slips out of grasp and comes to mean whatever
people want it to mean, 'a hodgepodge of conflicting and over-
lapping meanings'.

Where there is no clear or obvious wrongdoer, forgiveness can
become a matter of one-upmanship. I was struck when Fr Michael
told me once that forgiveness can sometimes be an accusation. In
other words, if you tell someone 'I forgive you', then you're telling
them they are responsible for doing something wrong. This can
be a very serious accusation, whether levelled within intimate
relationships or intergroup conflicts.

There is a famous example of this passive-aggressive application
of forgiveness in literature. It takes place in Charles Dickens' *David
Copperfield*, when Uriah Heep infuriates the blameless David by
telling him that he forgives him. 'You forgive me!' David retorts
indignantly. 'I do, and you can't help yourself,' replies Uriah
mockingly, '... you can't help being forgiven. ... I'm determined
to forgive you.' David is increasingly enraged by Uriah's manipu-
lative offer of forgiveness.[7]

It's hard to imagine any scenario whether in fiction or real life
where the person being forgiven wouldn't be infuriated by such a
disingenuous and condescending expression of forgiveness. With
the assumption made that the 'forgiver' is right and the 'forgiven'
wrong, even a small argument is likely to fester and grow. In
situations where forgiveness is weaponised like this, or where the

wronged and the wrongdoer become indistinguishable, I have long
been drawn towards Rumi's neutral field beyond judgement. The
thirteenth-century Persian poet, mystic and scholar wrote: 'Out
beyond ideas of rightdoing and wrongdoing, there is a field. I'll
meet you there.'[8]

Perhaps Rumi's field is less valuable when there is a clear culprit, but it feels vital for the everyday rough and tumble of human
relationships. I recently heard the British psychotherapist Robin
Shohet talk at a conference for relational coaches about this subject.
'Being right is a dangerous state of mind to be in,' he said, 'because
it gives us the justification to do terrible things. Every time we
put ourselves up, we put someone down. By being right we make
someone wrong. We "other" people so quickly and readily because
it gives us a boost and a moment of satisfaction.'

Over the years I've learnt an enormous amount from Jo Berry
about what it takes to rehumanise 'the other'. Jo is an extremely
impressive woman whose pioneering work in conflict transformation stems as much from her experience of violent extremism as
it does from having raised and home-schooled three daughters on
her own. In 1984 Jo's father, Sir Anthony Berry MP, was killed
along with four others in an IRA bomb at the Conservative Party
Conference in Brighton. The person responsible for planting the
bomb was Patrick Magee, an IRA activist who was later impris-
oned for fourteen years until in 1999 he was released under the
terms of the Good Friday Agreement. Ever since then Jo has been
in dialogue with him. At their very first meeting in Dublin in
2000 she listened calmly and courteously to what he had to say.
'At first it felt like political justification, but I was there to listen
and understand and did not want to change him or blame him,' she
says. 'If I'd gone in angry Patrick would have stayed in this place
of justification. It is very clear to me that when the wounded start
to feel righteous, we stop being curious about the other person and
that lack of curiosity can then turn into dehumanisation. It was

my empathy that disarmed him because there was a moment when there was a very clear change in Patrick and he said the words, "I don't know who I am any more. I have never met anyone so open as you. Can I hear your anger and your pain?" At this point he no longer spoke from the "we" of the IRA. He became much more vulnerable and human and wanted to know about my dad. It began to dawn on me then that he was now seeing my dad as a human being.'

Years earlier, immediately after the bombing and long before her first meeting with Patrick, Jo would frame her story around one of forgiveness because as an ardent believer in non-violence she was determined not to hate the man who had killed her father. However, as the years passed, she changed her position on forgiveness. This wasn't just to avoid the vitriol and death threats she had been receiving from some members of the public who were furious at the idea of a terrorist being forgiven, but also because she now realised that using the language of forgiveness didn't work for her as a way of communicating human empathy. It seemed to reduce the relationship to a transaction, to a power imbalance where something was owed by one to another; and she understood, therefore, that if she were to embrace this way of seeing things in her dialogue with Patrick Magee, it would award her all the moral power and thus become the defining expression of their unequal relationship.

Jo describes this moral condescension built into forgiveness incomparably well: 'To say I forgive you is almost condescending – it locks you into an "us versus them" scenario keeping me right and you wrong. That attitude won't change anything. But I can experience empathy, and in that moment there is no judgement. Sometimes when I've met with Patrick, I've had such a clear understanding of his life that there's nothing to forgive.'

In the prisons where The Forgiveness Project has delivered RESTORE – a group-based programme that supports prisoners in their process of change – the subject of forgiveness always elicits intense discussion. A recognition of the value of forgiving is often juxtaposed with a wariness around the dangers of forgiving prematurely. One prisoner likened insincere forgiveness with simmering anger, saying, 'I say I do but I don't really forgive, I just store it up inside and use it at a later date.' What underlined this burden to forgive was rage, knowing that what had happened was not alright.

On 12 February 1993 Mary Johnson's only son, twenty-year-old Laramiun Byrd, was murdered after an argument at a party. The perpetrator was sixteen-year-old Oshea Israel, who later received a 25-year prison sentence for second-degree murder. Mary's faith is strong, and she believed it was her Christian duty to forgive. So, when during the trial Oshea's mother asked for forgiveness, Mary told the whole court that, yes, she had indeed forgiven. I first met Mary in 2013 when we were both speaking at a forgiveness symposium in Minneapolis. Here she explained to me: 'But I hadn't actually forgiven. The root of bitterness ran deep, anger had set in, and I hated everyone. I remained like this for years, driving many people away with my story of pain and anger.'

Exhausted by intrusive thoughts, for many years Mary felt a hostage to her pain until, one day, she came across a poem which talked about two mothers – one mother whose child had been murdered and the other mother whose child was the murderer. 'It was such a healing poem,' she said, 'all about the commonality of pain, and it showed me my destiny.' As a result, twenty years after the murder of her son, Mary put in a request to the Department of Corrections to meet the man who had killed him. She recalls: 'Never having been to a prison before, I was so scared and wanted to turn back. But when Oshea came into the room I shook hands with him and said, "I don't know you and you don't know me. You didn't know my son and he didn't know you, so we need to lay down a foundation and get to know one another." We talked for two hours during which he admitted what he'd done. I could see how sorry he was and at the end of the meeting, for the very first time, I was genuinely able to say that I forgave Oshea.'

When Mary left the prison that day, she told me that she never again felt hatred, or animosity, towards Oshea. It seems inconceivable, and certainly it's extremely unusual, but she's not the first person who I've heard describe this movement towards forgiveness as something so immediate and so profound that in a single moment anger and anguish are completely eliminated.

Most problematic of all, forgiveness can sometimes be seen to endorse an offence. When white supremacist Dylann Roof entered a church one Sunday morning in Charleston, West Virginia and shot dead eight Black parishioners, almost immediately some members of the victims' families declared they had forgiven. Like Mary, their forgiveness was driven by their Christianity and footage of them saying as much in court was transmitted in news bulletins across the United States. Many people were comforted by this wholehearted refusal to hate, but not everyone felt comfortable with the rush to forgive. A vigorous debate ensued, with some asking, 'Does Black forgiveness only serve to encourage white violence?'

Ta-Nehisi Coates touches on this same uncomfortable confluence in *Between the World and Me*. In an open letter to his fifteen-year-old son, he contemplates the callous police shooting of his innocent university friend Prince Jones. Angered at the ease with which the Black community forgave, he concludes: 'The need to forgive the police officer would not have moved me because even then in some inchoate form I knew that Prince was not killed by a single officer but that he was killed by a country and all the fears that have marked it from birth . . . I did not believe in forgiveness.' I first read this statement in the autumn of 2020, shortly after the Black Lives Matter movement had exploded on a global scale in the aftermath of the murder of George Floyd. It landed heavily with me. It made me feel a burden of responsibility, worrying that the forgiveness stories I have collected, which have been shared and promoted round the world (albeit with an emphasis on choice and complexity), might in certain circumstances make people feel yet another layer of oppression – namely the duty to pardon or the pressure to forgive. Coates powerfully sums up here why those of us working in the field of forgiveness need to tread very carefully, because where there is structural injustice, we also have the moral obligation to work to transform and dismantle these institutions of power.

The term 'forgiveness boosterism' was coined by Jeffrie Murphy in 2003 and refers to the way in which forgiveness has been adopted as a technique and imperative in therapy – in other words the view that advocates forgiveness of those who have wronged us as the only way to move on from the offence. I get dispirited by the polarised arguments and absolute moral statements that surround the subject of forgiveness and have no time for the belief that if hurt people don't practise forgiveness, they will be ruined in some way. The internet is awash with this kind of oppressive narrative, for instance a recent report on CBN News entitled 'The Deadly Consequences of Unforgiveness' states: 'According to Dr. Steven Standiford, chief of surgery at the Cancer Treatment Centers of America, refusing to forgive makes people sick and keeps them that way.'[9]

No one can deny the link between forgiveness and physical and mental wellbeing. There is plenty of evidence to show that holding on to unresolved resentment for perceived transgressions depletes immune function and causes physical stress to the whole body. It has also been shown that forgiving people score better on just about every measure of psychological wellbeing than people who do not forgive.[10]

However, I have an issue with forgiveness boosterism because by insisting that forgiveness is a cure-all, and that not forgiving will deplete you in some way, it leaves little room for anger and resentment. It can also feel exclusive by suggesting that forgiveness is primarily for the mentally strong or the morally superior. It is not surprising to me, therefore, that someone like Jo Berry can't entirely relate to it and will only reluctantly refer to it because so often people frame her story as a forgiveness story. 'Forgiveness is an abstract term with no substance,' declared Colin Parry at The Forgiveness Project's second annual lecture in 2011. The lecture – 'No Forgiveness Without Justice?' – was given by former MP Clare Short, who had been an outspoken critic of the Iraq War. Alongside her I had invited three storytellers to share their personal experiences. I had chosen Colin, whose twelve-year-old son, Tim, was killed in the 1993 Warrington IRA bomb, precisely because he felt ambiguous about the whole idea of forgiveness.

Colin Parry is frequently asked whether he forgives and, just like Fr Michael Lapsley, he has always said that it is impossible to forgive if no one has come forward to claim responsibility for his son's death. He is clearly far more comfortable with the idea of reconciliation and has worked hard to build bridges in Northern Ireland and even met with senior figures within Sinn Féin. What interests me is that because Colin never talks in a bitter or vengeful way, many people just assume he has forgiven. A quick Google search reveals one church website in the UK using Colin's story as an example of 'forgiveness in action', and just recently I heard someone at an online Forgiveness Forum held by Templeton World Charity Foundation refer to Colin Parry's story as 'a wonderful example of forgiveness'. Perhaps it shouldn't matter. And yet I feel it does because Colin has always been so clear that he doesn't forgive the IRA, never has and never will. These assumptions feel lazy and go hand in hand with a tendency to simplify notions of forgiveness, rather than recognising the mess, nuance, complexity and ambiguity.

Rami Elhanan is a member of The Parents Circle – a joint Israeli-Palestinian organisation of over 600 families who have lost an immediate family member in the enduring conflict. Rami's daughter, Smadar, was killed in a suicide bombing in Tel Aviv in 1997 aged just fourteen. In a conflict that shows continual evidence of cruelty, some family members in The Parents Circle use the redemptive and rebellious practice of forgiveness as a way of preventing them from hardening against life, but Rami isn't one of them. Nor has he hardened against life. He says of the person who killed Smadar: 'I don't forgive, and I don't forget ... but the suicide bomber was a victim just like my daughter, grown crazy out of anger and shame.' Rami is a gentle man with immeasurable compassion, but he doesn't use the word forgiveness as far as I'm aware. He has reconciled with the pain and made meaning out of the tragedy, but his message is focused on building a sustainable peace with citizens on both sides of the divide, citizens who are united by the common human experience of losing a loved one through violent conflict.

Forgiving your harmer can be costly if the circumstances that led to the harm don't change. For example, in one scientific study of newlyweds, an associate psychology professor at the University of Tennessee found that men and women who forgave their partners' transgressions ended up with partners who only behaved worse.[11] The take-home message was that forgiveness may lead to more abuse. These dynamics suggest forgiveness can be dangerous, particularly in cases of domestic violence where pleading for forgiveness is part of the cycle of abuse and promises to change are used to manipulate the partner into staying. Similarly in child physical and sexual abuse, abusers are known to consistently show remorse and ask for forgiveness and yet they also frequently continue to abuse.[12]

In September 2021, an independent public inquiry examining evidence from thirty-eight religious groups in England and Wales, including sects from Christianity, Orthodox Judaism and Islam, found many of these groups were morally failing children in the way they treated allegations of child abuse.[13] Religious leaders were reluctant to see those in their midst at fault, with the reputation of the organisation held higher than the needs of victims. The inquiry also found that when leaders did respond to allegations of abuse, frequently they relied on religious dogma as a way of dealing with it. On the BBC's *World at One* programme, the secretary of the inquiry, John O'Brien, singled out forgiveness as being a major problem in this unfortunate dynamic, because, he said, 'religious institutions used the concept of forgiveness of people who have committed this dreadful crime as a way of keeping it within the organisation.'

It is for these reasons that forgiveness may be refused on ethical grounds. A good example of this is cited by Christopher C. H. Cook and Wendy Dossett in a chapter about addiction and forgiveness from the richly diverse *Forgiveness in Practice*. Cook and Dossett quote from one particular addict, a woman who was raped, and the significant point here is that forgiving is something she deliberately refuses rather than something she fails to achieve. Her position is that while in some circumstances forgiveness may be desirable for psychological health, it is her moral duty not to forgive because to forgive her abuser would imply potential forgiveness for *all* abusers. 'I don't forgive my rapist. I would be wrong in my view to do so. I'm not just an individual. I'm a woman, and I stand in solidarity with others (regardless of gender) who have been abused,' she says.[14]

Tara Muldoon, a survivor of sexual assault who has used forgiveness as part of her recovery, reached out to me several years ago to tell me about an organisation she had founded in Canada called *F-You: The Forgiveness Project* – a youth-driven social change initiative promoting forgiveness as tangible and attainable. A few years later Tara emailed again, this time in despair about what she described as a 'massive cultural hurt'. There had been a very public trial of a Canadian celebrity accused of sexual violence against at least twenty women, although only three had gone to trial. He had just been acquitted and the level of anger among women, especially survivors, was visceral. 'Everyone is triggered, and no one knows what to do. I feel like it has set back work we have done but most importantly, the city feels hopeless around the justice system. We feel defeated. I know forgiveness isn't appropriate right now.'

On another level forgiveness often gets a bad name for the simple reason that it can be made to seem too easy. The former archbishop of Canterbury, Rowan Williams, warned against the dangers of forgiving too readily in 2011 when he told the *Radio Times*, 'I think the twentieth century saw such a level of atrocity that it has focused our minds very, very hard on the dangers of forgiving too easily ... because if forgiveness is easy it is as if the suffering doesn't really matter.' In the play *Angels in America* by Tony Kushner, which focuses on the cruelties of AIDS and was revived by the National Theatre in 2018, a character makes the point that forgiveness lies half-way between love and justice and that it 'doesn't count if it's easy, it's the hardest thing.' It's an argument that needs to be heard by those who claim forgiveness is a soft option that only encourages bad behaviour.

The Algerian French philosopher Jacques Derrida comes to the provocative conclusion that forgiveness is only effective if it is difficult because in his view the only wrongdoing that calls for forgiveness is that which is unforgivable. By this he means deeds and wrongs so appalling that they can never be understood, over-looked or undone, and therefore cannot be fixed by restitution, reconciliation, apology or justice. In his words, 'Forgiveness is not, it *should not be* normal, normative, normalising. It *should* remain exceptional and extraordinary, in the face of the impossible.'[15] This is the most difficult type of forgiveness because it calls on the victim to forgive the most extreme offences without any possibility of their pain being alleviated by the perpetrator's redemption. Forgiveness in this sense might be a way out of hell, a lifeline, a last gasp when nothing else can bring relief or comfort. This is the zenith of unconditional forgiveness which Derrida, were he alive today, would have an interesting time defending against the likes of Matthew Parris or Professor Griswold.

Ray Minniecon, whom I met in South Africa at a conference on forgiveness and reconciliation in 2014, is an Aboriginal pastor and human rights activist from Australia. The first thing I noticed about Ray when I sat down to talk to him was a heaviness in his eyes – the kind of eyes that you know have been witness to much cruelty. With his roots in the Kabikabi and Gurang-Gurang tribes of Queensland, Ray now lives in Sydney and has dedicated his life to supporting members of the Stolen Generations. The term Stolen Generations refers to the tens of thousands of Aboriginal and Torres Strait Islander children who from the late 1880s until the 1970s were forcibly removed from their families by government agencies and church missions in an attempt to assimilate them into the culture of white Australia. The children of the Stolen Generations were taken from their families to be adopted by white families or forced to live in state boarding schools where they were often subjected to appalling abuse of every possible kind. It's hardly surprising that the intergenerational effects of these forced-removal policies continue to this day, with some children of the Stolen Generations suffering neglect and abuse at the hands of parents who themselves were denied competent parenting.

Somehow Ray escaped the fate of many of his friends. 'But as a child I lived in fear,' he explained. 'My parents told me that if the police tried to pick us up we should run like crazy. There were times when the black police car would come into the missions and I'd hear women screaming from one end of the community to the other for their children to run into the bush and hide. I was one of the lucky ones who never got caught.'

His father was a Christian pastor earning a small income from cane cutting in Queensland. The family moved from farm to farm during the cane season and when the season was over would return to the designated reserves or missions. In those days Aboriginal people had no recognition and were not allowed into towns. Ray listed for me a catalogue of indignities his people were subjected to, rules implemented with impunity by successive governments. Aboriginals had never been counted in the census, so no one knew exactly how many killings or massacres there had been; the government had control over every aspect of their lives; they were made to live on reserves; they weren't allowed out after six in the evening; they were not permitted to mix with white people. It was the government who would determine if someone could marry and *who* they could marry; how much money they had; who they could work for and where they could work. Aboriginals were also restricted in their capacity to get involved in any political agendas and forbidden to speak their languages or practise cultural traditions.

With the plight of the Aboriginal people becoming a significant political issue these policies eventually changed, but one set of problems was replaced by another, said Ray: 'As we came out of these reserves and foster homes we were forced to live in new urban environments where we now had to face the daily onslaught of racism. I joined the rest of the young people who didn't have the wherewithal to counteract this racism and like them found the only way to relieve the pain was to get drunk and take drugs. It was also a heady freedom for us. Living without restrictions meant for the first time we could do whatever we wanted to do.'

It was his parents' strength of faith that eventually led Ray to follow in his father's footsteps, leaving behind the protective oblivion of narcotics and instead drawing back into spirituality to find a new and different direction for his life. This was also the time that he became politically active. Many years of research into the government's forced removals and 'breed out the black' policy opened his eyes to injustices that none of his community knew about because they hadn't had access to newspapers or reports. Soon he was able to see the official records of the Stolen Generations and for the first time learn about the extent of the historic injustices that had taken place. He learnt how assimilation policies had resulted in high levels of chronic illness, psychotic personality disorders, loss of personal and cultural identity, social isolation, criminality, suicide, self-mutilation, not to mention the effects of systematic racism as a result of the continued denigration of Aboriginal society and values.

'The terrible pain you still see on the streets today shows how the brutality of our history is continuing into the present,' Ray told me as he passed his brown porkpie hat tensely from one hand to the other – a hat onto which he had attached numerous enamel pin badges, each signifying a different campaign either won or lost. The conversation then moved on to the difficult subject of forgiveness. Difficult because while it might be relatively easy to get your head round forgiving an individual for harming you, how on earth do you forgive a government, an administration, a whole population of bystanders? Is it even right to bring forgiveness into the frame when connected with such wholescale and systematic cruelty?

I found what Ray had to say about forgiveness and healing both revealing and very sad. He told me that he now considered forgiveness as more important than healing because, he said, 'I have come to see healing as a meaningless word for Aboriginal people, because we possess a wound that cannot be healed. Rape of the soul is so profound – and particularly for the Stolen Generations who were forcibly removed from their parents, communities and culture.' His story perfectly illustrates Derrida's theory, because nothing in Ray's past has been or ever can be restored through apology or restitution. There is no possibility of justice for the crimes committed on his people. And yet forgiveness can bring some relief. 'I struggle with forgiveness, but I know I have to practise it every day to relieve my bitterness,' he told me. 'It's a moment-by-moment thing because I can walk into a shop and have a person do racist acts without them even knowing they are racist because it has become so engrained; and when that happens, I have to walk away and deal with my rage and anger. I have to learn to say, "Okay, Ray, forgive that person." If I didn't forgive then the past would always be present and always there to haunt me.'

3

ISOLATION

'Nothing binds you to the object of hatred
more than your own aversion.'

YONGEY MINGYUR RINPOCHE

Eva Mozes Kor was a Romanian-born American child survivor of
Auschwitz. Eva, along with her twin sister Miriam, only survived
the concentration camp because she was part of a group of pairs of
twins who were used for sadistic pseudoscientific medical experiments. During their time in Auschwitz, Eva and Miriam were
starved of food and human kindness. Three times a week they'd
be placed naked in a room for up to eight hours to be measured,
probed and studied by the Nazi doctor Josef Mengele, also known
as the 'Angel of Death'.

On 27 January 1945, four days before the twins' eleventh birthday, Auschwitz was finally liberated by the Soviet army. Following
nine months in a refugee camp, Eva then returned to her village
in Romania to discover that no one from her family had survived.
Later she went to live in Israel, eventually making the United
States her home. For many years none of the twin survivors spoke

of what had happened to them. The common conception was that to keep silent about the past might obliterate the enduring pain. It wasn't until 1978, after the ground-breaking NBC mini-series *The Holocaust*[1] was aired on television, that people began to ask Eva about these gruesome experiments, and as she started to confront her past, she was prompted to seek out Mengele's other twin survivors. Many came forward and Eva found that exchanging memories about the past and having her story acknowledged in public for the first time was both cathartic and liberating.

In 1993 Eva was invited to give a lecture to a group of doctors in Boston and was asked if she could bring a Nazi doctor with her. At first it seemed an impossible request until she remembered that she had once featured in a documentary alongside a former member of the SS, Dr Hans Munch. She contacted Dr Munch in Germany, and he agreed to meet with her to film an interview for the conference. Eva was terrified at the thought of coming face to face with an officer from Auschwitz – terrified by what he might do to her and terrified that her own rage might erupt. However, when it came to it, Dr Munch treated her with the utmost respect, answering all her questions. 'I asked him if he'd seen the gas chambers. He said this was a nightmare he dealt with every day of his life. I was surprised that Nazis had nightmares too.' Later, when she was looking for a 'thank-you' card to send to him, the idea of a forgiveness letter came to her. 'I knew it would be a meaningful gift, but it became a gift to myself as well because in the writing I realised I was not a hopeless, powerless victim anymore.'

The card was so appreciated that two years later Eva invited Dr Munch to join her for the fiftieth anniversary of the liberation of Auschwitz. Here he signed a document about the operation of the gas chambers while Eva read out her document of forgiveness.

That Eva eventually came to forgive first the German people, then her specific Nazi torturers, and eventually the whole Nazi regime seems unimaginable and only begins to make sense as part of a continuum that began with her silence, denial and loathing. One coping strategy for responding to trauma is to take refuge in the safety of denial. Denial suppresses the pain and allows you to deal with only as much grief as you can take at the time. Retreating into the shadows of silence or darkness initially can bring much-needed comfort, but it is also a lonely and frightening place. It was only by speaking publicly and explicitly about her experiences in Auschwitz that Eva finally found relief from the pain that had been accumulating over the years. She would often say that while she may have been liberated from Auschwitz in 1945, true liberation didn't come until five decades later when she finally and unconditionally was able to forgive. Forgiveness for Eva – like for so many others I've met – became a survival mechanism when all other strategies had failed or ceased to work. Indeed, Eva came to describe her forgiveness as a kind of 'miracle medicine' in that it was free and had no side effects, although she would also say, as a kind of provocative caveat to those who found the idea of forgiveness harmful or counter-intuitive, that it was 'as personal as chemotherapy'.

In her later years, Eva Kor identified as a 'forgiveness activist', but she also made every effort to stress that she forgave in her name alone. And since her death in 2019, her son Alex has continued to stress this same point whenever he speaks about his mother's legacy. This is because Eva's book *The Twins of Auschwitz*, along with the film she featured in, *Forgiving Dr Mengele*, plus her frequent public comments about forgiveness, sometimes made her unpopular with other Holocaust survivors as well as with members of the Jewish community. This was particularly the case towards the end of her life in relation to the jailing of SS guard Oskar Gröning. At the time of the trial, Eva publicly spoke about walking across the court room in Lüneburg, Germany to embrace him.[2] She believed that his admittance of 'moral guilt' and his plea for forgiveness was sufficient repentance, and she stated publicly that he would be of far greater value to society outside prison than inside. By sharing his story in schools and education facilities, she argued, it would provide a powerful antidote to the dangerous lies flaunted by Holocaust deniers.

Like other vocal and high-profile forgivers, Eva Kor was a polarising figure in her lifetime, praised by some as a visionary peacemaker and reviled by others as a scandalous traitor to her people. For twenty-five years, this indomitable woman faced the fury of her peers but continued to advocate for the healing power of forgiveness as the one true path to shedding victim-hood. Reclaiming her personal power, said Eva, was her 'ultimate revenge' against those who had sought to destroy her.

In our society the incentive to get even is socially reinforced and therefore it is not uncommon for people who forgive their attackers, tormenters and antagonists to meet with disapproval and disbelief, whether from family, friends or society. Shad Ali, who was the victim of a vicious racial attack in Nottingham and one of the most warm-hearted men I ever met, often spoke about this to me before his untimely death from an unrelated illness in 2017.

'Forgiveness for me began the day after the attack when I woke up in my hospital bed feeling remarkably at peace,' he said. 'But I was surrounded by family and friends who were all distraught – particularly my male friends who wanted retribution. For me forgiveness came from wondering how on earth someone could inflict that kind of pain on another human being without feeling anything.'

For a long time Shad's family and friends couldn't understand why he would want to forgive his attacker, but Shad was resolute, even to the extent that for many years he battled with the authorities to get a restorative justice meeting set up so that he could meet his attacker. Restorative Justice, Shad always said, had restored the humanity in both of them.

By now Shad's wife and friends had come round to accepting his unswerving commitment to forgiveness. I think what they had probably found hard was the immediacy of his decision. I have indeed rarely met anyone who has embraced forgiveness after such a deep trauma so quickly and so wholeheartedly. Normally it takes years, sometimes decades – with people only lining themselves up to forgive after a long and difficult process where grief and bitterness have left them spent and looking for another way forward.

Shad often said that part of his reason for forgiving so quickly came from the gratitude he felt on waking up alive in hospital. He was determined to use that gratitude by taking positive action, which for him meant forgiving a man he didn't know and who at that point was still on the run from the police. It was a decision he made to feel better in himself despite the fact that no one close to him initially supported what he was doing.

If Shad felt angry, it was never at his attacker but more at the criminal justice system that for years put up roadblocks that delayed him meeting his attacker. But Shad is unusual here. Most victims go through extensive angry periods as part of coming to terms with the pain, so anger should not be dismissed as part of the forgiving process. Indeed, Marian Partington said 'forgiveness began with murderous rage' as she described the decisive moment when she realised that she too was capable of killing should rage consume her. The poet Pádraig Ó Tuama hits the nail on the head when he says, 'Anger is a magnificent and important defence and if forgiveness is ever to happen there needs to be a level of safety. And sometimes anger is a reminder to ourselves that safety hasn't been achieved yet, so anger is the protection.'[3] Undoubtedly, therefore, a season of anger is often necessary when confronted by pain or injustice. The difficulty comes when lasting anger or overwhelming self-pity become so engrained that they lead to cycles of self-destructive behaviour.

Ray Minniecon said that while he could manage, control and

understand righteous anger, because it was part of human nature and had at its core a desire for fairness, he had concluded that when anger turns to bitterness herein lies the problem. 'I've experienced that kind of bitterness and it buckles and twists you up, causing you to lash out,' he said. 'I have to be careful when this happens not to fall into that trap. I've fallen into it before, and it takes a long time to get back on my feet again.'

Forgiveness is often interpreted as a moral choice whereby a victim relinquishes their vengeful instincts and abandons hate. Certainly, forgiveness must include this intention, but on the other hand it's perfectly possible to set aside hate and the desire for revenge and still not forgive. Primo Levi, the Italian Jewish author and Holocaust survivor who died in 1987, was adamant about the need to rid himself of 'the bestial vice of hatred', but he didn't and couldn't forgive. In *The Truce*,[4] the sequel to Levi's harrowing Holocaust memoir, *Survival in Auschwitz*, he writes about the liberation of Auschwitz and in an afterword to the book responds to common questions from readers. One of the questions asked is: 'In your books there are no expressions of hate for the Germans, nor the desire for revenge. Have you forgiven them?' Levi's answer is instructional:

I regard hatred as bestial and crude, and prefer that my actions and thoughts be the product, as far as possible, of reason. Much less do I accept hatred directed collectively at an ethnic group, for example at all the Germans. If I accepted it, I would feel that I was following the precepts of Nazism, which was founded precisely on national and racial hatred. I must admit that if I had in front of me one of our persecutors of those days, certain known faces, certain old lies, I would be tempted to hate, and with violence too; but exactly because I am not a fascist or a Nazi, I refuse to give way to this temptation ... No, I have not forgiven any of the culprits, nor am I willing to forgive a single one of them, unless he has shown (with deeds, not words, and not too long afterwards) that he has become conscious of the crimes and the errors, and is determined to condemn them, to uproot them from his conscience and from that of others, because an enemy who sees the error of his ways ceases to be an enemy.[5]

Nevertheless, relinquishing resentment or the desire for revenge is probably the most important requirement for forgiveness. Certainly, for those whose healing can be viewed in a restorative context, it is frequently cited as fundamental to someone's ability to finding a semblance of liberation from pain. According to many of the victims of serious crime I've spoken to, it seems that vengeful instincts are either driven out in the full roar of battle because they threaten to consume, or they fizzle out before ever having materialised for the simple reason that the victim cannot bear to further the cycle of hate. It is much the same rationale that is sometimes adopted when relatives of murder victims speak of opposing the death penalty. Nietzsche's words from *Beyond Good and Evil* are worth taking into consideration here too: 'Beware that, when fighting monsters, you yourself do not become a monster … for when you gaze long into the abyss. The abyss gazes also into you.'

Forgiveness can be useful for those facing traumatic grief because it diminishes the impulse for revenge, which otherwise might keep a person trapped in a state of compulsive hatred, mirroring the very cruelty that is so detested. Marian Partington indicated some of this to me once when referring to the restorative work she was doing with lifers and other dangerous prisoners. Alluding to the pit of despair she had felt after discovering how her sister had been kidnapped, tortured and murdered, she confessed she had felt 'a connection with all those who are tortured by the imprisoning hell of their own minds.'

In 2002 Robi Damelin's son David was killed by a Palestinian sniper while serving in the reserves of the Israeli army. Robi recalls the exact words that came to her when the authorities arrived at her door to break the devastating news. 'Do not take revenge in the name of my son,' she found herself saying, instinctively understanding that there was nothing to be gained through retaliation. Aqeela Sherrills, the former LA gang member whose story we will look at in Chapter 8, had a similar reaction after his beloved eighteen-year-old son, Terrell, was killed in gun violence. This father, who had helped negotiate a peace truce between Los Angeles street gangs, relinquished his vengeful impulses for entirely pragmatic reasons knowing full well where vengeance would lead. 'I'm no novice to violence and death having witnessed it all my life,' he said, 'but nothing ever prepares you for the loss of your child. I pretty much raised him as a single father from the age of three. He was an unbelievable kid. After rushing to the hospital to be told that he hadn't made it, I thought, *What is the gift in this tragedy?* Then, when I heard his homies were gathering in the projects and going on a mission to avenge Terrell's death, I stopped it.'

Aqeela wasn't surprised that the sheriff's department never followed up the case and that the young man who had killed his son was never caught. The injustice could have sent him spiralling into revenge but instead he responded to his son's murder by prising his heart and mind open. 'I had this opportunity to retaliate, but I decided that revenge shouldn't be Terrell's legacy,' he said. 'Instead, I chose to have valuable conversations with the community about why revenge doesn't work. And when I found out that the perpetrator was a seventeen-year-old kid, I forgave him. I forgave not because I condoned what he did but because I don't believe that people *are* their experiences. The things that we have perpetrated and the things that have been done to us don't define who we are, they only inform who we are becoming. I didn't see him as a perpetrator. I saw him as a victim too because this black boy was a victim of a culture that doesn't see him as human – a victim of a culture that lacks compassion. You can only kill someone if you have a callous heart, so I want to know why this young man had such a callous heart. It's not enough simply to catch him and throw him away.'

Letlapa Mphahlele, who during South Africa's bitter anti-apartheid struggle became director of operations for the Azanian People's Liberation Army (APLA), said something to me once that will always stay with me. It stays with me because it was such an honest, unflinching explanation of where revenge can lead. He was talking about his days in APLA when he believed that terror had to be answered with more terror and so the only valid response at that time was to authorise high-profile massacres on white civilians in the same way that the apartheid government authorised high-profile massacres on black civilians. But years of reflection had led him to think differently: 'Where would it have ended?' he asked. 'If my enemy had been cannibals, would I have eaten white flesh? If my enemy had raped black women, would I have raped white women?'

We seem to live in a world which is far more vengeful than it is forgiving, although perhaps this is because retribution uses more oxygen than kindness and when meted out is far more hazardous. As human beings, our thirst for revenge has evolved from a prime-val predisposition to respond to harm and threats with aggressive retaliation. Homer's Achilles completely understands revenge's eruption when he describes 'that gall of anger that swarms like smoke inside of man's heart/And becomes a thing sweeter to him by far than the dripping of honey.'

Revenge narratives imbue the Old Testament, disrupt the natural order in classics from the Greek tragedies to Shakespeare, and form plots and subplots in just about every modern-day work of literature and film genre.* Revenge is played out in politics too, with ancient rivalries often coming to the surface when weak governments fall. One example of many is when the failed communist government in the former Yugoslavia collapsed, leaving space for old ethnic hatreds to erupt; the result was the Bosnian war. Governments often adopt the revenge impulse for popularity or strategic reasons. America's invasion of Afghanistan in 2002 was, for instance, a clear act of revenge for Osama bin Laden's 9/11 attack. Many intractable conflicts and civil wars are fuelled by acts of revenge, or, to look at it another way, by the moral incentive to seek justice. The death penalty is the state exacting revenge for murder, by taking a life for a life. There is of course a purpose to revenge, and it's true to say it can sometimes work as a deterrent. Threats of revenge can scare off rivals and adversaries and are sometimes critical to the survival of a person, group or nation.

But while the idea of revenge can seem attractive, with the phrase 'just deserts' promising something tempting, fundamental to the human urge to take revenge is an equation that doesn't always add up, namely that your misery can be eased and your injuries salvaged if the person who has wronged you is made to suffer. I witnessed a small example of this a few years ago at Holloway Prison when a young female prisoner was taking part in our RESTORE workshop. The group was talking about how betrayal can lead to acts of revenge, and she told of how her husband had been unfaithful and so she had retaliated by writing to her rival's children to tell them what their mother had done. Initially she had felt elated at causing such embarrassment and distress, but that feeling hadn't lasted long. 'You see,' she said, 'she

---

* But I'd also like to suggest that the theme of forgiveness is surprisingly prevalent too. Naturally my ear is attuned to it and in my experience it's rare to find any novel, TV drama series or feature film that doesn't include a character struggling to forgive or be forgiven at some point.

may have deserved it but after I did that I didn't feel any better. In fact, I felt worse.'

I have learnt a lot about revenge from psychotherapist Robin Shohet, whose fascination with it and understanding of how destructive it is led him to hold two conferences on forgiveness, both at the Findhorn Foundation spiritual community where he has lived for much of his life. In 2011 Shohet and I were both invited to speak at the Les Journées du Pardon conference in France. Here, in a monastery close to the Swiss border, and in front of a large crowd of mostly French people, he explained what had originally drawn him to look at the subject of forgiveness. He had been asked to write a book on revenge with his friend and colleague Ben Fuchs, who was also a psychotherapist. As a result, they had started collecting stories from Northern Ireland, Israel/ Palestine, from couples who had divorced acrimoniously and from families locked into conflict. He was also planning to draw on his own ongoing struggle with enduring resentments. Shohet is far from a vindictive person, but he has a mischievous sense of humour and has never been afraid to talk about his dark side publicly. At the same time as writing the revenge book, in order to create additional material, he set up a number of workshops which turned out to be an eye-opener. 'There was much laughter at these workshops as we recognised we were all "at it" in gross or subtle ways,' he said. 'Gossiping, put-downs, "forgetting", being late, not doing the dishes, sulking, withholding, refusing to acknowledge someone, envy, infidelity, being a failure, being a success even. None of these in themselves is necessarily vengeful, but all could be seen through the eyes of revenge in certain contexts.'

The book on revenge was never written: instead Shohet and Fuchs held their first forgiveness conference at Findhorn in 1999. In the process of writing and researching they had come to believe that ultimately revenge was a 'dead end'. 'And I mean that in both senses of the phrase "dead end", in the sense of the quote, "He who plots revenge should dig two graves" but also I discovered that revenge was a way of attempting to restore power which did not ultimately work. Being obsessed with revenge keeps people tied to both the wound and to the person who has done the wounding.'

What I have always appreciated about Shohet's approach to these two antipodal topics of revenge and forgiveness is that he recognises absolutely the lure of revenge and will never judge people for gravitating in that direction because he has done so frequently himself. 'One of the biggest pulls, I think, is that revenge can give a sense of identity,' he says. 'In *The Count of Monte Cristo*, Dantès says, "Don't take away my hatred. It is all I have." In my therapeutic work, I have seen that the forming of an identity around revenge is one of the most powerful reasons for holding on to it. Fighting for a cause can give life purpose, involve a sense of camaraderie and belonging, an opportunity to claim the moral high ground fighting against the oppressors.'

Shohet recognises that building an identity around our wounds and the need to be right can lock us into a revenge dynamic. I love the following passage from his essay on revenge in *Forgiveness in Practice* about how people take revenge to avoid feeling self-hatred: 'Some time ago I went to a therapist to complain about what I saw as my wife's attacks on me. I knew intellectually that in my mind I was attacking her for what I saw as her attacks, but still felt wounded. The therapist listened patiently as I built my case and just calmly said, "It has nothing to do with her, it is your own self-hatred." I knew she was right. How we judge and talk about others is often a reflection of how we treat ourselves. When the internal critic is too painful to bear, we project its wrath outward and find scapegoats who provide targets for our intolerance.'[6]

James Roose-Evans, the British theatre director, priest and writer on ritual and meditation, now in his tenth decade, has had a lifetime's experience of dealing with the typical sporadic ruptures in relationships. In a blog post he urges that when someone savages us or treats us badly, instead of being angry and hitting back, we reflect on where this other person is coming from and what unresolved conflict has unleashed such rage or jealousy in them; or, even to ask ourselves, 'What is it in me that has provoked such a reaction?' He also writes of the importance of always being open to the possibility of reconciliation and shares a personal story. 'In any relationship there will be occasional pin-pricks. The secret is not to over-react. It is always fatal to respond in kind ... I think of a woman friend of many years and a close colleague, who once wrote to me a four-page letter, demolishing my entire life, character and work. I reflected on why she had exploded in this way and then wrote to her, saying, "The bridge is down but would you like to come to lunch and let us rebuild the bridge?" She came to lunch. No reference was made to her letter and outburst, but it was clear that she was relieved that the friendship was not broken.'

Chanel Miller is a sexual assault survivor who has attempted to both tackle and untangle her story through writing it down. I only heard about her for the first time when Miller was interviewed on BBC Radio 4's *Woman's Hour* programme in 2020. She was in London to promote her memoir *Know My Name*,[7] a book that has been described by the *Washington Post* as 'a gut punch' but also 'blessedly hopeful'. The memoir is Miller's attempt to shine a light into the darkest places of humanity and lay bare, in intimate and courageous detail, a terrible chain of events which began on a January night in 2015 when she was sexually assaulted by a Stanford student outside a frat party on the university campus. She was later found lying near a dumpster close by, partially clothed and unconscious.

By the time the case went to court Miller had taken on the name of Emily Doe, partly to protect her identity and partly to rid herself of labels. She didn't want people to know that she was the woman who had been described by defence lawyers as an intoxicated, unconscious 'body' found by a dumpster, while her attacker, Brock Turner, was being commended for his athletic achievements. 'My pain was never more valuable than his potential,' she writes in her memoir. In the end, a jury found Turner guilty of three charges: sexually assaulting an intoxicated victim, sexually assaulting an unconscious victim and attempting to rape her. He served just three months in prison and at no point demonstrated contrition, regret or remorse.

At the sentencing hearing in court, 'Doe' addressed Brock Turner, reading her impact statement directly to him and beginning with the unswervingly plainspoken words: 'You don't know me, but you've been inside me, and that's why we're here today.' Horrified by the short prison sentence Turner received, she was then prompted to release her full impact statement for the world to see. It was published on Buzzfeed and immediately went viral, gaining 11 million views in four days.

Only in the process of writing *Know My Name* did 'Doe' reclaim her real name to tell her story. The secrecy of maintaining two separate identities had become an exhausting burden which she no longer was prepared to carry for the sake of anonymity. And so it was that in 2019 Emily Doe became Chanel Miller. As I listened to the *Woman's Hour* programme, I heard Miller speak passionately about wanting to use her story to help others. She presented herself as a survivor with a purpose who knew that the more she spoke out, the more she would be seen, and the more she was seen the more this would encourage other survivors to either speak out themselves or at least be able to rest in the knowledge that she was speaking for them.

Throughout the trial Miller's assailant dismissed and minimised what he had done. 'Erasure is a form of oppression,' she said in the BBC interview, referring to the fact that Turner has never claimed responsibility for his actions. She appealed, as if directly to him through the air waves: 'I encourage him to learn and one day understand what he did, and to step out of privilege.' Privilege, she said, meant never having to examine your own actions or the effect they have on other people.

In her memoir, Miller describes times of titanic rage, but in her contemplations on hope and resilience she concludes, 'revenge is a tiny engine' and she seems to find room for forgiveness. This is not the kind of forgiving made feasible through apology or reconciliation but forgiveness as a desire for the burden to somehow be lighter. In *Know My Name* she writes: 'From grief confidence has grown; from anger stemmed purpose. To tuck them away would mean to neglect the most valuable tools this experience has given me. If you've worried if I've forgiven him I can only say that hate is a heavy thing to carry, takes up too much space inside the self. It's true that I'll never stop hoping that he learns. If we don't learn what is life for? If I've forgiven him it's not because I'm holy. It's because I need to clear a space inside myself where hard feelings can be put to rest.'

In her BBC podcast *The Flipside*, the journalist and campaigner Paris Lees says something similar: 'Someone made me very unhappy growing up. They never apologised or sought my forgiveness but a few years ago I realised that my deep yearning for revenge was actually making me feel really bad and that needing that person to apologise, in order for me to forgive them, was actually giving them more power over me today because my ability to move on depended on something I wanted them to do. And I thought, *I don't need you to be sorry or to acknowledge what you've done, I can forgive you anyway*, and that was incredibly empowering.'[8]

While forgiving your enemy may make you feel better, it's not always a popular choice with those around you. Therefore, in facing the possibility of being ostracised by friends and family, forgiveness can become intensely private. Sometimes it is held so close to the chest that it might only be observed through a small conciliatory gesture or a gentle word of reassurance. But forgiveness can also be spoken out loud and shared widely to the point that it becomes a public act of resistance, as in the case of Eva Kor and even Figen Murray.

Four weeks after 29-year-old Martyn Hett was killed in the 2017 Manchester Arena bombing, his mother, Figen Murray, was on national television talking about forgiveness. It was a statement that she needed people to hear. The attack that killed twenty-two people, including many children, had been caused because of a terrible lack of tolerance and compassion, she said. Thus, the only way she knew of shifting this dynamic in a positive direction was by demonstrating the very values and principles that had been so lacking when her son was killed.

The first time I spoke to Figen it was in the spring of 2021 when the Independent Public Inquiry into the Manchester Arena attack was well under way. Figen was attending court every day, at the same time as campaigning for Martyn's Law – a piece of suggested legislation to ensure that security in public venues becomes mandatory. She explained to me that she had forgiven the suicide bomber because she profoundly believed that the cycle of hate had to be broken. Also, being able to step back from the trauma of what had happened had helped her see the larger picture, and this in turn had prevented her heart from being completely overwhelmed by darkness. After the bombing she had also embarked on a masters' degree in counter-terrorism because she said she needed to put meaning into the tragedy. Part of this finding meaning was trying to understand how it was possible that people who came from loving families and had loving relationships could possibly come to believe that killing children was the right thing to do. 'I also forgave because Martyn was such an open-hearted person and he wouldn't have liked me to become immersed in anger or bitterness,' she said.

The realisation that she had to forgive didn't come immediately.

In the days after the attack, shock and anguish were followed by quiet acceptance – but not forgiveness. She had actually always considered forgiveness a rather lame concept that seemed to suggest people got away with things. What changed for her was seeing a photograph in the *Guardian* newspaper four weeks after the Manchester bombing. The story covered another terror attack that had just taken place in London at the Finsbury Park Mosque. A man had driven his van into pedestrians, killing one person and injuring ten others. The man had then run from the vehicle but fallen as an angry mob tried to surround him. The photograph showed what happened next – a human chain had been formed around the far-right attacker by an imam and four other worshippers. 'In all that chaos, in all that confusion and terror, these five men had decided without having time to communicate to link arms and protect him,' said Figen. This potent depiction of compassion stayed with her all day and seemed to soothe her grief. By the evening she had made up her mind that she had to forgive and that she would say so publicly.

Forgiveness has both saved and isolated Figen. Originally when she announced her forgiveness it was met with some resistance. Her husband stood by her but didn't feel the same way, some of her other children disagreed with her, and not surprisingly she was slated by trolls on social media. Although her family have now come to support her position and the trolls have mostly quietened, she wrote to me during the independent inquiry about the sense of separation she was still experiencing. 'I feel very much the odd one out at court sitting with the other bereaved families as I sense their bewilderment about my forgiveness. So many people don't get me, I'm afraid. I often fear that people see me as naive and soft but I am neither. I thought about it very deep and hard and long and I know for me, personally, it was the right decision to make.'

Many people who seek to draw a line under the dogma of vengeance find themselves in this problematic and isolated place where promoting compassion can be seen as an act of betrayal. Ivan Humble is a former member of the English Defence League (EDL), who has spoken frankly about his feelings of displacement after leaving the far-right movement that for so long had given him a sense of belonging. Yet his Twitter handle @NewDayStarts indicates this is a man who has remade himself by embracing a way of being that he would previously have denounced.

I first met Ivan on an overcast September morning in one of London's most popular communal garden squares. It was the day after he had given a talk to a group of trainers on a programme aiming to identify young people vulnerable to radicalisation. I had already watched a number of videos about Ivan on the internet which told of how his racist views had been formulated, cemented, and eventually undermined. I was intrigued to meet this impassioned anti-hate campaigner, who with his soft voice and guarded interior was now carefully treading a new path. Having found a quiet spot to sit down with our mugs of tea, Ivan started to tell me how he had been drawn into the far-right movement. It was 10 March 2009 and radical Islamic preacher Anjem Choudary, along with eight other Muslims from a splinter group of the banned extremist organisation al-Muhajiroun, had interrupted a homecoming parade of troops in Luton. As soldiers from the Royal Anglian Regiment paraded through the town, Choudary and his supporters yelled 'Terrorists!' at them and held up placards with the words 'Anglian soldiers go to hell' and 'Butchers of Basra'. The police were out in force to protect Choudary and Ivan watched in disbelief as two members of the public protesting against the preacher were arrested. It was no surprise to him that the EDL was formed that day. Within weeks Ivan had volunteered to be the admin person for the group's webpage.

'As a single dad – lonely, depressed and self-medicating on cannabis – social media quickly became my social life and the EDL my community,' he explained. 'I had finally found a sense of belonging, although I'm afraid to say that my children suffered because I was online night and day. I was totally obsessed, working my way up the ranks of admin to regional organiser for East Anglia.'

In 2010, Ivan organised an EDL demo in Peterborough. By now he had stereotyped all Muslims as being radical extremists like Choudary and so when the community mosque used a local newspaper to reach out and invite the EDL to have a conversation with them, he was surprised. Convinced that some kind of trap was being laid, Ivan and his colleagues ignored the request. However, it planted a seed in Ivan's head. 'Why did they want to talk to us,' he wondered, 'after we'd gone there saying terrible things and terrorising the Muslim community?'

A few months later Ivan was in a neighbouring town taking his two children Christmas shopping when something else happened to shift his perspective. While he was waiting for his daughter in the shopping centre, he spotted two Muslim women wearing hijabs walking up the stairs. Never having been so close to Muslims before, he followed them up two flights to a prayer room where immediately a Muslim man came out to greet him. Ivan nervously blurted out that he was a member of the EDL and had come up to see what was going on. 'I was expecting (perhaps even wanting) conflict but instead this man – a white Muslim convert called Khalil – gave me a hug and said, "Fantastic, I've been wanting to meet someone from the EDL for a long time."'

The response was disarming, and left Ivan floundering for something convincing to say. Instead, he agreed to return the following day to talk with Khalil. In fact, there followed a further nineteen meetings over the next six months during which Khalil gave Ivan repeated opportunities to challenge and test his faith until finally Ivan capitulated, realising that Khalil's Islam, which was both compassionate and peace-loving, was quite different from the Islam of Anjem Choudary. Not long after this conversation, Ivan met another Muslim called Manwar Ali, who also went on to have a great influence over him. Manwar is a scholar and a former pioneer of violent Jihad in Afghanistan, who was now living in Ipswich having dedicated the remainder of his life to deepening his understanding of Islam and rejecting radicalisation and extremism. Manwar had come to Ivan's attention because he had recently bought an abandoned church and it was rumoured that he was going to convert it into a mosque. A protest was being organised by the East Anglian division of the EDL but Ivan made the decision that first he must meet the Muslim scholar to tell him that the people of Ipswich did not want his mosque.

When the two men met, Manwar immediately reassured Ivan that the church was not going to be converted into a mosque, but rather into a centre for the entire community, no matter what their faith. This was the beginning of Ivan's second sustained dialogue with a Muslim, and when in 2012 Ivan's sister died, followed six months later by the death of his father, it wasn't his EDL family who were there for him but his new friend Manwar. 'I began to think that my hate might be misguided,' he told me. 'But then something really bad happened – Lee Rigby was murdered.'

On the afternoon of 22 May 2013, a British army soldier, Fusilier Lee Rigby, was attacked and killed by Islamist extremists Michael Adebolajo and Michael Adebowale near the Royal Artillery Barracks in Woolwich, south-east London. Rigby had been off duty that day when the two men ran him over in their car. Adebolajo and Adebowale then jumped out onto the road and in front of horrified passers-by proceeded to use knives and a cleaver to hack the off-duty soldier to death. With their grim deed accomplished, they calmly announced to the horrified onlookers that they were waging war in the name of Islam and that they had killed Rigby to avenge the killing of innocent Muslims by the British armed forces in Afghanistan and Iraq.

This was the kind of incident that could have easily jeopardised Ivan's slow but steady pull away from the far-right. However, perhaps sensing this, both Manwar and Khalil rang him the following day to apologise for what had happened in Woolwich, adamant that the killers did not represent true Islam. By now Ivan had heard enough through his conversations with both men to know this must be true. But there was something else playing out in his mind as well:

> After Lee Rigby's death there was a big surge in support for the EDL and hate crimes against Muslims increased. I couldn't help but wonder if some of the perpetrators were members who I'd recruited and radicalised. Silent walks were being organised by the EDL across the country in support of Lee Rigby and so I asked Manwar if he'd take the risk to walk with me. He agreed. As I went to meet him that day I saw his daughter, and then his wife, followed by twenty-five other Muslims. His daughter held a big box of roses and was handing them out to people. It was very emotional. I received a lot of praise that day for reaching out, but Manwar got attacked by some groups within his community who viewed him as a traitor. Suddenly I was hit by immense guilt for my part in all this. How could I hate Muslims when I'd been welcomed by so many of them?

The realisation hit hard. In January 2014, feeling by now disappointed and starting to get disillusioned with the EDL, Ivan opened up his laptop one day and posted on the group's website page: 'I'm done. I'm out.' Just as victims of terrorism are vilified for not hating their terrorists, the same is true of those who decide to quit hate groups. From the moment Ivan Humble left the EDL, he found himself the target of vicious criticism. 'That was when I changed from being the hater to the hated,' he said. 'I was accused of being a Muslim convert and a Muslim lover. I understand why people hate me. Hate is fear of the unknown and I've stirred up something and given them conflict in their minds.'

These days Ivan's life has taken a new direction. Determined to challenge violent extremism and build bridges between hostile communities, he travels the length and breadth of the country (often with his teenage daughter by his side) to attend public speaking events and lead training workshops, which have in time provided him with an entirely new and unexpected place of belonging and sense of meaning. 'Hate always hurts the hater the most,' says Ivan. 'Since leaving the EDL I've been meeting with Muslim communities and trying to sort out the misconceptions that my misguided hate led me to. Even though it's been tough for both me and my children, it's much more rewarding doing things this way than standing on the street shouting abuse at someone.'

So many of the survivor narratives I've collected and shared through The Forgiveness Project highlight shame, silence and secrecy as reactions to trauma. This brings to mind the prescient words of the American author and anthropologist Zora Neale Hurston, from her autobiography *Dust Tracks on a Road*: 'There is no agony like bearing an untold story inside you.' I like to think that one of the services that The Forgiveness Project has provided over the years is to give a voice to the silenced by creating spaces and platforms through which to share these untold stories.

Scottish stand-up comedian Billy Connolly, speaking to RTÉ Radio in Ireland, demonstrated the relief felt by victims when others bear witness to episodes of trauma and shame. Referring to the abuse he had suffered by his alcoholic father between the ages of ten and fifteen, he said, 'I got rid of it by talking about it. I just unleashed it on the public and it's theirs to deal with now. I'm glad I did.' The comedian's abuse was first revealed in a biography written by his wife Pamela Stephenson in 2001, some years after his father had died. But it wasn't until twelve years after that that he first talked openly about how the only way he'd found to live with the historic abuse was to forgive his father. In 2013, in an interview with the BBC, Connolly told reporter Kirsty Wark that sexual abuse was 'a very odd affair ... Mine is very, very typical – you don't tell anybody about it. Everybody wonders why people who are abused don't rush off to the police or the authorities or an aunt or an uncle and tell them. But it just doesn't happen because you feel you've taken part in it.' He also acknowledged to Wark that the abuse hadn't stopped him from loving his father, even though for years he shouldered the guilt and shame. 'I loved him, and I kept loving him, and I love him today. And you know, forgiveness is a great thing – the power of forgiveness is immense, and you can forgive dead people as well.'[9]

Like Connolly, one of The Forgiveness Project storytellers, Geoff Thompson, has experienced the same suffocating prison of shame following abuse, as well as the same deep sense of freedom after being able to share what happened and ultimately forgive his abuser. Having been sexually assaulted by a trusted adult at the age of eleven, Geoff often says it was the grooming that damaged him more than the abuse itself, leaving him with feelings of shame and self-disgust. As the years passed and he endured debilitating bouts of depression, his anger turned inwards. It was only when he got a job as a bouncer that he managed to find some physical outlet for his rage. But, he says, his yearning to fight threatened to turn him into a 'monster' until training in the martial arts unexpectedly led him down a different path.

It was at this point that he embarked on what he has described as an 'internal inquiry', challenging his shame, his self-abuse and all the negative beliefs about himself that were making him so unhappy. At this point he started to explore his fears by writing about the abuse, and having utilised the power of self-expression he began to exorcise his rage; the big realisation being that while he longed to reclaim the pure place of his childhood he'd never get it back through vengeance or violence. In other words, his abuser could only be defeated with compassion.

Geoff explains exactly how he came to meet and forgive his abuser and what that meant to him in terms of the reciprocal nature of human engagement.

One day I just found myself confronted with this guy as I was in a McDonald's. As soon as I saw him, I knew innately that if I was physical with him in any way, I would entangle myself more. I would create more reciprocity because whatever was in him would be fed by my rage and whatever was in me would also be fed by it. I suddenly saw that I was being given the chance to have a conversation. I had built this carapace, this armoury around this very wounded, insecure child and when I saw him that eleven-year-old was evident again. So, climbing out of that McDonald's chair was like climbing out of a dugout and going across no man's land; it felt like life and death to me, but I knew that if I walked away, I would lose a vital opportunity.

By this time in my life I'd completely disfigured myself. I had been a pretty boy, very androgynous, but after the abuse I'd put myself into a place where I had got a broken nose and cauliflower ears. I was very heavy. I kind of disfigured myself unconsciously to get rid of all the prettiness and now, as I stood in front of him, I said, 'You won't recognise me but you abused me and you need to know that I forgive you,' and I told him it twice. I had to really affirm it, once for him and once for me. Then I watched him dissolve in front of me. I watched his power dissipate as I forgave him.

4

THE OIL OF PERSONAL RELATIONSHIPS

'All friendships of any length are based on a
continued, mutual forgiveness.'

DAVID WHYTE

Karsten Mathiasen is a Danish storyteller and circus performer who views life as a series of lessons. The 'catastrophe', he tells me, happened many years ago when he was a young father and had taken his Icelandic pony to the western peninsular of Jutland to learn some new tricks from a famous horse trainer. On the last afternoon before returning home to Zeeland, as Karsten and the trainer turned on the television to catch up with the news, they watched in horror as the Twin Towers of the World Trade Center collapsed nearly 4,000 miles away. 'Little did I know,' says Karsten, 'that my own life was also about to collapse.'

The nature of Karsten's catastrophe can't be compared to the horrifying public spectacle of what happened in America's worst terror attack, but in relation to Karsten's private life it was a devastating body blow. When he arrived home his wife told him that she had fallen in love with another man, who she now intended to see at least once a week. Wanting to make everything seem normal for the sake of his young son and daughter, he went along with what his wife wanted, but in private he cried bitterly.

Karsten recounts his story with the purpose and precision you'd expect from a storyteller, shaping his experience into a kind of fable with a strong narrative arc and a persuasive moral ending. He continues: 'One day, my wife said, "Do you want to hear the truth?" "No!" I answered, because I knew I couldn't stand to hear it. Things then got worse, and at Christmas we had to tell the kids that their mother was leaving. I have never heard children cry in such a heart-breaking way.'

Later, when Karsten told his closest neighbours about the impending divorce, they shared a little of their wisdom with him. They told him they knew of two couples who had got divorced. The first couple separated peacefully and became like a big family with their new partners and bonus kids. The other couple quarrelled about everything and lost a lot of money by taking legal action and had remained bitter enemies ever since. Karsten was in no doubt which was the better way to behave. He desperately wanted to swallow up the hurt for his children's sake. However, peaceable action doesn't always follow good intentions and in the coming months his sorrow soon turned to rage.

This rage wasn't directed against his wife, but at her new man, Torben. The magnitude of his feelings shocked him and when he found himself fantasising about killing Torben he decided to ask for help. 'So, I contacted a psychiatrist about these murderous thoughts,' he says. 'He advised me to roll a blanket together and beat it with a stick, imagining I was beating Torben. But my desire to harm Torben grew. I wanted to really frighten him, and so one day I telephoned Torben and told him I wanted to kill him. He was very silent down the telephone. Eventually I hung up but the following week I telephoned him again to say, "I won't kill you, but I feel like tearing one of your arms off!"'

Karsten's revenge fantasies continued for several weeks until one day his children came back from visiting their mother to tell him that actually Torben was a really nice guy. Knowing that his vindictive crusade would only ever divide the family, Karsten tried once more to overcome his vengeful instincts. 'A week later I phoned Torben again,' he says, 'and this time I told him, "I won't harm you, but I'd love to come to your office and smash your computer with an axe." I imagined this with great pleasure.'

Still, Torben said very little. There is something to be learnt here about how personal relationships can be reconstructed when the person being subjected to an onslaught of abuse is not drawn into it but rather remains attentive and patient. Because Torben did not react aggressively but instead listened to Karsten's anguish, eventually the dynamic shifted and Karsten's anger started to fade until finally he was able to pick up a pen and paper and write to his rival, promising he wouldn't bother him again. It was a truce, but not yet peace.

Then, once again, his children prompted him to think anew. It was the week leading up to Thanksgiving, and Karsten's daughter had started worrying that the whole family would not be celebrating together that year. Karsten understood how important this was for her and therefore realised he now had to do something radical. So, he picked up the phone and dialled Torben's number – this time with an invitation to meet him for a coffee in Copenhagen. Karsten was the first to arrive. 'When I saw this man come through the door, I found him handsome and friendly,' he recalls. 'He had a gypsy-like appearance, which I liked and I knew from that moment on that we would become friends. Later at the Thanksgiving party we sat together and had a good conversation. Next, I invited Torben to come to a garden party for my daughter's birthday. Not only did he come, but he even brought his mother. That was a good way to start creating a bigger family.'

When Karsten's neighbours heard about this sudden and

unexpected rapprochement they offered some more wise counsel, reminding Karsten that 'he who conquers himself is greater than he who conquers a town.' It marked the start of a close friendship between Karsten and Torben which was to last for many years.

Like all real stories, this one doesn't have just one ending. Some years later, Karsten was walking with his daughter in the woods when he noticed she was angry. When he asked her what was wrong, she told him she had recently asked her mother why she had fallen in love with another man and her mother had revealed that when the children were still very young their father had had a relationship with another woman, and because of this she had vowed not to hold back if she ever had the chance to follow her heart. Standing there now in the woods, Karsten's daughter turned to him, visibly upset, and asked, 'How could you betray me, a little child, just one year old?'

The memory still stings. 'This came like a hammer blow,' he says. 'I suddenly realised how much of a skeleton in the cupboard this old love affair of mine had been, even if my wife seemed to have forgiven me. How could I explain to a seventeen-year-old girl what lunacy can possess a man! We kept walking in silence. Then I asked, "Can you forgive me?" And she replied, "Yes", and we walked home hand in hand. At first, I thought I was the great forgiver, but in the end, I was the one to ask for forgiveness.'

Karsten's story explains exactly why I'm involved in forgiveness work. It beautifully illustrates the possibility of finding renewal in the dimmest of places, proof if you like that love can grow from hate and that kindness can ease bitterness. From the vantage point of middle age, Karsten now surveys his family story with deep gratitude: 'We lived in peace with our extended family until Torben developed cancer. It was so hard to see this good and wise man shrink and fade away. At his deathbed, as Torben was lying with his eyes closed and not able to speak, I sat holding his hand in mine and told him a story about forgiveness between a father and his son. I knew Torben had had a troubled relationship with his father. After the story, he squeezed my hand. That was the last time I saw him. I have to admit that when he went out of my world, I cried the way I did when he came into it.'

There is much to learn from this story, if for no other reason than it's not clear-cut. Karsten is 'the great forgiver' but also he is a father who must ask for forgiveness; some might view Torben as a 'home wrecker' but he is also the archetypal peacemaker. The story shows how important it is to express vulnerability if we want to heal ourselves and mend fractured relationships; it also illustrates how easily wounds get passed down through families, and how revenge fantasies can be both overwhelming and transmutable. Karsten's story reminds me of what South African Ginn Fourie says of her relationship with Letlapa Mphahlele, the man who ordered the terror attack which killed her daughter: 'Vulnerable feelings, when expressed to other people, have the potential to establish lasting bonds.'

Just as with the bigger and more extreme stories The Forgiveness Project has collected, forgiveness in daily life is an extraordinarily useful tool that has the ability to repair broken relationships and mend broken hearts. Families are fragile and if we are unable to even consider applying a forgiving lens to a personal conflict, then it's likely to lead to relationship breakdowns and family estrangements. Talk to just about anyone and you will probably discover a multitude of unresolved hurts that fester within families, or grievances that have ripped friendships apart.

I'm referring here to what C. S. Lewis described as 'the incessant provocations of daily life'; when we fall out with people who we care about – our friends and relatives who may have been in our lives for years, people we've loved and laughed with, sometimes married, our life-long friends, our close colleagues. I have lost count of the terrible stories I've heard about family members estranged from each other. Of course, this is not the same deep anguish suffered by people like Wilma Derksen or Figen Murray, but nevertheless it produces a different kind of carnage.

I was recently sitting in a small café in the pretty harbour town of Conwy in North Wales. At the table next to me sat two elderly men, clearly close friends. I was alone and it was impossible not to overhear much of their conversation. After a while I noticed one of them craning their neck looking out of the window. 'That's my granddaughter,' he said, pointing at a young woman pushing a buggy. I expected him to get up and call her name, but he didn't and she passed by. 'So you don't speak to her because of her mother?' I heard his friend ask. 'That's right, and I don't even know if the baby is a boy or a girl,' came the reply. There was silence and I looked away, but I could see that both men were visibly upset. It struck me then that while this intimate moment was incredibly sad, it was also incredibly common – just one more example of a family split apart, something that happens in every corner of every country in the world.

Just sitting here now, and without having to think too hard, my mind easily jumps to three similar stories. None of these people are friends of mine but all are known to me. In one case, a bitter divorce has led a husband and wife to drag their four teenage children into their conflict. The children have now been drawn so far in that they have been forced to take sides. Two of the children have sided with their father, while the other two have sided with their mother. Despite living in the same Cornish village, neither faction speaks to each other any longer and any thought of reconciliation looks increasingly unlikely.

Another similar example is of two sisters who ran a business together along with both of their husbands for nearly twenty years. The two families lived close by; their lives were interlocked and deeply connected. The five cousins shared parties, holidays and school friends. But when the business hit hard times, problems arose around finances and the husbands blamed each other. Nowadays the two families no longer speak. The grandparents have been left distraught, heartbroken to see their once harmonious family fall apart so spectacularly.

The final example involves a 53-year-old woman whose elderly mother died two years ago and who has fallen out with her brother because of issues to do with the lasting power of attorney and their mother's will. Her brother's children, all in their thirties, have written their aunt angry letters accusing her of stealing money, but she maintains the money was always meant for her. The woman, who is single and has no children of her own, now has no extended family either.

In each of these three cases, family members hold parallel perspectives often poles apart, and the chance of finding peace in the tug of war of who is right and who is wrong feels as remote as solving the intractable conflicts of the Middle East. None of these examples probably sound that unusual. I am sure most people will be able to think of their own. Some may even have experienced the sudden severing of a relationship themselves, whether self-driven or forced upon them.

I don't even remember exactly what went wrong between me and Robert, one of my closest friends from university. And even if I could remember, it wouldn't help to explain anything any better. The only thing that I know for certain is that I did or said something that caused him distress and much consternation. In a nutshell, he felt betrayed by me and, as a result, from one day to the next he cut off any communication. I knew he had had other friends whom he'd eliminated from his life – just as you might sever a dead branch from a tree – but naively I didn't expect it to happen to me. We had become very close friends over a period of years. He had stayed at my house, sleeping on the sofa bed in my sitting room on numerous occasions whenever he came from Scotland to visit London. He got on well with my three children, would drink beers late into the night with my husband and we even all went on holiday together. So, it tore me up to suddenly have no contact with him as well as no explanation as to what had gone wrong. I berated myself for having been stupid, insensitive, or disloyal.

I very much relate to what the author and philosopher Alain de Botton wrote on Twitter a few years ago when he came up with an imaginative remedy to solving these kinds of misunderstandings. 'Once a year, grudges should be disclosed without shame to resolve the horror of people one has upset without meaning to,' he suggested. It is maddening and perplexing when you've wronged someone, and they won't accept your apology, and in particular when you don't know what you've done wrong, and can't have any dialogue. No matter how many times I said sorry to Robert, my words of regret were ignored. As a result, I started to feel less sorry and increasingly resentful. Every now and again, as the months became years, I'd imagine he must be over it by now and send off another friendly text or postcard. I had always believed I could resolve any personal conflict, reconcile with any friend, and I was eager to make amends.

The problem was that the harder I tried to redeem myself the more my attempts became a kind of grovelling humiliation as I handed all the power over to him. In the end, and only after several years, did I learn to let go completely. This meant first giving up attempting to repent, then accepting that the friendship was over, and eventually ceasing to care. The simple learning for me here was that people have the right to change their minds about who they want to stay close to. It was a weird kind of forgiveness I felt for Robert – if indeed it was forgiveness at all – but certainly I let go of all my angry upset feelings about having been so unceremoniously disposed of by a friend without any opportunity for dialogue. Whether Robert has forgiven me, however, is a whole other matter. I think probably not, and I suspect that, unlike me, he can remember every last detail of whatever my crime was.

Forgiveness is difficult for people who are at loggerheads, unwilling to compromise, move on or forget. Psychotherapist Ben Fuchs explains that for some people, forgiving and letting go of a grudge 'can be very unattractive because it means giving up a hard-won sense of power ... It also means giving up the moral high ground that comes from identifying myself as the person betrayed and you as the betrayer.' The particularly difficult nature of these intractable conflicts is that both parties so often feel they are equally 'right', equally justified, and equally hard done by.

It seems that within the maelstrom of human relationships it is often harder to forgive the smaller wrongs of loved ones than the greater wrongs of strangers. Perhaps this isn't surprising since love is only ever half a step away from hate and any serious conflict with people who we care about is likely to involve accusations of betrayal, rejection, favouritism or unfairness. This in turn is likely to leave us feeling raw and tender, exposing old wounds or creating new ones. And if we feel wronged or betrayed, we all too easily don the armour of moral indignation to protect ourselves. Hardened positions are then adopted, and lines drawn, with the ultimate punishment being to act as if the other person doesn't exist. Rather than edging forward with vulnerability to find common ground, both parties hold their positions firm, taking comfort in nursing their festering wounds.

When someone is caught in the middle of such a heated battle – whether between warring nations or squabbling siblings – it's best to let indignation and righteous anger have their day. Forgiveness doesn't thrive when you are hell-bent on survival or determined to triumph at all costs. As we've seen, a season of anger is important because it helps the wounded build resilience and is an essential part of the recovery process. What is clear is that if you are deeply hurt or overwhelmed by sadness, any talk of forgiving may not be helpful but rather may be a trigger to tip you straight back into rage.

Once someone has been hurt within what was once a loving relationship, they will often do everything in their power to get even. I have witnessed a number of errant spouses punished so heavily and relentlessly by their deceived partners that it is these vengeful impulses which in the end destroy the marriage more than the infidelity itself. I don't want to minimise the hurt that betrayal causes, the chasm of pain that it creates, the shattering of a world that once seemed so safe and secure, but anyone who has lived a few decades will know that life is full of unwelcome surprises and people are unpredictable. As Ben Fuchs writes, 'We grow up with the myths about life: of romance, dreams of how relationships should be but ... reality is very different, bringing a betrayal of the myth.'[1]

Forgiveness unquestionably helps us to navigate this disarray because developing a more forgiving mindset can also help create a chink in our adversary's armour, which, eventually, potentially, can lead to a change of heart. But what is a forgiving mindset? If someone is feeling sad, angry or disappointed by someone else's behaviour, a forgiving mindset might mean adopting a worldview that accepts that while people may have diametrically opposed opinions to your own this doesn't make them bad or wrong. Having a forgiving mindset will mean you feel the anger and hurt but somehow will be able to respond out of compassion rather than rage. It will mean blame isn't your default position, you'll be able to act from a nuanced place, have an adaptable mind and move beyond your own hurt feelings to embrace the hurt feelings of others. It means imagining what it is like to be someone other than yourself. Indeed, almost two and a half millennia ago, Plato concluded that 'The highest form of knowledge is empathy, for it requires us to suspend our egos and live in another's world.'

American psychology professor Dr Kathleen Lawler-Row had much to say on this subject. A couple of years before Lawler-Row's death in 2013, journalist Harriet Brown quoted her in a thoroughly absorbing article published on oprah.com.[2] What Lawler-Row said has struck a lasting chord with me. Reflecting on what having a forgiving disposition means, she concludes, 'You're more flexible, less black-and-white in your expectations of how life or other people will be. If there's one thing that characterizes people who have experienced forgiveness, it's that kind of larger perspective: I can't predict what life will hand me, but I'm going to respond to it in this way.'

I have never really understood the black-and-white, all-or-nothing, good-versus-bad way of looking at the world. It feels so inflexible and final. However, I also know that when a relationship becomes too malign, dangerous or toxic, the wisest thing you can do is walk away. Desmond Tutu is interesting in dispelling the commonly held belief that forgiveness means reconciliation. In a short video he made in 2014 to promote the online Tutu Global Forgiveness Challenge and *The Book of Forgiving*, co-written with his daughter Mpho Tutu van Furth, he explains, 'If someone is constantly abusing you, being ready to forgive doesn't mean you have to be a masochist. If you have had someone who repeatedly hurts you, it is far better to release the relationship than to renew it.' In other words, you can turn your back on someone and still forgive. As a key figure in South Africa's post-apartheid reconciliation movement and from his work as chairman of the Truth and Reconciliation Commission, Desmond Tutu understood more than most about the value of justice and accountability when it comes to reconciling with harm, but he also knew from the many stories of atrocity he bore witness to that choosing to forgive flows from a softening and an opening of the heart. This requires a deeply held awareness that those who have hurt us will not, or cannot, necessarily behave as we expect and want them to. Inner healing therefore requires a creative and ultimately a uniquely personal response.

As Tutu acknowledged, sometimes estrangements are necessary.

Toxic behaviour passed down the generations will just create more damaged people if preventative action isn't taken. For instance, if a mother has hurt her daughter so badly that in adulthood the daughter realises the only means to repair the damage is to block contact, both to protect herself and to protect her children, then this is probably the best form of redress. Harriet Brown's article probed this very dilemma when the author attended a workshop on learning to forgive led by forgiveness expert Dr Fred Luskin. Brown was there to report on the process, but also to try to resolve her own personal wounds from having a mother who had deeply hurt her.

This is how she describes the end of the workshop as she confronts Luskin about what to do when none of the methods to overcome her resentment towards her mother have worked – whether therapy, writing, medication, talking to her mother, or not talking to her mother.

At the afternoon break, I snag Luskin for a few minutes to pose a question: It's one thing to forgive something that's happened, that's over and done. But what if the person who hurt you in the past keeps hurting you over and over, in the present? He interrupts before I get the last words out. 'It's not happening now, this second,' he says in an offhand way. 'So try again.'

I take a breath, unclench my jaw, and pose a different question: 'How can you keep yourself safe with a difficult person?' In response, Luskin smiles – the first genuine smile I've seen from him all day. 'That's the right question,' he says, beaming. 'That gets rid of the blame and the enemy.' And keeps the focus where it belongs, on me. 'You can probably answer that question yourself,' he says.

My answer, I tell him, is to keep my distance from my mother, talking to her maybe once or twice a year. He nods encouragingly. 'Now, can you do that with an open heart?' he asks.

I sit back in my chair and consider – deeply, seriously, honestly – what that would mean: No more bitching about my mother. No more whining to friends for sympathy. No more self-pity. Thinking of my mother with as much compassion as I can muster, but not necessarily getting any closer to her. Accepting our relationship as it is rather than wishing it were different.

Forgiveness, I begin to see, is not about pretending you don't feel angry or hurt. It's about responding out of kindness rather than rage. It's about letting yourself feel the full spectrum of emotions – grief and anger and hurt, but also kindness and compassion. Even toward someone who's hurt you deeply.

Social worker Honor Rhodes has run interventions for families for over thirty-five years and understands the difficulty of using a for-giveness lens on work that deals with tangled family relationships, not least because when contemplating forgiveness there is often a tendency to cast players into roles of the wronged and the wrong-doer. She writes about this in *Forgiveness in Practice*, in a chapter entitled 'Families, Forgiving and Withholding Forgiveness'. The complexity lies in the fact that often the wronged and the wrong-doer are one and the same person. It was during her early days as a social worker in east London that Rhodes realised that issues of betrayal and disrespect, guilt and a desire for mercy were at the heart of the troubles of many families. Consequently, she began to think more seriously about the role of forgiveness and became aware that whereas everyone has experience of forgiveness, there are very few tools that can be used by professionals.

During her working life Rhodes has increasingly edged for-giveness into her work, while realising that for some families it is unattainable. Her work then focuses on what can be achieved in its absence. She writes of one such example which I think is helpful when considering how to mend and repair family ruptures if forgiveness is not an option.

'A good enough position in one family I met was the acknowledgement that a wrong had been done to them; they had been badly swindled by a trusted friend. They would never be reconciled to the betrayal and were never going to be compensated but they wanted to be able to talk about the episode without the level of rage and turmoil that had surrounded it and that had affected the children badly.' Rhodes then supported the family to manage their distress by creating a different narrative around the hurt. She helped the parents to find a 'script' or a story that could be used to explain what had happened and help them feel less broken by it. 'The act of telling their betrayal and recovery story helped reduce the pain it caused them and gave them a sense of choice and agency. This was important in helping them to imagine that in future they could trust others without being betrayed.' In this example, understanding and acceptance can stand in for the more challenging practice of forgiveness.

Forgiveness can be such a sensitive subject that I've learnt to be very careful around offering advice to anybody suffering from a broken heart. A friend once emailed me saying she had discovered her husband was having an affair. She was stunned by the revelation and was feeling betrayed and profoundly hurt. Amid describing the extent of her pain and the details of what had happened, she asked me, 'Can I ever forgive him, Marina?'

I realise now that my friend was not actually seeking my advice, and this was more of a rhetorical question, but at the time I took it at face value and weighed in, suggesting that, yes, in time she might forgive her husband. In saying this I completely misjudged the tenor and mood of her cry for help, and my words came over as careless and crass. My email hit totally the wrong note in a way that is easy to do when pinging messages across continents rather than talking face to face. My friend was upset by my reply. I apologised sincerely but soon discovered that no matter what I said I could not take back what I had written. All my friend wanted was for me to listen to her; this was no time for wise counsel or any talk of forgiveness.

The result was a cooling-off period for our friendship lasting a couple of years. In that time her brief communications were distant and intermittent. A thawing only came when we met in London where she had come for her mother's funeral. Here, finally, we were able to talk about what had happened. She apologised for freezing me out and I apologised for having been so thoughtless. Then we stood back and, while surveying the landscape of our decades-long friendship, realised it was most certainly worth salvaging. In fact, we soon built back an even closer relationship. Talking about forgiveness had got us into knots – it was *not* the conversation to have had at that time, and I should have known better. And yet, because of this misunderstanding, our friendship became more precious and more resilient – a little like the Japanese art of Kintsugi, where broken ceramics are considered more beautiful in their imperfection having been artfully repaired with plant resin and powdered gold.

For a long time while collecting testimonies for The Forgiveness Project, I tended to avoid everyday stories of grievances and grudges. I had spent fifteen years as a journalist specialising in so-called 'human interest' stories and I was frustrated by the increasingly intrusive nature of this work as editors demanded ever more personal details about people's lives. For this reason from that moment I decided to concentrate on the more extreme stories of crime, violence, genocide and terrorism. Forgiving the unforgivable became my focus because I knew that these stories had the ability to intrigue and inspire.

But even though I have largely shied away from the everyday stories of familial hurts, buried within the big forgiveness stories are smaller, more common stories of estrangements, family rifts, bullying and neighbourly disputes.

For instance, there is the case of South African-born Magdeline

Makola, who was abducted in Scotland in December 2008 when she was working as a nurse at Edinburgh Royal Infirmary. Justice Ngema kidnapped her and then locked her in the boot of her Vauxhall Astra, which he later abandoned. Ten days later she was discovered by the police, apparently within hours of her death. What I find interesting about Magdeline's story is that while she was able to forgive her kidnapper for his heinous crime, there were others closer to her – who committed far more minor transgressions – whom she was never able to forgive.

Ngema was a friend of an acquaintance, who had once knocked on her door wanting to leave his bags in her flat. She had turned him away but then late one night just before Christmas he appeared again, this time wanting a drink. Magdeline explains what happened next: 'I was very naive and let him in. A moment later he had grabbed me round the neck ... then gagged and blindfolded me. Before I knew it, he'd dragged me over his shoulders and thrown me into my car. I was terrified.' She talks about the terrible hours and then days that she lay trapped and alone in the boot of her car with no idea of where she was or whether anyone would rescue her. She lay there despising Ngema – 'finding an anger I never knew I had' – until finally she knew she must calm down in order to preserve her life. In the end, convinced now that no one would rescue her, she prayed to God; no longer consumed by anger or hatred, she determined to die peacefully.

Magdeline was rescued on Boxing Day, severely frostbitten but elated; so thankful to be alive that she could feel nothing but joy. At the trial Ngema pleaded guilty but showed no remorse, which is why this is also a story of unconditional forgiveness brought on, as Magdeline explains, because her life was saved. 'Because of the joy of being found alive, I have never again felt any hatred towards Justice Ngema, but I have felt a deep sadness. We were both South Africans in a foreign country, and we should have helped one another, like brother and sister.' She also makes the important point that just because she has forgiven Ngema doesn't mean she could ever trust him.

The reason I mention this story here is not because of Magdeline having forgiven her unrepentant kidnapper but because of how the kidnap impacted on her friendships. She told me: 'The saddest thing of all for me is that after my ordeal some of my friends seemed more interested in talking to the media than in my well-being. With one close friend in particular I have felt so betrayed and hurt. This did more damage than being locked in the boot of the car. I now have a problem with trust.'

I first met Mathew Shurka in New York City having been alerted to his story via a newspaper article that had been shared on Twitter. There was a forgiveness aspect to this story and I wanted to learn more.

Sitting in Mathew's apartment on the thirtieth floor of a Brooklyn high-rise, he told me his story, laying the pieces of his life out in front of me with the reassuring benefit of hindsight. Cool and confident in demeanour, only an occasional tremor in his voice reveals a darker history. He told me how he had grown up in the suburbs of New York in the 1990s with his parents and two sisters as part of a close-knit Jewish family. They weren't particularly religious but every Friday there would be at least thirty people for Shabbat and Mathew never missed a single one. In his teens, as his sexuality began to emerge, he found himself attracted to other boys but was terrified of admitting this to anyone, let alone himself. So determined was he not to be gay, that he was willing to do anything to prove his masculinity, and when friends used words like 'gay' or 'faggot', he joined in enthusiastically. However, being part of the in-group came at a price, as denying the person he was increasingly becoming caused growing inner torment. In time these feelings became so overwhelming that finally, aged sixteen, Mathew decided to come out as gay to his father. It was a cry for help, and he assumed that once he'd told his father he would have navigated the biggest hurdle of his life. However, it didn't quite work out like that. Mathew said, 'At first I was relieved by his response. He said, "I love you no matter what, and I'm going to support you." But my father had his own fears of what it meant to have an openly gay son, and he arranged for me to see a therapist, a university professor who told me there was no such thing as homosexuality and that I had the option to have the same feelings for girls as I had for boys. It was the start of five years of conversion therapy. I was convinced by now that I was psychologically damaged and so turning straight became a matter of life and death for me.'

Also known as 'reparative therapy' or even the 'gay cure', the term conversion therapy describes a range of practices designed to attempt to change, suppress or divert a person's sexual orientation and reduce same-sex attraction. While some, mainly religious, people still hold by the theory, it has been widely discredited, with multiple medical associations and experts condemning the practice and attesting that LGBTQ identities are not diseases to be cured, 'changed' or eradicated by psychological therapies.[3]

For Mathew, the specific treatment he underwent was particularly cruel. He was told that because he was young there was a good chance he could be cured and therefore he must separate himself from his mother and two sisters, which meant that while they still lived in the same house, he wasn't allowed to have any interaction with them in case he picked up feminine mannerisms. He was told to get a girlfriend and to spend as much time as possible with the other boys at school in order to encourage 'healthy' male bonding. When he struggled with intimacy with his girlfriend, he was prescribed Viagra. Mathew's mother reluctantly went along with what the therapist said because she too believed the advice of an expert. This malpractice lasted for five years, during which time home no longer felt like a safe and loving place for Mathew, who became convinced that if he was ever to lead a happy and healthy life he must completely smother his homosexual impulses. 'I became the police officer in my own home, which meant whenever my mother tried to talk to me, I'd insist, "Don't ruin this, I'm trying so hard!"'

As Mathew grew older, his confusion and resentment increased. He noticed his parents weren't getting along so well now; it was as if his conversion therapy had shone a light on the flaws of their marriage. By the time he graduated from high school he was experiencing extreme anxiety and having suicidal thoughts. Finally, something snapped, and the part of him that was trying to crush his true identity could no longer uphold the façade. And so, at the age of twenty-one, exhausted, Mathew found the courage to leave conversion therapy and to start leading his life as a gay man. By now his mother had seen the damage it was doing to her son and, having separated from her husband, fully supported Mathew in his coming out. But then, as so often happens when families are brittle, new lines were drawn and fresh battlegrounds surfaced. As Mathew explained: 'The year that my mother and father began their divorce I took the side of my mother. They were arguing over family assets which were in my name. So, I drew up my own lawsuit against my father. I wanted revenge and would have done anything to hurt him. During this time my father moved back to his native Israel; I wasn't sure if I'd ever see him again.'

Even though by now Mathew had come out to friends and family, there was still a part of him that believed he had failed because the therapy hadn't worked. His self-esteem was in tatters; he slept fitfully and was restless in every aspect of his life. It took another four years with help from a psychotherapist to undo the damage and get him back to how he had felt before the conversion therapy. Later, through the personal and professional development training programme the Landmark Forum, Mathew began to find his sense of self, coming finally to the realisation that there was nothing about him that needed fixing or curing. In 2014 he launched a campaign called Born Perfect, a survivor-led national movement working with legal experts to pass legislation outlawing conversion therapy and end the harm it was doing to LGBTQ youth and their families.

But the story doesn't end there. Part of the Landmark's programme is to encourage participants to make amends where conflict has torn relationships apart. Encouraged by this emphasis on finding resolution, in 2012 Mathew decided to take a calculated risk. The first thing he did was buy a plane ticket to Tel Aviv. After that, he contacted his father to tell him that he was on his way to visit. They hadn't spoken for five years. Matthew told me what happened next:

> That first evening I was in Israel we went out to a restaurant and after the meal my father suggested we went for a walk. Since we hadn't spoken in five years he didn't know if I had continued conversion therapy or if I was now openly gay. He asked if I had come out. I replied, 'I've met inspiring role models, received lots of love and support, and yes, Dad, I'm out.' In that moment he went right back to the position he'd always taken. 'It's a mistake. You'll get hurt,' he said. My first reaction was to be angry, but this time I just listened. He rambled on for ten minutes, giving the same speech I'd heard so often. For the first time I could see he was begging me to save my life. In the past I'd always perceived him as this horrible man who didn't understand or care for me, but now I just saw a father who loved his son. So I kept calm and when he'd finished I hugged him and kissed him on the cheek. Then I looked him in the eyes and said, 'Don't worry, Dad. There's nothing to worry about. I know what the world is, and who I am, and I promise you I will take it as it

comes and I will live a beautiful life.' My father looked at me, stunned, and then just said, 'OK.'

Mathew was twenty-four when he got his father back and ever since then they have reconstructed a tender and loving relationship. Forgiving his father helped to shift the last residue of stress he felt about his sexuality, even to the extent that he now was able to get a full night's sleep. 'I wasn't present in my life for all those years when I was angry with my father,' he said. 'Being angry is exhausting and time-consuming – it took me away from what really mattered to me, pursuing my dreams and living a life that I love.'

Mathew's story is an example of how forgiving a family member requires walking into hostile territory and seeing the world from another's point of view. There is no doubt that this is incredibly difficult, especially when a relationship has broken down or been eroded through distance or disapproval over the years. Relationships with parents are so often fraught with sadness and disappointment that forgiveness is a frequent preoccupation. I was very struck by what the French composer and music producer Jean-Michel Jarre said in an interview titled 'Letter to My Younger Self' in the *Big Issue* magazine in 2018.[4] He was describing his fractured relationship with his film composer father, whom he had never known well. This was largely because when he was five his parents had divorced, and his father went to live in America. He saw him rarely after that and as he entered his teenage years the separation cemented: 'For a teenager it's very difficult . . . if you're in open conflict with your dad you have someone to rebel against and that can be good. When you have nobody it's like a black hole. It's very difficult to go through it and I really suffered quite a lot about that. I carried a sense of melancholia because of his absence.'

Years later, Jarre came to terms with his impaired relationship with his father, able to make peace with the pain of not feeling loved. What he describes is both unfamiliar and unexpected:

'These days I'm really cool about how it went with my father. Now I think, we only have one father and one mother and no matter what they have done to you, you have to accept it and stop questioning it and stop suffering. He probably had a handicap in his heart which came from his own parents. I understand that. And he was not able to express love. That was sad for him. When he passed away I stood in front of his dead body and said, "OK, I forgive you." And I said something which came out of the blue – I said, "Forgive me for not being able to be loved by you." This idea, of asking forgiveness from someone who has hurt you, it's a very good process. I felt much better after that.'

To return to the poet and philosopher David Whyte, I think Whyte encapsulates what Jean-Michel Jarre is describing in his philosophic musings in *Consolations*, where he looks at the under-lying meaning of everyday words. The opening paragraph of his three-page contemplation on Forgiveness reads: 'Forgiveness is a heartache and difficult to achieve because, strangely it not only refuses to eliminate the original wound but actually draws us closer to its source. To approach forgiveness is to close in on the nature of the hurt itself, the only remedy being, as we approach its raw centre, to reimagine our relation to it.'[5]

'To approach forgiveness is to close in on the nature of the hurt itself' – this is what Jarre did. The essence of his hurt was not feeling loved by his father and so he places himself in the frame, accepting that there must also have been something in him that had blocked their relationship from growing. As the words come out at his father's deathbed, the feelings of woundedness and deep sadness that he had harboured for so many years start to shift, and he is able to feel love in his heart again. As Jarre approaches the 'raw centre' of the pain he is able to find a remedy by reimagining his relation to it and thus transform it. Further into his beautiful Forgiveness meditation, Whyte explains more: 'To forgive is to put oneself in a larger gravitational field of experience than the one that first seemed to hurt us.' Albert Einstein famously described this paradigm shift when he said, 'No problem can be solved from the same level of consciousness that created it.'

The former professional football player and television person-ality Ian Wright says something very similar in his 2021 BBC documentary *Home Truths*.[6] The documentary takes the shape of a quest for answers as Wright shares his personal narrative of growing up in a physically and psychologically abusive home. In the final leg of his journey to understanding he meets with those who have themselves abused others and begins to contemplate the difficult relationship he had with his now elderly and very frail mother.

He describes a chaotic childhood, living in one room with his mother, stepfather and older brother, and frequently having to witness his mother being abused by his stepfather – the only escape being when his brother would cover his ears so he couldn't hear. He describes a cycle of abuse as over time the victim – his mother – becomes the perpetrator, passing the abuse down to him by physically and emotionally hurting him, and frequently telling him that she wished she had terminated him before birth. He acknowledges that his traumatic, loveless childhood has con-tinued to affect him throughout his life, leading him to take it out on others by being violent on the football pitch. 'You get stuck emotionally with things that happen when you're a child,' he says. 'When you feel you're not wanted it will cause a problem when you're older.'

Towards the end of the documentary Wright meets with those who are trying to change their violent behaviour and who tell him about their own complex and often oppressive childhoods. Understanding much more now about the cycle of abuse, he starts to contemplate the very real possibility of finding forgiveness for his mother. Forgiveness is positioned here as a transformational tool, something that can pull Wright away from being a powerless victim and which is finally able to break the cycle of trauma. In the closing minutes of *Home Truths* he says this about his mother: 'I'm slowly and surely forgiving her, simply because I have to accept that whatever her journey was she's probably not been able to deal with that like I've been able to deal with it.' Thinking about what his mother has been through, Wright concludes, 'I can forgive. I have to find it within myself because I've got to move on – for my own kids. I've got to try and make sure that they are OK.'

The inherited nature of violence, and indeed of forgiveness, has frequently been discussed in the prisons where The Forgiveness Project works. One woman described watching her seventeen-year-old daughter viciously attack a much older woman. It was a clear illustration of how anger and hatred could be passed from one generation to the next and the woman resolved to find a way to prevent this behaviour continuing. In her workbook she described how she felt after attending the course: 'It has made me feel that the hate I feel for others is not worth my pain. I have now seen through others if I let the hate go the pain will ease.' Another woman commented in her workbook: 'I would like to forgive my husband for getting me sent to prison, I can't do it right now but when I am home I will do everything I can to forgive him so I can parent my boys without hate in my heart and make sure they grow up into well-adjusted men as my hate will give them hate and I don't want them to hurt how I hurt.'

In Hanya Yanagihara's darkly brilliant novel *A Little Life* there is a scene which powerfully illustrates how a parent's unconditional love elicits a forgiving heart. The central character, Jude, who has struggled to live a normal life after years of horrific childhood sexual abuse, develops a close parent–child relationship with one of his professors, Harold, who later with his wife adopts the adult Jude. Unable to accept that he is lovable, the novel's infinitely damaged central character occasionally finds himself caught in the eye of a tantrum. When one evening, just like a three-year-old,

Jude hurls a plate of sandwiches against the wall and expects to be heavily berated, Harold instead tenderly wraps him in his arms: a powerful indication that to be forgiven should always be the prerogative of the child. Yanagihara's description of Jude's softening is unflinching: 'And he cries and cries, cries for everything he has been, for everything he might have been, for every old hurt, for every old happiness, cries for the shame and joy of finally getting to be a child, with all of a child's whims and wants and insecurities, for the privilege of behaving badly and being forgiven, for the luxury of tenderness, of fondness, of being served a meal and being made to eat it, for the ability, at last, at last, of believing a parent's reassurances, of believing that to someone he is special despite all his mistakes and hatefulness, because of all his mistakes and hatefulness.'

The privilege of behaving badly and being forgiven is exactly what every child's first lesson in forgiveness should be. As Katherine Bucknell observes in her introduction to the collected letters of writer Christopher Isherwood and the artist Don Bachardy, 'A lover who betrays is harder to forgive than a prodigal son who wanders and returns. The prodigal son receives unconditional love and is always welcomed home, whatever the emotional cost.'[7]

5

FORGIVENESS FROM THE INSIDE OUT

'Some of the things you do when you're young
are unforgivable to you when you're old.'

NIALL WILLIAMS, *This Is Happiness*

Lis Cashin has thought long and hard about what it means to forgive herself. At the age of thirteen, during the hot, dry summer
of 1983, her life changed forever when in a freak accident at her
school sports day she threw a javelin which veered off course and
killed her friend.

I first met Lis, now in her fifties, when interviewing her for *The
F Word Podcast*. Sitting across from me as we sipped green tea, she
shared her story with a befitting mix of confidence and humility. I
already knew from reading her memoir that she had spent decades
processing an event that in a single moment had ended her childhood. I was interested in the lasting impact of that devastating day,
and where on her long path to healing self-forgiveness belonged,
most particularly self-forgiveness for an accident committed by a
child under the supervision of adults. If you look at the facts – and
an inquest placed the responsibility squarely with the school – Lis

was only doing what she had been told by her teachers when, with a single throw, disaster struck.

In Lis's own words, this is how the day unfolded on 15 July 1983:

Sammy, my friend, and a couple of other friends had been put into the field to mark the javelin throws ... One of my friends had just gone off to get an ice cream and so Sammy had stepped in as well as another girl, and they were both standing just by the white line to the right of me. So, I did as I was told, waited for my name, took my run up and threw the javelin as hard as I could because I really wanted that medal. At first it was going straight but just at the last minute it veered off to the right almost as if the wind had taken it, although I was told later there wasn't any wind, but that's how it looked. Sammy was distracted for some reason ... she wasn't looking and there was this moment of horror realising it was heading towards her.

That evening, waiting at the hospital, Lis's mother broke the news to her that Sammy's deteriorating neurological condition meant she was not expected to survive. 'And that was when everything just collapsed really for me,' said Lis. 'It was so defining in that moment. Nothing could ever be the same again after that.'

Having grown up in a Catholic environment where the commandment 'thou shalt not kill' never came with the proviso 'except if it's an accident', guilt became the defining characteristic of her life, isolating her from both friends and family. Her stepfather told her never to mention Sammy's name again; her doctor didn't think the incident significant enough to include on her medical records; and when the police implied some kind of blame by asking if she had quarrelled with Sammy that day, she became convinced she would end up in prison. Little wonder that by the time Lis was offered an appointment with a psychiatrist she turned it down, fearing it would prove to everyone that she was 'crazy' and prevent her from ever getting a job. While she was told that all the teachers at her school were keeping an eye on her, in reality no one actually spoke to her about what had happened. 'I felt like I was in some sort of goldfish bowl. It was horrendous, just amplifying the guilt that I was feeling . . . I never thought I would be able to let go of this self-blame because the javelin had left my hand and it hit Sammy. I never thought I would ever be able to change that feeling.'

During the years that followed Lis worked hard and played hard. Outwardly she looked capable as she took on various corporate roles, but inwardly her life was in chaos as she tried to obliterate the memory of what had happened through drugs and intensive clubbing. But all her efforts to push the trauma back into a box didn't work, and at the age of twenty-eight she had a complete breakdown. It was this psychological collapse followed by an unexpected personal breakthrough at a work training course that led her finally to realise she had the power to influence her thoughts. Then, aged thirty-two, while travelling in India she experienced a 'spiritual awakening' on a beach after someone gave her reiki and for the first time she felt connected to 'something outside myself'. This took Lis down a more spiritual path, trying out various healing therapies to help her release the pain she was still holding. But it wasn't until years later, after reading the ground-breaking book on trauma *The Body Keeps the Score,* that she came to understand the meaning of post-traumatic stress disorder (PTSD) and for the first time realised that she had been living with the condition for thirty years. In her memoir *This is Me* she writes, 'For someone with an anxiety disorder like PTSD, shame-based thoughts such as "What's wrong with me?" keep us focusing on our "wrongness" and this in turn stops us from exploring what's really driving our anxiety, such as a traumatic incident. This is what I experienced following The Accident. I became focused on my "wrongness", which stopped me from having to face up to the underlying trauma, which felt too over-whelming to process.'[1]

Many months of intense compassion-focused therapy followed. 'I had to relive the whole experience. It was incredibly painful, but it really helped me to shift,' she explained. 'I realised that under-neath everything I believed I was evil and that I deserved to be punished. What I got to re-experience through the therapy was that I was actually an innocent thirteen-year-old going to school that day, who had just done what she was told and then something devastating had happened.'

Although years of therapy have eased her distress, as Lis retold her story to me in the safety of The Forgiveness Project's office in central London, she was clearly thrown back to the time of the accident and quickly overcome with emotion. I asked if she was able to continue and she insisted that she was, explaining that when she first started sharing her story publicly it had always re-traumatised her and, for this reason, she had stopped telling it. It was only after embarking on compassion-focused therapy that she was able to reckon with her painful past. From then on telling her story no longer perpetuated the trauma but rather had the cathartic impact of releasing it. Most importantly, because she began to see how her story was helping people who had caused damage in their own lives, there was now a purpose to the telling.

When I asked Lis whether the adult Lis has been able to forgive the thirteen-year-old Lis, she replied emphatically:

Definitely, definitely! After the therapy it was almost like my heart was breaking for myself because I had been holding on to all of this blame and guilt and punishing myself and self-sabotaging all that time in so many different ways. Now, suddenly I realised I had a right to be safe at school that day. I wasn't messing about. There was nothing I did wrong and yet Sammy was dead. And actually at that point I realised the school had a responsibility. So it started with forgiving myself when I thought I had done something wrong, but when I realised that I was only a child who hadn't meant to harm anyone, on another level what I really felt then was self-compassion, understanding that actually there was, in a way, nothing to forgive myself for. That was the level that I progressed to which was actually just pure love and compassion for the child, for me, on the school playing field that day.

Through the years, unable to be gentle to herself, it was actually Sammy's parents who had been able to offer Lis most kindness. From the day their daughter died they held no blame, realising it might just as easily have been their own daughter throwing the javelin that afternoon. Right from the beginning they stressed that it had been a terrible accident and made every effort to ensure that Lis's name was kept out of the press. Years later they even gave Lis permission to write her book and when she told them she was planning to dedicate it to Sammy, Sammy's mother tenderly told her, 'I think you need to live your life for you now.' It was, says Lis, the greatest act of compassion. 'I don't know if actually I would still be here alive today without their kindness because if they had somehow blamed me through the years this would have been a whole different story.'

In the absence of wrongful behaviour there should be nothing to forgive, and for a blameless offence no reparation due, and yet I wonder if Lis has sought to make amends by choosing not to have a family of her own. I thought about this when she told me that not having children had been a conscious decision. 'With children I think I would have just been so worried all the time,' she said. 'I love children and I do have children in my life, but I don't think it would have been healthy to have had children myself. It wouldn't have been good for the child, or for me.'

Curiously, being forgiven by her victim's family initially did not alleviate Lis's feelings of guilt. Recently, I heard very similar sentiments expressed by a young Australian man who had caused a fatal car accident. He told journalist and campaigner Paris Lees for her BBC podcast *The Flipside* how receiving forgiveness from the family of his victim did not help him feel better about himself. I'm interested by this because having worked with prisoners in secure facilities, and with ex-offenders and former violent extremists, I have frequently heard how being forgiven can restore and repair. This means that, on one level, crippling remorse cannot be assuaged by being forgiven because those who take full responsibility for what they have done will always think 'I don't deserve it', especially in the initial stages of trauma. But it's important to ask, what might these people's lives have been like if they hadn't been forgiven? How much worse potentially might the trap of shame have become? And as Lis acknowledged, she wouldn't be where she is today without the continuing support and kindness of Sammy's parents.

Dr Masi Noor, with whom I worked to help create The Forgiveness Toolbox (a set of skills enabling people to transform the impact of harm and violence) and who co-authored *Forgiveness is Really Strange* with me, summed up why self-forgiveness is so very hard when he was also interviewed for *The Flipside* podcast. 'It might be harder to forgive oneself because forgiving oneself requires [us] to work at a deep identity level,' he said. 'As human beings … we have a deep profound psychological need to be seen as morally sound. We defend our moral integrity and yet here you are almost naked … You can see the consequences of your wrongdoing and it's irreversible. And so, in that sense, self-forgiveness is very, very challenging indeed.'

Masi also made a point that I'd not heard mentioned before, namely that perhaps we find self-forgiveness so hard because we don't want to live in a society where individuals easily find their way to forgiving themselves, 'because then anything goes'. It made me think of an experience of my own which I once talked publicly about at a *Real Stories Told Live* event in north London. The response from the audience was interesting – most people could easily put themselves in my shoes and imagine doing the exact same thing, but one person told me afterwards in no uncertain terms that I was wrong to have let myself 'off the hook' and had no right to forgive myself. Perhaps he was worried that my response might create a society 'where anything goes'. Nevertheless, regardless of what this man said, the fact remained I was able to let go of the guilt and self-blame for this incident because I believe what happened was a terrible mistake and because ever since I have made great effort to take care around animals and household appliances.

The story goes like this. When my children were still at school, I killed our six-month-old kitten, Mossy, by accidently trapping him in the washing machine. I still clearly remember going to unload the machine that morning and wondering how my daughter's black fleece had somehow got in among all the whites . . . and then suddenly realising my catastrophic mistake. I was utterly distraught, so much so that my husband commented at the time that I'd cried more about the cat than I had about my grandmother who had recently died. The fact that I had been wholly responsible for the death of this beloved family pet sat heavily with me for days. My inconsolable children blamed me, and I blamed myself while also feeling enraged by those who seemed to find the whole thing a laughing matter. The worst of it was, I'd seen the cat around my feet minutes before turning the machine on and had meant to check, but then the phone had gone and when I returned I totally forgot. It had been so completely preventable; it was such an utterly stupid mistake and there were no mitigating circumstances. Perhaps I had been stressed; obviously I was very distracted but none of that was an excuse. I didn't think I'd ever get over it, let alone be able to forgive myself.

And yet, exactly a week to the day after this awful event, I woke up one morning feeling lighter, knowing that my thoughtless and reckless actions would not burden me for the rest of my life. I understood that this feeling of reprieve came from being able to forgive myself. I was able to reason that what I had done was an accident, that I had not meant to kill our cat.

A few days after I killed Mossy, a boy at my children's school died when he was knocked over by a car on his way home. It was an appalling tragedy for the family and deeply shocking for the boy's friends and for the school. Alongside the outpouring of grief that came from the local community, some people felt some sympathy for the driver too. I have no idea of the circumstances that led to the accident, but whatever they were, that driver's life is likely to have been scarred forever. Who knows if they could ever forgive themselves? Indeed, this raises the question: does anyone have the right to forgive themselves if the person they have hurt doesn't forgive them?

In *The Lost Art of Forgiving* by Johann Christoph Arnold, the author tells a story which left a lingering impression on him, probably because it is every parent's worst nightmare. When he was growing up in Paraguay, his former teacher, a man called Delf, was backing a truckload of firewood into his driveway one day as his two-year-old son, who was playing outdoors, ran to meet him. Delf did not see him until it was too late and ran him over. Delf's wife, Katie, was busy in the house when her husband came inside, carrying their little boy limp in his arms. You might assume Delf's wife would never forgive him, but in the book her response to the question of forgiveness is comforting: 'There was never any question about forgiving my husband, as I knew I was just as much to blame. Likewise he did not blame me, only himself. We stood in our sorrow together.'[2]

Arnold then goes on to describe how Delf came to be his teacher and how he struggled to forgive himself. 'The accident haunted him for years,' he writes. 'From then on, he went out of his way to make time for children – time he could not spend with the son he had killed. Looking back, I remember how his eyes often glistened with tears and wondered what it was that made them come. Was it that he saw his son in us? Was he imagining the boy his toddler would never become? Whatever the reason, it seems that Delf's determination to show love to others was his way of making up for the anguish he had caused himself and his family by unintentionally taking a life. I am convinced that it saved him from brooding, and from nursing his feelings of guilt. Through loving others he was able to forgive himself and regain a sense of wholeness and peace.'

Self-forgiveness is made possible therefore only when we can accept our bruised heart as a part of ourselves, and not as our defining or worst characteristic. It occurs when we can feel and show love to ourselves and others again. And it is about understanding that moving outwards towards a shared humanity may save us from endlessly nursing inner feelings of moral failure.

Mercifully most of us will not experience the trauma of accidently killing someone we love; but we are all likely to have harmed someone, either physically or emotionally, whether on purpose or accidentally, and we are likely therefore to have felt regret for what we've done. When this happens, guilt will kick in, most likely followed by feelings of remorse and a desire to make amends, which may or may not lead to reconciliation and reparation. Shame may also follow, cementing these emotions so that we intrinsically feel bad about ourselves. While the memory of what we did will normally retreat as the busy-ness of our lives takes hold, from time to time something will come up to remind us of what happened, and the feelings of self-blame and remorse are likely to resurface all over again.

So much about self-forgiveness comes back to shame – that most fundamental, unavoidable and disturbing of human experiences. We feel ashamed of our weaknesses, just as we feel guilt about our wrongdoings, and we go to great lengths to avoid, transform and conceal these feelings from ourselves. A broad distinction between guilt and shame is that guilt results from our actions and behaviour, whereas shame is associated with the way we see ourselves. It is often said that with guilt we feel bad about what we have done whereas with shame we feel bad about who we are. Guilt therefore is a trait that involves remorse and regret and can promote conciliatory behaviour, whereas shame is a sensation that worms its way deep inside us and is harder to resolve. As Gerschen Kaufman writes in *Shame: The Power of Caring*, 'Shame is a wound felt from the inside, dividing us both from ourselves and from one another.'

Lis's story illustrates perfectly how self-neglect and self-blame can eat away at your self-esteem, derailing ambition and sabotaging relationships. Since shame triggers an avoidance defence which shows up as concealment and self-deception, self-compassion is its antidote because it can lead to a change of heart. In fact, I tend to think of self-forgiveness as a movement of compassion both towards the other and towards the self, the recognition that if we don't deal with our regrets and failed promises, they may overwhelm us.* Therefore, forgiving ourselves requires not only coming to terms with our own dark side, but also embracing our own vulnerability.

Looking back at our past actions, it is easy to be ambushed by the limits of our regrets. Prospero's advice in *The Tempest*, 'Let us not burden our remembrance with a heaviness that's gone', suggests that regret becomes a heavier burden to carry as we grow older. The author and former bishop of Edinburgh, Richard Holloway, has much to say on this subject. Now in his ninth decade, Holloway acknowledges in *Waiting for the Last Bus: Reflections on Life and Death*

---

* A study involving 657 LGBT individuals looking at forgiveness, shame, and self-esteem found that the participants who harboured fewer feelings of shame and the highest amount of forgiveness had the highest levels of self-esteem. Specifically, self-forgiveness was directly predictive of self-esteem. (Darrell C. Greene and Paula J. Britton, 'The Influence of Forgiveness on Lesbian, Gay, Bisexual, Transgender, and Questioning Individuals' Shame and Self-Esteem', *Journal of Counselling and Development*, 91/2, (2013): 195–205.

that the view from the summit of life can be challenging at times. Describing how as a bishop he frequently would have to attend to the old and the dying, he writes, 'I have sat at the bedside of people eaten up with regret because of mistakes they made in their lives. Wrong roads they took; relationships broken and still unrepaired; troubled children who blamed them for their own failures.'

For me self-compassion or self-acceptance is almost inter-changeable with self-forgiveness, but in *Forgiveness in Practice*, Stephen Cherry, author and dean of King's College, Cambridge, points out an important difference. He argues that the power of self-forgiveness is that it is a moral word. The implication is that whereas self-acceptance is about cultivating self-love, self-forgiveness is more about overcoming self-hatred, and for that it is ultimately about transformation. 'The reason why self-forgiveness is better than self-acceptance as a term is that "self-forgiveness" admits in its vocabulary that something that cannot be ignored is wrong and that it needs to be put right,' claims Cherry.[3]

One of the most acute and prescient reflections on self-forgiveness I've come across is from the poet and philosopher Pádraig Ó Tuama in his immersive reading of Dilruba Ahmed's poem 'Phase One', presented on the Krista Tippett *Poetry Unbound* podcast. This is such a salient explanation of what it means to hold yourself hostage to blame, and, as Ó Tuama says, the intuition of the poem suggests that forgiveness is freeing, opening us to be present to a shared humanity. He points out that on first reading this poem, it is as if the poet is writing about someone else, perhaps about the daily irritations of a spouse or perhaps a close friend, but then he realises it could only be a person speaking to themselves because they are so intimately aware of everything they hold against this person. It is a stunning example of what Ó Tuama sees as the essence of poetry, asking you to be brave and to go into the moments of your own failure. And it is a beautiful example of how poetry can give words to a more forgiving voice. 'Phase One' begins like this:

For leaving the fridge open
last night, I forgive you.
For conjuring white curtains
instead of living your life.

For the seedlings that wilt, now,
in tiny pots, I forgive you.
For saying no first
but yes as an afterthought.

The poem continues at a pace with the regrets and irritations of everyday life named and expunged. This person grants themselves forgiveness for all the things that so many of us will be able to relate to – for leaving windows open in the rain, for loving too much, for only singing when no one can hear, for showing contempt for a parent who deserves compassion. The poem ends like a hymn reciting the reciprocal nature of self-forgiveness, with the words:

I forgive you. For growing
a capacity for love that is great
but matched only, perhaps,
by your loneliness. For being unable

to forgive yourself first so you
could then forgive others and
at last find a way to become
the love that you want in this world.[4]

The word 'forgive' is repeated thirteen times in the poem and the phrase 'I forgive you' appears six times. It's as if this poem is trying to create a refrain, suggesting self-forgiveness is something we need to return to over and over again because if we're holding these misgivings against ourselves, it becomes very difficult to find connection with others. As Ó Tuama says, 'It needs to be a mantra, it needs to be a thing we say to ourselves in order to get out of our way, in order to be able to love.'

Sometimes there's a concern that a focus on self-forgiveness is somehow selfish, but according to Ó Tuama it's the exact opposite, because self-forgiveness is to remove yourself from always being the centre of the drama. In the podcast he says:

> What I think self-forgiveness does, is to recognise that if we're holding enormous things against ourselves, it can be very difficult to be present and loving in those moments. If you're spending so much of your energy putting yourself at the centre of your story and hating yourself, it can be very difficult to be present with other people because we do tend to give to others what we've given to ourselves, and if we're constantly sharpening an iron against ourselves, well then we might be using that same iron against the people we meet, whether those are small encounters on the bus or encounters with a partner or children or somebody else that we live with or see regularly. So I think starting with yourself in this moment might be the beginning of having a place of practice where you can begin, then try with others ... You can begin to imagine being compassionate to them because you've had to do the hard work of being compassionate to yourself.

Arno Michaelis, a former violent white supremacist whose story appears in Chapter 8, told me recently how self-forgiveness was imperative to him becoming a valuable and peace-loving member of society. He also made it very clear that self-forgiveness was not about letting himself off the hook:

> My main driver for self-forgiveness is that if I am hating myself for the harm that I have done, I'm not going to be able to help other people stay out of hate groups. I'm not going to be able to

help people along the same path that I have taken. So, for me it is a very tactical process. And it by no means even implies that the harm that I have done is okay or that it's forgiven or that it's off the table. I'm going to carry the harm that I have done to my grave and I should. But, if I let that harm continue to harm me, I don't believe that I'm honouring my victims. I think the way to honour the people that I've hurt and the people who've been hurt by the broken white kids that I set loose on society is to fix broken white kids and give them a lesson that there's a better way to live their lives and I can't do that if I beat myself up.

In an interesting 2002 study into autobiographical narratives of forgiveness and unforgiveness, researchers Zechmeister and Romero found that self-forgiving offenders were more likely to report attempts to apologise or make amends to their victim than were offenders who did not forgive themselves. They also found that offenders who forgave themselves reported more positive consequences and fewer lasting negative consequences of the wrongdoing than offenders who had not forgiven themselves.[5] Jeffrey Blustein, a philosopher and medical ethicist, argues, 'One cannot forgive oneself for what one has done if one is not prepared to take responsibility for it.'[6] Certainly, in my experience of working in prisons, offenders who take responsibility for their crimes are better able to reach a point of self-forgiveness, and even then most feel they do not deserve it.*

In one of the finest and slimmest books written about forgiveness,

---

* Some perpetrators will emphatically reject the notion of self-forgiveness. When I asked Manwar Ali, the Muslim scholar who befriended former EDL member Ivan Humble, if he could ever forgive himself for the harm he had caused while fighting in Afghanistan or for the hurt he had caused his family, he said, 'Maybe I don't want to forgive myself, because if I did, then what would motivate me to carry on? If it's all washed off and cleansed, then how do I carry on helping others make reparations? Or stop them from making the same mistakes I made?'

Richard Holloway concludes that the hardest place to start with forgiveness 'is in the struggle with our own guilt ... most of us seem to be quite good at forgiving or understanding human weakness in people we love, at sticking with our friends through the painful consequences of their mistakes. It is much more difficult to apply the same generosity to ourselves.'[7]

I have come to the same conclusion myself through witnessing the painful struggle of many people trying to forgive themselves, perhaps because shame can so easily become ingrained, but also because of our own harsh inner critical voice. When I was collecting personal stories from America in 2005, I flew to Georgia to meet with Celia McWee, who has sadly since died. All I really knew on arrival was that two of Celia's adult children had been killed in unrelated but equally barbaric incidents. In 1980 her daughter, Joyce, had been murdered by her son-in-law in a 'crime of passion', while in 2004 Celia's son, Jerry, had been executed on death row. As we settled down to talk, I learnt that Celia was a staunch opponent of the death penalty as well as a strong advocate of the power of forgiveness. I wondered if the focus of this interview might therefore be on a mother forgiving the state of South Carolina for her son's execution or on a mother forgiving her son-in-law for the murder of her daughter. Celia did indeed speak about both these things, but what stood out for me was what she said about self-forgiveness. 'Although I seem to forgive easily, the person I can't forgive is myself,' she told me.

I had invited Celia to come and talk alone with me in my hotel room in Atlanta. I knew we needed time as well as privacy. Almost immediately she asked if she could lie on the bed. It wasn't that she was unwell; she was just exhausted from carrying the burden of loss for so long. When I asked what it was that she couldn't forgive herself for, she explained that Jerry had been happily married for seventeen years until he fell in love with a 22-year-old woman and walked out on his family. His wife was heartbroken, and Celia, upset and angry at the callous way he had treated them, refused to speak to him. In time Jerry got a divorce and remarried, but when he ran into financial difficulties, his new wife left him. Alone and without money, he now moved into a run-down apartment in the projects with a teenage boy who had a history of crime and drug-taking.

What then happened was the cause of Celia's greatest sorrow. 'One day Jerry came to my work. We said hello but I was still angry and didn't ask if he wanted to talk. I thought, *If you're going through a hard time, then good, because now you're being punished for what you did.* To this day I'll never forgive myself for not responding in a more caring way, for not reaching out to him. A few days later Jerry took a gun and went with this new friend to a convenience store where he shot a man dead. I'll never know why he did it, but I'm certain he was thinking of his brother-in-law when he pulled the trigger. The following day, the two of them went to visit their roof contractor boss and Jerry's young friend shot and killed the poor man. After that Jerry alerted the police. He told me later, "I was very much afraid the killing would have continued."'

As soon as Jerry was arrested, Celia vowed to stand by her son whatever it took, and for thirteen years every Sunday she would drive three hours from Augusta in Georgia to Ridgeville in South Carolina, to visit him in prison. Jerry strongly regretted what he had done and believed he deserved the death penalty, but when one day he called from prison to tell his mother he'd been served his execution date, she collapsed in disbelief. All she could think was that she was glad her husband was no longer alive as he wouldn't have been able to bear the pain.

I have seldom witnessed such palpable grief as when Celia told me what happened next:

Jerry didn't want me to witness the execution, but I fought tooth and nail to be there. I couldn't let him die in front of a room full of strangers. There were just two of us watching – myself and a relative of the roof contractor. The wife of Jerry's victim wasn't there, and I would say she's the most sympathetic person I've ever known. She never publicly denounced what my son did, nor did she ever call for his execution. Just before the lethal injection, Jerry turned to take a good long look at me and then blew me a kiss. After that he closed his eyes, and I watched the blood drain from his face. I don't know what could be harder than watching your son die like that. A mother does not see a thirty-, forty-, fifty-year-old man strapped to that cross-like gurney. She sees the child she gave birth to, the child that in her eyes never grew up. I deeply resent a government that kills its own citizens – its own children. It still feels so raw and so painful, and yet I feel no hatred or blame – neither for my daughter's husband, nor for those who killed my son. My anger is entirely directed towards myself for turning my back on my son when he needed me most.

Convinced that she could somehow have averted Jerry's downward spiral into violent crime, Celia seemed utterly broken by the realisation that she hadn't been able to act with the unconditional love of a mother for a child. I could feel the weight of her pain and hoped that by sharing her story with me for *The F Word* exhibition in America it would educate the public against the death penalty as well as help Celia find new meaning in her experience. Over the years I have heard many people speak of their pain and regret for things they have done or not done, but I don't recall ever witnessing such profound remorse as in the heartbreak of Celia McWee, a mother unable to reconcile with her actions at a moment of crisis in her son's life.

*

Like Celia, there are other people I've met through The Forgiveness Project who have done things that they deeply regret and for which they say they will never forgive themselves. However, lack of self-forgiveness doesn't necessarily mean they are overwhelmed by feelings of shame or regret, and indeed may take the form of sincere repentance.

Take Chen Alon for example, who joined the Israeli Defence Force (IDF) to defend Israel against the first and then the second intifadas – the Palestinian uprisings against the Israeli occupation of the West Bank and Gaza. While taking part in multiple violent sieges against the Palestinian people, he came to hate what he had signed up for, questioning how he could possibly consider himself a loving father and yet be prepared to brutalise and dehumanise Palestinian children. 'I began to realise that in the de-humanising of the *other*, you begin to de-humanise yourself,' he told me. Worn down by the relentless nature of the Israeli-Palestinian struggle, Chen eventually became a *refusenik*, embracing his newly found peace activism with enthusiasm. When I met him in Tel Aviv in 2010 during a visit to Israel to collect stories from members of the Combatants for Peace organisation, to which he belonged, he made an interesting observation about how easily enemies demonise each other: 'When I decided to publish my name as a *refusenik*, I went to warn my parents because I knew it would be a big scandal,' he said. 'My mother's reaction was to say, "Isn't that dangerous?" I thought this was strange because in the army I'd been under constant attack and in far more danger. There is a common thought in Israeli society that Palestinian mothers care less about their children because Palestinian mothers send their children to commit suicide attacks. And yet Israeli mothers are willing to sacrifice their children in exactly the same way by sending their children into the army. The mindset is no different.'

When I asked Chen about self-forgiveness, he dismissed the notion of forgiving himself as erroneous and told me a story instead: 'One day I was in Ramallah telling my story to Palestinians and a person in the audience asked me directly, "Are you asking us to forgive you?" I said, "No, I don't forgive myself, nor do I ask for forgiveness." For me, telling my story is not about asking for forgiveness but about taking responsibility. This is not just about words and emotions – it's also about action. I will only be able to achieve self-forgiveness by creating alliances with Palestinians, and this means being allies in a non-violent struggle against injustice and oppression.'

Taking responsibility and feeling remorse can therefore become the driving force for reconciling with regret. A little while ago I happened to receive a letter from a woman I don't know who told me that she had embarked on a very difficult process of self-forgiveness. Amber wrote: 'I have spent many years searching for healing, progress, development, improvement and yet always have ended up feeling STUCK.' She explained that guilt, shame and accompanying sorrow had overwhelmed her after she had 'rejected' her two young sons at the ages of four and six. This had happened at a time in her life when she was unable to cope with parenting and so leaving her children in the care of others had seemed in everyone's best interest. However, over the following years, regret had taken a firm grip from which there seemed no turning back. 'I imagined their victimhood was sealed and therefore mine too,' she explained. 'I imagined I must always be guilty because their past would always be a part of their present and future, as it was mine.'

She went on to describe the trap of not forgiving yourself, which can bind you to a place where no resolution is possible and where you are simply fixed to one spot, stuck with your own sorrow day after day. She said that for years she had tried to conceal her actions from herself and others, avoiding people and their 'normal' lives and endlessly ducking innocent questions about children and parenthood.

Amber's reason for writing to me was to try to explain how you can row back from debilitating feelings of waste which keep you forever stranded in the guilt of your behaviour. She wrote of an astonishing sea change. Perhaps because unyielding regret became too exhausting, eventually she made a promise to herself to investigate what self-forgiveness might feel like and how she could use the emotion of remorse creatively in order that it could become a positive force in her life. The letter does not explain exactly how she did this, but it appears that by being prepared to embrace her vulnerability and culpability, by stopping making excuses for herself and no longer blaming herself, this intention was enough to profoundly alter her perspective in places where she'd previously been so stuck. The letter ended with her saying, 'Feeling remorse gives us permission to release ourselves, perhaps even forgive ourselves; for how can we pay back in the world if we are crippled by low self-esteem, low self-respect and a belief that we are unworthy of participating in a happy, useful existence?'

Remorse thus becomes not a prison of shame but a spur to create value around us. Self-forgiveness was freeing for Amber because it wasn't dependent on whether her sons forgave her or not. It came from an innate understanding that life is complex, we mess up, we make decisions we regret, we hurt people we love. This illustrates the complex geography of forgiveness which acknowledges that life is morally complicated, that good people do bad things, and that bad things happen to good people.

For those stuck in self-pity or paralysing shame, there may come a time when the only means of freeing yourself from such tight constraints is through moving towards self-forgiveness. Holocaust survivor Eva Kor may be best known for forgiving her Nazi per-secutors, but for me the most touching part of her story was when she described the inevitability of her push towards self-forgiveness.

We had just met for the first time. It was 2008 and I was attending a conference on conflict transformation in Würzburg in southern Germany where Eva had been invited to speak. We were sitting talking in the gardens of the conference hall when she grabbed my hand, held my gaze, and told me that key to everything in her healing from trauma had been her ability to forgive herself. I looked at her a bit confused, not fully understanding what exactly a victim of the worst excesses of human cruelty would have to forgive herself for. But then, in a way that wonderfully illustrates the multidimensional, intricate arc of forgiveness, she explained: 'The day I forgave the Nazis, privately I forgave my parents whom I hated all my life for not having saved me from Auschwitz. Children expect their parents to protect them; mine couldn't. And then I forgave myself for hating my parents.'

In a similar vein, but under very different circumstances, Gethin Jones had to find his way to forgive others before he had the capacity to forgive himself. Gethin spent his youth in and out of care homes, spending long periods of time in secure units and then prisons. It was only after reaching rock bottom and injecting heroin into his neck that his drug worker started to talk about recovery. Up until then he'd only ever focused on the unkind staff who'd caused him pain, but now, all of a sudden he could see how some staff also wanted to help him. And then there was his mother to consider, whom he hadn't seen for ten years. Gethin explains: 'My breakthrough came with the help of a counsellor called Alan. I still had huge resentment for my mum who was the foundation of all my resentments ... Alan asked me one day, "What was your mum's life like, Gethin?" I'd never thought about this before but of course my mum had been in children's homes in the 1950s and '60s. I started to think about this young girl with learning difficulties abandoned by her parents. And as I imagined what that must have been like for her my resentment just washed away. It was a massive release and I no longer hated her.'

For Gethin, forgiveness started with forgiving the system, then forgiving his mother and eventually forgiving himself.

Self-forgiveness, however, was the hardest part because by now he had three children and was tortured by thinking of all the hurt he'd caused them. But then someone on a 12-Step Fellowship programme told him he would never change the past; he would only change the future by changing his behaviour today. 'It made real sense,' Gethin says. 'For the first time I took ownership of who I'd been, and I decided that every single day from then on I would strive to be the very best version of myself. It doesn't always come easily, and I still feel anger, but the heartbeat of my change is that I no longer want to hurt myself or anyone else.'

In effect Brenda Adelman lost both her parents in a ruthless act of domestic bloodshed. Brenda's mother was an award-winning artist and photographer when in 1995 she was shot and killed by her husband in her Brooklyn home. Brenda's father pleaded guilty to involuntary manslaughter and ended up serving two and a half years of a five-year prison sentence. Soon after the catastrophe, and wanting desperately to heal, Brenda began to investigate every nook and avenue of what it meant to forgive, initially not anticipating that self-forgiveness would play such a key role in making her feel whole again.

The first time I met Brenda was in London in 2010. She had travelled from her home in Los Angeles to perform *My Brooklyn Hamlet*, her sixty-minute one-woman stage show based on her life story. As the lights came down, I sat in the back row, feeling a little nervous for Brenda and not really knowing what to expect. But it wasn't long before I was totally captivated by this raw, dark, often funny, but entirely redeeming piece of theatre which skilfully combined process and personal narrative with a twist of Shakespeare.

After the show, I met up with Brenda in the garden of a nearby café and here we talked about how she had become immersed in the theory as well as the practice of forgiveness. I felt immediately drawn to this quirky and creative woman who had used therapy and the arts to weave a path through trauma. She had even taught radical responsibility and self-forgiveness to at-risk youths and women in prison; she had produced an e-book with her three-step forgiveness process, led workshops at spiritual communities and designed an online forgiveness course. A little way into the conversation she pulled out from her jacket pocket a small black-and-white photograph. In it 10-year-old Brenda is standing between her mother and father, holding their hands tightly and staring joyously into the camera. Her parents look like a couple in love. She told me that she now rarely spoke about her mother because while the loss was still intense there was no need – the relationship had been extremely loving and she felt the comfort of her mother's presence in her life every day.

Five years later I met up with Brenda again – this time in my brother-in-law's apartment in Santa Monica – to continue our conversation about forgiveness. She told me she thought she had forgiven her father immediately after her mother's death, but she knew now that was only because she was in denial and couldn't bear the thought of losing her father, along with her mother, on that one night.

'I thought I had to; it was the thing to do but I didn't really understand what that meant. In forgiving him too soon I actually was denying my truth. I needed the time to hate him and work with my anger in a healthy way. After my mum's death I felt this deep sense of shame and despair. I felt like damaged goods. What did it say about me if this is what had happened to my parents? The only thing that helped to transform these negative emotions was writing my story. I was doing an acting course in LA at the time and so I wrote and performed a fifteen-minute personal piece, at the end of which I noticed people crying. I was amazed because instead of being judged for what I'd revealed I received a standing ovation and so much empathy and compassion.'

Holding the family's pain meant suffering an existential collapse until she realised that if she were ever to recover, she must find compassion not just for her father but also for herself.

For a long time, I didn't know how to forgive as I assumed forgiveness was about reconciliation and I didn't want my dad back in my life because he had showed no remorse. However, during the process I realised forgiveness also meant resolving inner conflict and clearing my heart of hate; it meant that if I thought about my father my day wasn't wrecked anymore.

The missing step was embracing my anger in a healthy way. But I still felt a deep level of anger at myself for not having saved my mother and for trusting my father, which was demonstrated by my over-eating. I had so much self-judgement and you can't really forgive someone else unless you've forgiven yourself. Self-forgiveness appeared as an issue because every time I thought I had forgiven my father I would be triggered again. I did years of working my process on every level to forgive him even when he moved in with and married my mom's sister. I took a master's degree in Spiritual Psychology, during which time I recognised how with each negative thought directed at my father I was re-wounding myself. I took an in-person anger workshop. I went to a therapist. I went to workshops. I journalled. I wrote. I forgave my judgements consciously. I went to the top of a mountain in Los Angeles and carried out a ceremony of release using one of my father's hats which I threw over the mountain side. With this simple ritualistic gesture something was released inside of me. From that moment I wasn't burdened anymore.

Even though her father has since died of a heart attack Brenda knows she has forgiven him because she has complete peace in her heart whenever she thinks of him and can still feel love for the good times they shared together.

Brenda has also wondered if perhaps it is harder to achieve self-forgiveness than to forgive others because forgiving yourself requires you to address and make peace with your own shame. 'Because life happens and so much of the self-loathing happens silently in our head, we aren't letting it out to be seen, and eventually released, like we do with let's say anger at a loved one, a boss, a partner, a parent, a child. So, we have this voice that repeats, over and over again, for instance: "Why didn't I stand up for myself in this situation?", "Why did I eat that?", "Why didn't I go to the gym?", "Why can't I lose weight?", "Why did I make that investment?", "Why did I hire that person?", "Why didn't I hire that person?", "Why can't I get well?", "Why doesn't he love me like I love him?", "Why did she take advantage of me?" Every day we have these voices that we usually silence and don't share with others: and so they get stronger. The shame or guilt around them turn into a story that feels real. And so by bringing these internal voices and judgments into the light of conscious awareness ... that is where the healing can take place and the self-forgiveness is experienced.'

Author and mental health campaigner Rachel Kelly believes that self-forgiveness can be the key to unlocking this harsh inner critical voice that many with anxiety and depression experience.

As someone who has herself suffered from severe depression, she came to understand how cultivating an inner voice of forgiveness was a gentler approach to recovery than focusing on bolstering self-worth and resilience. In an email exchange with Kelly, I asked her about the connection between compassion and judgement in relation to mental health. She replied: 'For years now the world of positive psychology and self-help has held up self-esteem as the holy grail of good mental health. But the self-esteem model is flawed: boosting self-worth is no bad thing in and of itself, but it tends to be based on needing to feel above average/better than others and borders on the narcissistic and competitive, which can lead to feelings of inadequacy. Rather, recent research shows cultivating self-compassion has a far bigger impact on assuaging feelings of anxiety and/or depression.'

Two hours after addressing this viewpoint for the sake of this book, I was scrolling through my Twitter feed when I came across a quote from someone which precisely and eloquently echoed what Kelly had been saying. The person had posted: 'I dream of never being called resilient again in my life. I'm exhausted by strength. I want support. I want softness. I want ease. I want to be amongst kin. Not patted on the back for how well I take a hit. Or for how many.'

It seems that 'resilience' – this catch-all term for overcoming challenging situations – has suffered a bit of backlash recently. On the Australian current-affairs programme Q&A, indigenous singer and songwriter Mitch Tambo pleaded for empathy and for the stories of the Aboriginal people to be heard. 'I'm crying out for healing for my people because we hear that term all the time, "you're resilient, you're resilient" but that doesn't mean we want to be resilient. We want to be free. We want to be trauma-free.'[8]

The author Bea Setton, aged twenty-seven, wrote to me recently about a subject closely related to self-forgiveness: self-love. She was saying that in her opinion it required self-love to be able to be self-critical and to improve. She had noticed that her generation were not good at self-forgiveness because they were not good at self-reflection or overcoming their own judgement of themselves or their actions. 'I think that there is something about endless self-indulgence for my generation,' she wrote. 'I don't want to sound like a reactionary critic or anything – I love my generation too – but criticism is so unbearable to us, we only want mercy and forgiveness, and shirk away from any judgement or truly critical self-analysis. I always think there is something about self-hatred that is a protection mechanism against the anger of others. It's like, I hate myself so much already, I can't take anything anyone else says on board.'

This broad, bold speculation interested me because

self-absorption certainly seems the defining trait of our time. Unable to handle the anxiety of dealing with difference, our social media feeds reflect the comfortable echo chamber we have created for ourselves. We become locked in our own small worlds, increasingly unable to empathise with people who are different from us. This means that when contrary views are put forward it disturbs our fault lines. Self-forgiveness requires being comfortable with our own failures and mistakes, as well as being prepared to look inwards to find self-compassion among the brokenness and messiness of our interior lives. It would not be a surprise to me, therefore, that for younger generations blighted by crippling anxiety, caused by complex pressures and widespread expectations, self-forgiveness and self-love are often hard to unearth.

In Anne Lamott's powerfully redemptive meditation *Hallelujah Anyway: Rediscovering Mercy* she addresses the countless mean-spirited and grudging tendencies by which we let ourselves down. We should begin, she suggests, by facing 'the great big mess of ourselves'. Exploring where to find meaning in life, she writes of letting go of judgement and absolving the unabsolvable, and asks: 'So why today is it absolutely all I can do to extend mercy to myself for wanting to nip an annoying relative's heel like a river rat? Forget extending mercy to this relative, who has so messed with me and my son – she doesn't even know she needs my mercy. She thinks she is fierce and superior, while I believe she secretly ate her first child. Horribly, she is perfectly fine. I'm the one who needs mercy – my mercy. The need for this, for my own motley mercy, underpinned most of my lifelong agitation, my separation from life itself.' Recognising how alike we are in our imperfections, she says, teaches compassion and is a sizable part of self-forgiveness.

Self-forgiveness often involves a resolution to change and to behave differently in the future. You may set out conditions for yourself – for example, I will only forgive myself if I change or make reparations. I will only forgive myself if I am forgiven by the person I have hurt. The change I made after killing my cat was that I never again failed to check the washing machine before putting a wash on when we had a pet living with us, and my reparations were to get another cat and allow this cat to have kittens: 'a life for a life' as my children insisted in order for me to be forgiven by them. But more than reparation to others, reconciliation with the self is necessary in self-forgiveness. There are many ways we inflict harm on ourselves and let ourselves down, for instance failing an exam because we didn't study hard enough, frightening off a potential partner by being too controlling, or not being able to give up smoking or alcohol due to addiction. We might suffer from guilt and shame because of our inability to stop engaging in self-destructive behaviour. Self-forgiveness requires embracing human fallibility and placing the transgression – whether against oneself or another – in a larger perspective. In short, it means realising that one is merely human.

6

POLITICAL FORGIVENESS

'The only antidote to the irreversibility of
history is the faculty of forgiveness.'

HANNAH ARENDT

Stacy Bannerman tells her story with the smouldering conviction
of a lifetime peace activist. 'Most Americans now consider the
Iraq War a mistake; that mistake destroyed everything I loved,'
she says, enunciating each word deliberately and slowly to drive
her point home. The 56-year-old residing in the New River
Valley of Virginia is the author of *Homefront 911: How Families of
Veterans Are Wounded by Our Wars*, and for the past twenty years
has campaigned to break the national silence about the frequency
and severity of combat veteran domestic violence.

Stacy's story has always interested me because while it is certainly another example of forgiveness in the private sphere (in
her case finding compassion for a violently abusive husband), her
experience also led her to explore forgiveness in the collective
of public life, in particular forgiving a society she had grown to
despise for having encouraged the wars in Afghanistan and Iraq.

In this sense, she has come to see forgiveness as a vital path to national healing.

In 2010, Stacy's husband retired after twenty-seven years of service in the military, returning to live with her in the family home in Oregon. 'But the war wasn't done with him,' she says, explaining how he soon developed post-combat trauma, started shooting crystal meth and eventually became violent towards her. As his symptoms worsened, she became his caregiver and an advocate for veterans and their families. At first, she constantly excused his abusive behaviour; and even when he strangled her to the point of unconsciousness, still she tried to love him back to life. Attempting to understand what was happening to her husband, Stacy started reading studies on PTSD in war veterans. Her research led her to conclude that the problem went much further than creating hordes of mentally unstable veterans. While stressed soldiers suffered high levels of psychological injury that could last a lifetime, the evidence was showing the same was true of the families left behind. Many were bearing psychological injuries at nearly the same rate as the returning troops.

'Eventually it became too dangerous, and I filed for divorce,' she says. 'I put our house up for sale, and in July of 2015, fled the only home I'd ever owned and placed my horse and two goats at an animal sanctuary. I moved into a travel trailer in a mobile home park, where it took everything that I had to get out of bed in the morning. My sense of self was all I had left but then I became victim to identity theft by a female crystal meth drug user who my husband let move into our house after I moved out. In less than 90 days, I was stripped of my home, marriage, companion animals, health care, social and economic status, and of my identity too.' Finally, when Stacy was able to authorise the sale of the marital home, her husband threatened her with an M4 semi-automatic weapon and then tried to take his own life in a suicide-by-cop attempt.

By now all the research Stacy had done on the impact of war trauma was pointing to the fact that the majority of violent and abusive veterans were more victim than perpetrator. 'As I mourned and tried to make sense of things, I would think about my identity thief and how bad things must have been for her to want to become me. And so I began to understand how, if you felt you were all alone in the world, it would be easy to start shooting meth to stop the pain. And because I understood, I found I was able to forgive my identity thief, and my ex-husband too who was unable or unwilling to deal with the demons of combat trauma and crystal meth. I realised, too, everything that had happened to us was a consequence of the primary cause: the Iraq War.'

Stoked by the strength of the persecuted, Stacy adopted the rhetoric of moral outrage. While President George W. Bush and his advisors may have technically been responsible for so much of the ruinous war in Iraq, she also blamed the 76 per cent of the American people who wanted the war, and the 99 per cent who sacrificed nothing for it. She blamed them for the deaths of all the soldiers who had been killed in Iraq, or who killed themselves on return, and she blamed them for the deaths of the many military spouses who had been murdered by their veteran husbands.[1] It was only when her campaign of blame developed what she herself identifies as an alarmingly vengeful twist ('I found myself wanting everyone who supported that war to suffer') that it caused her to pause and think again. At this point, Stacy came to realise that the most difficult work of forgiveness still remained: forgiveness on a macro level, forgiving the society in which she lived and her fellow American citizens.

'After I lost everything, I had to forgive everything, or I would live the rest of my life controlled by rage and the desire for retribution,' she explains. 'I had to decide that being reconciled to what had happened was more important than being right about why it should never have happened. Grace or something like it began to fill the cracks in my heart, and instead my motivation became to cause no more suffering in the world.'

She also began to understand the psychology behind the call to war, namely that the grief felt by so many Americans in the wake of the September 11th terror attacks may have fuelled rage and the desire for retribution. Therefore, she asked herself, hadn't she also succumbed to one more turn in mankind's endless cycle of attack and counter-attack, and thus committed much the same offence?

What was critical to Stacy's change of worldview was a powerful encounter that took place at a healing centre in Ashland, Oregon in 2016, where for the first time she shared her story with a group of strangers in a circle of support. As she spoke of her anger and disappointment, the women squirmed in their seats but also listened intently. Afterwards, each in turn responded with compassion and understanding. 'They told me how ashamed they felt knowing they'd done nothing to try to stop the war, knowing they hadn't behaved like the people they wanted to be. They apologised and told me how sorry they were for all I had lost. I saw the weight of what they carried and said how sorry I was for what they too had lost. They saw me in all my aching humanity, and I saw them in theirs. I knew that I could have been them, and they me, and there was nothing left to forgive.'

Stacy's sharing of her story with the women in Ashland is an example of how the micro can become macro and how an intensely personal experience can be transformed by embracing a larger perspective. Stacy's focus now changed direction as she began campaigning for public platforms upon which America's 'better self could stand', advocating for something like an American Truth and Reconciliation Commission on the war in Iraq. Those called to testify would include politicians and pundits who championed the war, grassroots and spiritual leaders, as well as those who were harmed and their affected communities. All would come together to create solutions to promote reconciliation and the restoration of relationships in much the same way that South Africa's Truth and Reconciliation Commission sought to develop a shared national narrative of human rights abuses under apartheid by telling the stories of both victims and perpetrators.

This may seem an implausible suggestion, but in the United States there have been many calls for Truth and Reconciliation models to resolve historical conflicts such as racial injustice, genocide, slavery and more recently even as a means to bring healing after Trump supporters stormed Capitol Hill on 6 January 2021. None to date have come to anything because of the failure to find consensus. For Stacy, as the years have passed and the possibility of constructing such a resourceful container for bearing witness grows further away, the trauma and the damage done by the war does not. Setting up a Truth and Reconciliation process continues to be her life's work because she believes it is the only way of 'facilitating forgiveness, and advancing atonement' so that America and the generation of Iraq War veterans and their families are less likely to carry the hurt and anger forward, seeding future generations with the traumatic legacy of war.

Over the past years, international law and theories on reparations, apology and conflict studies have increasingly placed more attention on forgiveness, and related concepts of mercy, pardoning and reconciliation, as a means of drawing a line under past wrongs. And yet on today's bloody stage of interethnic rivalries, brutal terrorist attacks, and wanton acts of destruction to the planet, the prospect of forgiveness and reconciliation often seems fanciful and incongruous, even inadvisable. One of the difficulties when considering forgiveness in the social or political realm is that some or all of the moral transactions may have to be conducted by substitutes for those who are no longer alive or who are unable to be held personally accountable. Forgiveness therefore becomes more symbolic than actual.

It is easier to apply forgiveness when the offender is within sight.

For instance, you might forgive the heroin-addicted burglar who breaks into your home if you view addiction as an illness. Or you might forgive your older brother for claiming all the valuables from your deceased mother's home because you understand he had a stronger connection to her than you did. Or you might forgive a close friend for having lied because you understand how she couldn't face the shame of telling the truth. And, if you agree with Eckhart Tolle's declaration in *The Power of Now* that 'The greatest catalyst for change in a relationship is complete acceptance of your partner as he or she is, without needing to judge or change them in any way,'[2] you might even forgive the person you love most for almost anything. Anyone who is able to shift their perspective and feel compassion for damaged people will probably have experienced something like these incidents of forgiveness at some point in their life.

The parallels between personal and collective forgiveness are sometimes stark. If you compare a conflict between neighbours over the positioning of a garden fence with conflict between neighbouring countries over disputed borders, the two situations may seem incomparable in terms of human cost, but there are likely to be striking similarities when you look at what caused the hostility in the first place: misunderstandings, past grievances, expansion by stealth, abandonment of dialogue. Also, ancient tribal hatreds between nations filter down over the years, often grimly mirrored by the prolonged antagonisms and fallouts within families. It was only the other day that my elderly Irish neighbour, who has lived in my area of north-west London since 1979, told me that he hadn't spoken to his family in Ireland for decades because, as he put it, 'they continue to regard all of us who came to live and work in England with homicidal hatred. We are "English scum" who have gone to the other side.'

It may be imprecise to compare my neighbour's domestic predicament with the sustained and intractable conflict between

Israel and Palestine, and yet when thinking of these polar cases I am drawn to John Milton's grave pronouncement in his epic poem *Paradise Lost*. Published at the end of the seventeenth century, the poet and champion of civil and religious liberties wrote: 'Never can true reconcilement grow where wounds of deadly hate have pierced so deep.' Perhaps this is an invitation to us all to look inward to ensure our own 'deadly hate' doesn't pierce so deep as to make things irreparable.

Political forgiveness aspires to the ideal of righting an historical wrong or enabling hurt communities to move beyond their painful past, perhaps even in forgetting. In collective terms it involves a group, or the representative of a victim group, offering forgiveness as a pragmatic road to finding peace, perhaps as Ireland's President Higgins said in 2020 on the centenary of the Sack of Balbriggan, 'If forgiveness and forgetting did not exist, we would be trapped in the past where every previous action would be irrevocable and where the present is dominated, burdened even, by preceding events and memories.'

And yet I find myself often sceptical of the possibility and even potency of forgiveness in the context of large-scale collective wrongs because the toxic consequences of such conflicts can proliferate across communities and generations, often descending into what Hannah Arendt famously called the 'unforgivable' – crimes against humanity that can neither be forgiven nor punished. Forgiveness is a largely intangible process and doesn't fit comfortably for me as a means of repairing collective wrongdoings, whereas acts of apology, acknowledgement, reparation and reconciliation can be studied and measured because they rely on public expression for their efficacy. Dr Eileen Borris, who has done a great deal of work on political forgiveness, makes the same point. 'I often speak of forgiveness on a political level and I'm sure when people hear these words they automatically think that to forgive means to let people off the hook, including our political leaders.

That is not what political forgiveness is about. On the contrary, a political forgiveness process must begin with truth-telling and accountability. This is the critical first step. Without this healing is impossible.'[3]

Lack of justice is so often the complication when it comes to considering forgiveness for widescale cruelty, indiscriminate neglect or official incompetence. How can there be political forgiveness where justice has not been served and where truth is still suppressed? As the former Labour MP Clare Short asked when she gave The Forgiveness Project's second Annual Lecture in 2011: 'Is it justifiable to ask the victims of injustice to forgive without redressing the causes of injustice? Might anger at injustice, inequality and corruption be one of the forces that drives historical change and important social reform?' Also, in *Healing Agony: Re-Imagining Forgiveness*, author and theologian Stephen Cherry sets out his theory of 'the good grudge', suggesting that 'as long as an oppressive situation persists then a grudge can be a good thing.' In this way, demanding fairness and holding on to the grievance becomes an act of humanity but it requires skilful navigation between knowing what is right and the trap of righteousness, because righteousness, as Jo Berry has said, can lead to demonisation as you place your own rights above the rights of others. It can easily harden the heart. Indeed, Stacy Bannerman admitted that in the early days of her activism, as she tried to bury her own grief and pain, she began to display symptoms of the very oppression she was fighting against. 'Many activists have done this,' she said, 'because we're organising from the wound. Righteous anger is a legitimate, powerful motivator. But when moral authority becomes moral superiority, it's easy to demonise and attack.'

Almost the entire world will have agreed when just ten days into the Ukraine War in early 2022, on Forgiveness Sunday – a day celebrated by Orthodox Christians – President Zelensky of Ukraine announced: 'Today is Forgiveness Sunday. But we cannot forgive for the hundreds upon hundreds of victims. Nor the thousands upon thousands who have suffered ... And God will not forgive. Not today. Not tomorrow. Never. And instead of forgiveness, there will be Judgement.'

There have been times I've found myself wanting to lean away from the subject of forgiveness, and never more so than when considering forgiveness within the political sphere. We have even contemplated changing the name of the charity, replacing the word forgiveness with empathy or compassion. I remember very early on in my work I was invited to speak on a panel at a festival in Gloucestershire exploring healing and reconciliation. On the platform alongside me were two women from the Congo who had been raped and brutalised during their country's civil war. They had received no justice, no reparations, and precious little acknowledgement. They hadn't even had their stories heard at a judicial proceeding. On the panel they were the first to speak and their stories overflowed with pain. There were tears and there was anger as they pleaded with the audience, and with the wider world beyond, to 'please, please listen to our stories'. I had prepared a few thoughts about the efficacy of collective forgiveness but now I looked at my notes and tore them up. Suddenly I was squirming at the discomfort of feeling like a spokesperson for forgiveness.

In no time at all the tone and content of my short presentation changed, and instead I spoke from the heart about a victim's right to feel rage at state-sponsored violence, and about how in the midst of conflict I didn't think forgiveness was a helpful response because at best it was likely to be premature and at worst it would be self-destructive.[4] I suggested that only in the aftermath of the divisions of war, when punitive justice had been exhausted or shown to be impractical, only then in the foothills of recovery might gestures of forgiveness become a part of mending broken relationships and building peaceful communities. But I stressed that forgiveness in these settings was rare and should always be a matter of personal choice or collective will. It was a timely reminder for me of just what a sensitive subject forgiveness was and how easily and unhelpfully it could be construed as an imperative for healing.

The event reminded me once again that forgiveness becomes problematic when talking about injustices which haven't been acknowledged, let alone rectified. The closest we can perhaps get to forgiveness in this sense is to think restoratively. An anonymous member of Actoras de Cambio (Actors of Change), a feminist human rights collective in Guatemala, doesn't talk about forgiveness but reframes justice away from being a punitive instrument to something that can bring healing though acknowledgement and action: 'Justice for me is someone who will hear me. Justice is someone who will help me heal. Justice is creating conditions against the repeat of harm,' she said.

Retributive justice, which usually involves the right to punish (perhaps a prison sentence, even the death penalty), may sometimes be helpful in allowing victims to move on but it is likely to fall short of fostering a satisfactory restorative process, not least because the criminal justice system can be cumbersome, time-consuming, expensive, and often just further traumatises victims and survivors. The elements needed for restoration include the kind of acknowledgement and accountability that focus on pain rather than guilt and listen to the voices of those who have suffered rather than the justifications of perpetrators or charges read by prosecutors.

In the documentary feature film *Beyond Right and Wrong: Stories of Justice and Forgiveness,* the Northern Ireland politician Lord Alderdice sums up the place of justice when considering historical human rights abuses. He says, 'If you simply hold tight to the requirement of justice come hell or high water, then you probably won't find it possible to move forward. But if you try to move forward without attending to the pain and the hurt of the injustice and the trauma of the past, your move forward will probably be illusory, and you will carry some of that difficulty into the future and into your relationships as an individual or as a community.'

I love Rami Elhanan's thinking around justice. The Israeli father who is a member of The Parents Circle and whose teenaged daughter was killed in a suicide bombing has said, 'Justice is a noble and important thing; you can't live your life without justice but it's not the only value in the book. If you think about a traffic light that's green, you have the right to cross the road, but a lorry may be speeding towards you. Certainly, it's your right to cross but you need to be sensitive and sensible to navigate justice and understand the reality on the ground. You need to be modest about the ability of your powers, to reach the other side where their justice is not the same as yours. The basic word for me is respect. Respect the other person. The minute you treat him or her as you want to be treated this is the opening for discussion about justice. Justice is important but respect more important.'

Duncan Morrow, a professor in politics at Ulster University, who has for the past thirty years worked to promote reconciliation in Northern Ireland, has spoken about the intractable nature of sectarian conflicts that have endured in one form or another for decades. There is often a problem with apportioning blame when it becomes forever more difficult to decipher whose story is the true story, whose story is the good story, and who started the conflict in the first place. In the context of ethnic and sectarian violence he warns about the limits of justice: 'Justice is dependent on the existence of an authority seen as just and when that is absent, or when opposing groups disagree as to who is the victim and who is the perpetrator, who then can bring justice?'

An example of an individual trying to use personal forgiveness to push the collective narrative in a new direction is that of Jude Whyte. Jude is a victims' campaigner and a Catholic from Belfast, whose mother, Peggy Whyte, was murdered outside the family home in 1984 by Protestant paramilitaries during Northern

Ireland's bitter sectarian conflict. These days Jude still lives in Belfast – while his children, having all grown up, have moved to England, Scotland and other parts of Northern Ireland. In his spare time he likes to take visitors on tours round his city to the peace wall and the political murals. He is one of very few people given permission to take visitors into both the Nationalist and Unionist parts of town, because he says, 'I'm considered to be this airy-fairy kind of guy who talks about forgiveness'. But Jude is far from airy-fairy. He is resolute about the rights of victims, angry at the persistent injustices, and would never push forgiveness on anyone. For himself, however, forgiveness has been a life-line, and in terms of the wider unresolved political situation in Northern Ireland he believes it could be a life-line too.

He grew up with his parents and seven siblings in a working-class, largely Protestant area in South Belfast and remembers a blissfully happy childhood before Unionist neighbours made it increasingly clear that his parents would now be targets of sectarian violence simply for having Catholic names.

The Whytes of 139 University Street soon became victims of hatred and discrimination. This involved raids on their home, direct job discrimination, harassment and humiliation at road-blocks, not to mention constant verbal sectarian abuse from officials who were supposed to protect them. And yet Jude's mother would always say she could never understand the madness that had taken over what had previously been such a friendly neighbourhood, and encouraged her children not to hate. Jude recalls:

The first time our home was bombed was in 1983. It was by a young Ulster Volunteer Force (UVF) man who lived a mile away. When he accidently blew himself up in the process it was my mother who comforted him and told me to get a pillow to put under his head. In my entire life if I've ever seen a victim it was him. He was alone and cold with only my mother to help him. A part of me thought the UVF wouldn't come back after that because we'd saved this man's life, but they did and this time they made no mistake. When my mother spotted the bomb on the window ledge outside the living room, she called the police. Unfortunately, it exploded as she was opening the door, killing both her and the young police officer, Michael Dawson, who'd come to investigate. The police were basically our enemy, but my mother had taught me to reach out to those in need and one of the first things I did was go to the house of the young police officer to offer our condolences. It was the beginning of the journey I'm now on.

In those days there was no counselling or trauma advice and initially Jude was consumed by inexhaustible hatred. He admits that during those years he was a bad father, a bad husband and a bad lecturer because his thoughts were only on revenge. He could feel the bitterness eating away at him until eventually he had a nervous breakdown. It was at this point that he knew if he were to save his family, his job and his sanity he had to change something fundamental inside of him. And so it was that he made a conscious decision to thread his painful memories into a new narrative of forgiveness.

'Forgiveness was for me both a pragmatic decision and an emotional feeling – it had nothing to do with religion,' he says. 'It meant that I lived a lot easier, I slept a lot better. You could say my revenge for the murder of my mother is my forgiveness because it has given me strength. I don't forgive on behalf of my mother but for the pain that was inflicted on me for the loss of my mother. And while my mother may not have given me permission to forgive, she did tell me to get a pillow for the UVF man who tried to blow us up.'

And yet Jude has now lost hope that reconciliation and peace can come to Northern Ireland. There is, he says, precious little forgiveness in such a toxic and segregated society, split along lines of identity. Jude puts the blame for this partly on people like him: people who were never members of the IRA, who never committed acts of violence, but still stood by when Protestants were killed and said nothing. 'Because I only protested when my own community were hurt, I'm as guilty as those who committed acts of violence,' he says.

More than 3,500 people died during the Troubles and over 47,000 were injured. It has also been estimated that a third of people in Northern Ireland were affected directly or indirectly by the violence, and many others suffered in Britain, the Republic of Ireland and Europe. Recent political history and the political fighting over trade and border issues following Brexit have shown that the legacy of this bitter civil war is still alive and very present.

Because the complex justice issues remain unresolved despite the best efforts of NGO organisations, lawyers and community leaders, there is a growing recognition that the criminal and judicial systems cannot and will not ever provide resolution. Roughly 1,700 unsolved murders exist and tens of thousands of other acts of extreme violence have left Catholics and Protestants alike with severe and life-changing injuries and little hope of redress. The Historical Inquiries Team set up to investigate these incidents was disbanded in 2014 due to shortcomings and budget cuts, meaning that few now believe that police inquiries and trials can ever bring justice. Jude has spent many years as part of a movement calling for a Truth Recovery Process. The proposal charts a system of conditional amnesties for former combatants that encourages them to come forward and agree to enter into a process of meaningful engagement with victims and survivors. This would, Jude believes, put victims at the centre of the process, provide more information than a court case ever could, and with any luck bring a measure of atonement and even reconciliation.

He has long believed that such a system could create the

conditions for accountability where people would feel safe enough to talk. However, he is increasingly pessimistic and has stood down from his role on the Victims and Survivors Forum on which he served for eight years, believing he can do no more and because the situation remains too politically charged. Somewhat despairingly Jude declares, 'I still know a lot of people for whom the totality of their existence is the events that happened several decades ago. It's time to move on, it's time to forgive. If the dead could speak to us now, they would say "forgive". But most people don't ever forgive because they see it as stampeding all over the memories of their loved ones.'[5]

What happens when a national scandal involving gross negligence has happened and no one has been held accountable? When politicians again and again evade responsibility? The fight for justice will be loud and furious and if there is any talk of forgiveness at this time it will be quiet and intimate, operating well below the radar of accountability. In June 2017 the Grenfell Tower fire disaster in London claimed the lives of seventy-two people. Every single one of those lives was lost due to negligence and systemic failures. There has certainly been no justice here, so where can forgiveness possibly fit in? Indeed, the only reference to it I've found comes from individuals asking for forgiveness – although not (yet) from those responsible for the conditions that led to the fire itself. For example, it was reported that some firefighters in the days that followed the fire left emotional messages at the foot of Grenfell asking for forgiveness from those they could not save. Other than this, in the case of the Grenfell fire – like so many other tragedies caused by negligence, corruption or racial discrimination – any talk of forgiveness feels hollow and even insulting. Additionally, the longer it takes for people to claim responsibility and the more difficult it is for victims to get justice, the further away any possibility of using forgiveness as a route to healing becomes.

In a heart-breaking interview to mark the fourth anniversary of the Grenfell Tower fire I heard a female survivor describe in a TV news report how the failure to hold any person or entity accountable was as bad as, and in some ways worse than, the fire itself. That's an appalling indictment and it reminded me of how a woman whose husband was murdered told me once that the criminal justice system in England – which delayed, obstructed and minimised her pain in court – felt crueller than the harm caused by the original crime. The failure so often of those responsible for man-made catastrophes to own up to their mistakes and their tendency to cover up and blame others indicates the darker side of human nature and is all too evident from the many public inquiries that have tried and failed to reveal the truth and bring justice.

When victims forgive those who have harmed them there is no doubt that it can help former adversaries live together in peace. However, you can never legislate for forgiveness. When I was in South Africa in 2003, I met one of the architects of the Truth and Reconciliation Commission who told me that 'for a brief moment – until we saw sense* – we wondered whether to make forgiveness a mandatory part of the hearings.' The Gacaca courts in Rwanda were a participatory justice system traditionally used to seek legal resolution and settle disputes in local communities, which after the genocide opened the door for repentance, forgiveness and freedom. Placing an individual within a collective process, participants would publicly confess their crimes and ask for forgiveness from the people who they had harmed or their

---

* Gillian Slovo wrote in an Open Democracy article, 'In my view, one of the hearing's most distasteful features was the occasions when the victims were encouraged to forgive those who caused them such great harm. This, I thought, was a political compromise being turned into a forced embrace of old enemies, in which it is always the victims, who had already given up their right to legal redress, were then asked to make the greatest sacrifices.'

families. While there may be a question over the authenticity of some of these public declarations of forgiveness, nevertheless many have said that the Gacaca courts were key to preventing revenge attacks and helped people to live together once again.

In my work with The Forgiveness Project it has always been important for me to examine the possibilities as well as the limitations of forgiveness. Irina Krasovskaya has no time for forgiveness in situations where justice is absent. Her husband, the businessman and dissident Anatoly Krasovsky, was abducted and murdered in Belarus in 1999. Krasovsky's body has never been found and no one has ever claimed responsibility for the murder despite overwhelming evidence of state involvement. Irina told me she didn't blame the people who pulled the trigger because they were just following the orders of government officials. She said:

> It's easier to forgive when you don't know who has hurt you because then it remains abstract. If you know who did it, but there is no acknowledgement and no accountability, then forgiveness is not possible. Forgiveness requires justice. The perpetrators need to be punished, imprisoned and publicly convicted. With justice I could forgive and then I could start to put the perpetrators far away from my mind. My future forgiveness also depends upon the government apologising and acknowledging that they participated in this crime. Then they need to promise to create conditions where these kind of crimes won't be committed again.

I thought of Holocaust survivor Eva Kor who forgave all those who in one way or another contributed to her torture. How much of Eva's ability to forgive was influenced by seeing Germany painfully reckon with its past for the world's scrutiny (albeit many years after the initial failure of denazification), while Belarus, described as 'Europe's last dictatorship', remains an authoritarian state with a dismal human rights record.

Only acknowledgement, sincere apology and reparations can help bring justice after this kind of iron fist oppression. Justice in turn can bring healing and peace of mind. Only then, as post-conflict societies struggle to recover, might forgiveness be seen as useful. Here collective mercy becomes an entirely pragmatic way to set aside ancient hatreds for the sake of broad community healing.

An example of this can be found in the West African country of Sierra Leone. Following Sierra Leone's protracted civil war, which was characterised by extreme brutality and widespread human rights abuses, the charity Fambul Tok (Family Talk) was founded to help bring harmony to divided communities and to revive communal traditions of confession, forgiveness and restorative justice. It was also founded out of frustration with the Sierra Leonean Truth and Reconciliation Commission, which was costing vast sums of money and struggling to achieve community reconciliation. As part of its mission to help build peace in Sierra Leone, Fambul Tok developed a system of forgiveness rituals which were usually conducted around village bonfires at night and on numerous occasions succeeded in reintegrating former rebels into their native villages. Many of these rebels had committed abhorrent crimes and were now once again having to live next door to the very families they had so grievously harmed. Civic reconciliation thus became a vital ingredient in preventing a repeat of the bloodshed, while mercy and reconciliation were seen as the most effective approaches for soothing old wounds and seeding new futures. Whereas the political motivation had been to fight and divide when civil war ravaged the country, now the incentive was to forgive because the villages needed cooperation and collaboration in order to survive.

Brima Koker was a member of the Revolutionary United Front Army that took up arms against Sierra Leone's government forces. He had lived in the Nyandehun region in the Eastern Province of Sierra Leone all his life but, like many of those who joined the rebels, he'd became so suspicious of his neighbours that he did not hesitate to burn his own village to the ground. He did this with the full knowledge that his own brother Vafi, who was the proud owner of two concrete houses, would lose everything. By the end of the war 50,000 civilians had been killed and Brima had fled to Liberia, only later to be returned to his village by Save the Children. Understandably Vafi's resentment ran deep, and he would have nothing to do with the brother whom he had come to despise.[6]

Brima explains what happened next:

> When Fambul Tok came to investigate conflicts in our community and to promote forgiveness and reconciliation, we all went to the open field at the bazaar to see whether we could reconcile. I was standing some distance away from Vafi; he wouldn't even turn in my direction. At times I sneaked a look at him to see how he was responding to the other people like me who were making confessions. Eventually I went up to him directly and asked for his forgiveness. I told him that everything that happened was due to the war and I prayed that he would find it in his heart to forgive me. I said that some of the things we did during the war were terrible and we shouldn't have done them, but that these had been unique circumstances and we were not in control of our actions or of what happened next.

Whether it was the power of the forgiveness ritual or whether it was because Brima had finally demonstrated sincere regret, Vafi didn't say, but it appears he was so moved by the ceremony that in front of the entire community he turned to his brother to reassure him that he would now offer him the gift of forgiveness. He knew also that this small sacrifice of personal forgiveness would lead to community healing, which was now the urgent desire of village elders, who saw forgiveness not as another form of coercion, as some had suggested, but as crucial in moving forward in the aftermath of the bloody civil war. As is common following sincere acts of reconciliation, the brothers soon re-established a close relationship, and indeed one that culminated in them working together for both their economic benefit and that of the village.

Brima's story is an example of how forgiveness can alter the power balance in post-conflict societies. Forgiving an injury is so often seen as a weakness but it can also be a strength because it holds the key to reintegrating the perpetrator back into the human community once again. The condition is of course that a moral path is followed and upheld; should it not be then forgiveness can be taken away again.

Pumla Gobodo-Madikizela, professor in the Faculty of Arts and Social Sciences at Stellenbosch University, South Africa, describes the kind of forgiveness bestowed on Brima by his brother Vafi as 'a kind of revenge, but revenge enacted at a rarefied level'.[7] These words come from *A Human Being Died That Night* – a groundbreaking book which examines forgiveness in the context of conflict and widescale atrocity. Gobodo-Madikizela's striking moral document, published in the decade following the end of apartheid, is based on a dialogue between the author and the notorious Eugene de Kock, one of the most feared and hated men from the apartheid regime who worked as the commanding officer of state-sanctioned death squads. The book, subtitled *A Story of Forgiveness*, raises questions around the value of remorse and the limits of absolution. There are no simple answers as to whether it is possible to forgive under such extreme circumstances, other than perhaps 'the recognition that in the past lies a nightmare and in the future, the possibility of regaining one's sympathetic instincts.'

Although the apartheid era may be slipping away into the pages of history books, from all of the many stories I've collected from South Africa, it's clear that there is still so much to be forgiven.

However, interpersonal forgiveness is there in abundance and many of these personal narratives involve restorative justice and victim-perpetrator liaisons, which have been set up in a post-apartheid endeavour to help secure lasting peace. However, as I heard Gobodo-Madikizela point out at a conference in 2014, although the apartheid era may be over, there is one vital piece missing for reconciliation in South Africa to ever truly happen. 'That is,' she said, 'the acknowledgement of white people (I'm leaving aside exceptions here) who deny responsibility for past atrocities. There is also the problem of the hierarchy of perpetrators, with some white South Africans comparing themselves with violators in other countries, and insisting, "We weren't as bad." Perhaps this is true, but the act of comparison blocks people from taking full responsibility and prevents them from opening their hearts to the hurt and pain of those who were oppressed.'

A few years later I heard a similar sentiment echoed by Deon Snyman, from South Africa's Restitution Foundation. He was saying how one of the shortfalls of the Truth and Reconciliation Commission was that it had only looked at extreme atrocities – the kind of excessive violations committed by men like Eugene de Kock. The Commission had chosen not to address the daily humiliations or the more common acts of violence under apartheid. This had meant that the stories of the bystanders who benefited from apartheid privilege – simply by being white – had remained untold. He concluded, 'for that reason white South Africans today do not see themselves as complicit.'

Kemal Pervanić is a survivor of the notorious Omarska concentration camp, which was set up by Bosnian Serb forces in the early days of the Bosnian war. The camp, nominally an 'investigation centre', was uncovered by British journalists in 1992, leading to international outrage and widespread condemnation. Kemal was transferred along with 1,250 survivors to a camp registered by the

International Committee of the Red Cross, from where he finally made it to England. But in his new home, the past would not let him alone. In his blackest moments he would fantasise about killing his torturers.

I first met Kemal in 2005 in Folkestone, where he was then living, having recently published his book *The Killing Days: My Journey Through the Bosnian War*. A Muslim by birth, these days Kemal chooses a secular narrative to distance himself from institutional religions. He has since moved to Poland where he now lives with his partner and son. We have met many times and Kemal has frequently given talks organised through The Forgiveness Project, especially for schools to mark Holocaust Memorial Day. Like many of the storytellers I've worked with and observed over the years, the events which caused the original harm may have changed or been diluted, but the conditions that created them haven't necessarily gone away. Like with others, for Kemal this can often be a cause of fresh pain and further challenge. I sense that his embracing of forgiveness may largely have been to avoid being worn down by the great magnitude of his past, an attempt to make peace with the horrors of war.

Ten years after the war, in 2002, Kemal first returned to his village with the express purpose of asking his former neighbours why they had taken part in ethnic cleansing. He even managed to meet up with two of his former teachers who had been guards at the Omarska concentration camp, responsible for herding, beating and in some cases sentencing their former pupils to death. One of them seemed full of regret and reassured Kemal that he had never wanted to participate in the Serb National Project, but the other, who had been an interrogator in the camps, had clearly enjoyed his role. He was looking for forgiveness, but at that time Kemal was in no mood to forgive because his former captor seemed incapable of understanding the gravity of his actions and was unwilling to show any remorse.

Back in England Kemal suffered a breakdown as his psyche fought to make sense of what had happened. Returning to his village had been harrowing – his home had been destroyed, the village covered in grass and rubble, and he'd come face to face with former enemies. But at the same time, he was starting to realise that having finally faced the trauma of his past, something fundamental had shifted and he was no longer filled with hatred. 'I didn't decide not to hate because I'm a good person,' he told me. 'I decided not to hate because hating would have finished the job they'd started so successfully. It would have poisoned me.'

Then something unusual happened. One cold January morning Kemal was taking a shower and not thinking about anything much when out of the blue he found himself saying softly, 'I forgive you.' Year after year he'd carried the memory of the perpetrators on his shoulders, so when this moment came it felt like a huge sense of release. 'It wasn't a conscious decision to forgive. Something just changed inside me,' he explained. 'Perhaps it was because my father's recent death had inspired me to make some personal amends. Or perhaps I forgave because I realised that death can come at any time and take away the opportunity for reconciliation.'

These days, nearly three decades after ethnic violence tore his country apart, Kemal continues to return to Bosnia in a bid to build reconciliation. Having founded Most Mira (Bridge of Peace) – a UK and Bosnian charity – he now sees his sole purpose as encouraging understanding and tolerance between young people of all ethnic backgrounds. At times it has been soul-destroying work. Personal forgiveness is much easier than creating a culture of forgiveness on which the foundations of peace can be built.

For this reason, Kemal has come to see forgiveness as something that is unconditional, dependent neither on apology nor repentance, but rather connected to a deep understanding of the root causes of violence as well as a fundamental acceptance of the fragility and fallibility of humanity. He has a strong sense that if he keeps waiting for an apology from those who committed or ordered the atrocities in Bosnia, he will be trapped in his own victimhood. He refuses to dehumanise the perpetrators, believing it to be dangerous as it suggests only monsters and demons can be responsible for such atrocities. 'People describe these people as monsters, born with a genetically inherent mutant gene. But I don't believe that. I believe every human being is capable of killing,' he says.

He is weary of trying to encourage people to reconcile. Peace in the former Yugoslavia is simply the absence of violence, but old hatreds simmer under the surface and all Kemal can do is accept that what they have now is better than what they had before. He knows as well that peace will only be maintained if they keep talking. Healing comes when both sides recognise that they share common wounds, but what happens when this commonality of suffering is denied or obfuscated?

Most people within or outside Bosnia don't like talking about reconciliation. I have grown accustomed to the survivors being reluctant to discuss this issue. What surprises me is the anger of certain outsiders who wade into the discussion like raging bulls, trying to gore everyone in their way. In the Bosnian language reconciliation literally translates as making peace, and some survivors say they didn't have a quarrel with anyone, hence no need for them to make peace – with anyone. Reconciliation is a very uncomfortable way of releasing pain which initially may increase the existing pain, but it's much better than remaining in this state of denial which is akin to claiming the moral high ground on shifting sands. Reconciliation can be personal or societal, or both. The individuals I just described obviously don't understand their personal need to reconcile themselves with their own past. It's a process which ultimately drives you towards acceptance of past events. It's about self-healing; it's about becoming an active citizen; it's about giving your past suffering some meaning.

In addressing forgiveness and justice you can forgive on a personal level and still strive to seek justice on a public level. Neville Lawrence, talking about the racial murder of his son Stephen Lawrence, has acknowledged that while he wanted all his son's killers to face justice, he has now forgiven them in order to release himself 'from the burden of hate'. Bereaved relatives of homicide victims in America can both be staunch advocates of the death penalty while forgiving the perpetrator who they still believe deserves to die for their crime. And yet, forgiving for your own wellbeing, when many others have been harmed by the same perpetrator(s), or when justice has been imperfect or even absent, can cause outrage in fellow survivors or bereaved families. We saw this with Eva Kor and the stern criticism from some Jewish communities she faced after she publicly forgave her Nazi persecutors.

While I might agree with Professor Charles Griswold when he suggests that true forgiveness occurs only between two individuals and that at the political level forgiveness is not appropriate as a tool for repair, nevertheless if you blur the lines just a bit there is another way of looking at this which I find equally compelling. Psychotherapist, author and creator of the Garden of Forgiveness in Lebanon Alexandra Asseily has written extensively about how the past will always haunt us if we can't lay to rest old resentments. She talks about the repetitive nature of conflict; about how conscious and unconscious grievances are received by each new generation through what she calls an 'ancestral bond'. Such enduring grievance stories passed down from teachers to pupils, from parents to children, through the media or by politicians, she believes can *only* be transcended through understanding, compassion and forgiveness. Stacy Bannerman refers to this in terms of creating an opportunity where hurt people are 'less likely to carry the hurt and anger forward for decades, thus seeding future generations with the traumatic legacy of violence.'

Forgiveness has the power to change the narrative, move the story along, and turn the page when nothing else can. When the original perpetrators are long dead, or when satisfactory justice is no longer possible, then forgiveness, mercy and pardoning may be the only strategy we have to help us reconcile with our past pain and prevent old wounds and historical resentments from festering down the generations.

7

The Hardest Word

'The only way we can have true reconciliation
is when we honestly acknowledge our painful
but shared past.'

ELIZABETH ECKFORD
(from the Little Rock Nine)

In 1993 Lyndi Fourie was killed in the Heidelberg Tavern Massacre in Cape Town, aged just twenty-three. Nine years later, her mother, Ginn Fourie, heard a radio interview with the man who had ordered the attack and, wanting answers, set out to meet him. During the apartheid era, Letlapa Mphahlele had been the director of operations of APLA, the military wing of the Pan Africanist Congress (PAC), and he was in Cape Town to promote his autobiography, *Child of This Soil*. This was to be the beginning of a relationship that has lasted many years, with Ginn and Letlapa travelling the world to tell their forgiveness story as proof of inter-personal reconciliation within a socio-political context.

While for Ginn forgiving Letlapa was a personal expression of her Christian faith, there was also a transaction to be made by way of restoring each other's humanity. Ginn describes what happened when Letlapa, after many years in exile, invited her to his homecoming ceremony in his village of Seleteng. 'He asked me to make a speech. It was here that I was able to apologise to his people for the shame and humiliation which my ancestors had brought on them through slavery, colonialism and apartheid.' The audience in the packed hall exploded into applause and after the ceremony a young Black man approached her wanting a photograph taken with her. He said, 'I have to have a photograph to take it back to my home, my family and my village, to show them that a white person understands.'

Conversely, Letlapa has always steered away from the territory of apology. This doesn't mean to say that he doesn't feel intense remorse for some of the consequences of his actions, but rather that he believes the struggle against apartheid was just and therefore apologising becomes a weak and futile gesture. Far more meaningful for him is to strive to make amends through restorative action. While he concedes that Ginn's forgiveness has been entirely responsible for the 'restoration of my humanity', he also acknowledges that it isn't easy to receive the gift of forgiveness, explaining that this is because there will always be a debt to pay. 'I wished Ginn didn't forgive me because as soon as she forgave me, I felt a burden of responsibility. It is easy to be *un*forgiven because you don't have to prove anything, but to be forgiven you get your humanity restored and at the same time you have to reciprocate and prove that you are worthy of forgiveness.'

When representatives apologise for historical crimes and grievances, it's not enough that the words of repentance are uttered; in order to be effective it must be a transactional process. The apology must be perceived by the victims as reflecting genuine sorrow or regret, and signalling a promise that the offence will not occur again. In addition, the remedy must, where possible, be a commitment to restorative acts and deeds of restitution.

David Cameron's formal state apology in 2010 for Bloody Sunday was considered sincere because he didn't shade around the edges, and when he said 'sorry' it sounded like he meant it. There was no attempt to qualify that a serious injustice had been carried out by the British Army. It was a recognition of the truth that thirteen innocent civilians had been killed on 30 January 1972. But the apology took thirty-eight years to come, and in the end was delivered by a British Prime Minster who was only five when the massacre occurred. Perhaps unsurprisingly, those more directly responsible – for example the British Army regiment and its commander – never apologised. Perhaps, just as Tony Blair could never apologise for the invasion of Iraq, it is almost impossible for someone to shoulder the responsibility of such a calamitous mistake. The weight of shame in the knowledge of so many lives ruined would be just too crushing to the human psyche.

Pastor Ray Minniecon, whose story I referred to in Chapter 3, has spent most of his adult life campaigning for truth-telling processes and accountability for the tens of thousands of Aboriginal and Torres Strait Islander survivors who make up Australia's Stolen Generations. Throughout his life Ray has worked tirelessly to bring to the attention of successive governments the effects on survivors of the forced-removal policies.

As soon as Ray started lobbying the Australian government to get support and reparations for his people, he quickly realised that like so many other institutions trying to support the Stolen Generations, politicians had no idea how to help Aboriginals heal from such a massive trauma. 'It's a huge issue,' he says.

The traumatic experience of being in these institutions is evident in every conversation I have with my people. The problem is that when they came out of the homes, they didn't have the tools to work out who they were in relation to where they were taken from. Many fell into crime and ended up in jail for years; few received counselling for their suffering. They still feel deeply that the Government needs to offer appropriate reparations to ease their suffering and their trauma. Most of all they need hope. I tell them that they never had control of their own lives, so I want them now to have control of their futures. If I'm able to give them this one small message, this single vision of hope, then they often have this incredible realisation of, 'Yes, I can do this. I can take control because who'll stop me!' They also use other creative practices to get through. Many become brilliant artists. One of the first guys I worked with in New South Wales wrote a book to tell his story. It was his way of reclaiming his narrative.

Australia does at least now have a National Sorry Day held on 26 May each year to remember, acknowledge and raise awareness of the history and the mistreatment of Aboriginal and Torres Strait Islander people. Just as important, in 2008 Prime Minister Kevin Rudd made a formal apology on behalf of the Federal Parliament to Australia's indigenous peoples, particularly to the Stolen Generations. It was an unprecedented acknowledgement of state brutality addressed to several generations of Aboriginal people, and for the first time officially informed non-indigenous Australians of the nation's dark history. The apology was a watershed moment because from then on the abuses suffered by the Stolen Generations stopped being a debate and became a fact. It meant that the injustices suffered by Aboriginals were no longer just a problem for indigenous people but a national burden for all Australians to carry.

Any thorough examination of public apologies given by individuals, companies and administrations will reveal that most ring hollow, with many of these faux apologies being a strategic defence in the face of defeat, with the subtext 'get off my back' never far from the surface. How do we ever know whether saying sorry is sincere or simply a power play? Probably only by seeing action being taken to improve the lives of those apologised to. This means those who are to blame must take responsibility. The trouble is that future-orientated promises, which may be made in good faith, are often not followed through when administrations change hands, or rigid and bureaucratic procedures take over the process.

In Australia, Kevin Rudd's public apology may have been a momentous gesture of optimism, but sadly it turned out to be little more than symbolic, as it didn't bring the healing and compensation that had been promised. National reparation schemes were largely abandoned, and indigenous communities complained of being shut out of consultation processes.

Nevertheless, it continues to remind Australians of this blemished chapter in their national history and it is important to acknowledge that, as Ray told me, when the official apology was spoken in Parliament on 13 February 2008 for all Australians to hear, it brought great comfort, hope and pride to the Aboriginal people. And I must say, having seen a recording of Rudd's apology filmed inside Parliament House in Canberra, it seems to have been an electrifying occasion. In front of a packed audience and broadcast live with huge crowds gathered beneath giant screens, Australia's Prime Minister held nothing back. In the film I watched Aboriginal men and women, sitting side by side in the Great Hall, as well as packed together on the grassy verges outside, listening in silent astonishment as their Prime Minister apologised for the laws and policies of successive parliaments and governments. I saw Elders clasping their hands tightly, many weeping openly and hugging those sitting close by. There seemed to be an air of disbelief as well as an overwhelming sense of relief. At the end of the twenty-minute apology, everyone rose spontaneously to their feet in rapturous applause: the standing ovation not so much for Rudd as for all Aboriginals who had suffered so much under this form of state cruelty.

Afterwards, as they filed out of the hall, I spotted some Aboriginal women wearing black T-shirts with the single word 'THANKS' printed in large white letters. Outside, a myriad of Aboriginal flags fluttered in the wind creating a carpet of colour. Then a white woman, who for many years had worked in the reconciliation movement, described what she had just experienced, her voice heavy with emotion: 'You could hear a pin drop as it was unfolding. Then of course the tears, and more tears, and more tears. The crying has never stopped. It's like it was just the beginning of a huge breath, an exhale of relief and emotion.'

Even though Kevin Rudd's speech never lived up to its promise, the formal apology was widely regarded as an historic gesture of reconciliation. It's also a powerful example of the power of repetition to drive a message home. Rudd doesn't say sorry once; he says it multiple times. And even if the outcome didn't turn out as many had hoped, nonetheless the apology in its sincerity is something which many leaders today could learn from. Here is a small section:

To the Stolen Generations, I say the following: as Prime Minister of Australia, I am sorry.

On behalf of the government of Australia, I am sorry.

On behalf of the parliament of Australia, I am sorry.

I offer you this apology without qualification.

We apologise for the hurt, the pain and suffering that we, the parliament, have caused you by the laws that previous parliaments have enacted.

We apologise for the indignity, the degradation and the humiliation these laws embodied.

We offer this apology to the mothers, the fathers, the brothers, the sisters, the families and the communities whose lives were ripped apart by the actions of successive governments under successive parliaments.

In 2013 when I spent five weeks in North America, my first stop was Winnipeg, close to the Canada–United States border. Here I learnt for the first time of Canada's own dark history of residential schools, which two years later, in 2015, would be condemned by a national commission as 'cultural genocide'.

The residential schools in Canada were created by Christian denominations – mostly the Catholic Church – on behalf of the Canadian government and were in operation for more than 160 years, with the last school closing in 1996. As in Australia their existence was an audacious attempt by the federal government to forcibly re-educate and convert indigenous youth, and then to assimilate them into Canadian society. Sacred ceremonies were outlawed as Aboriginal people were told that their traditional practices were devil-worship. Many of the children were forced to become Christians, forbidden from speaking their native languages, and abused sexually, mentally and spiritually. Just as in Australia, the schools disrupted lives and communities, causing a multitude of systemic and long-term problems among indigenous people that have filtered down the generations until today.

During my time in Canada, I visited the largest residential youth correctional centre in the province of Manitoba, built in the outskirts of Winnipeg. Having been told that Canadian jails were filled with the legacy of the infamous policy to 'kill the Indian in the child', I was not surprised to find that there was a massive over-representation of Aboriginal people in the Manitoba Youth Center (MYC). Because of this I was keen to meet and speak with Stan LaPierre, a traditional elder and the co-ordinator of Aboriginal Spiritual Care at MYC who was fighting a hard battle to help young people heal and reconcile with their past. His mission was to bring the healing methods and stories of identity to the young people, as well as administer sacred Aboriginal traditions through smudging (the burning of sacred herbs) and cleansing ceremonies.

As we sat chatting in his cramped afterthought of an office,

I noticed the room was full of books and traditional artefacts celebrating his Aboriginal ancestry. Clearly LaPierre was a much-needed father figure or *Mishomis* (grandfather), a spiritual counsellor and mentor. Pointing to the chair I was sitting on, he told me, 'That's where hundreds of Aboriginal youth in custody sit and tell me their secrets. I have heard thousands of secrets of sexual abuse, witnessed so much grieving from these young people. They sit and start to heal because they are prepared to tell me their stories. They need to free themselves of their past if they're going to have the energy to do something with their future.'

LaPierre then began to speak of his own story. When he was a young child his father abandoned the family and he was raised by a mother who didn't know how to parent. He described his mother as a Roman Catholic brought up in a religion that belonged to others. He himself later spent time in prison for drink-driving but for the past thirty years had been sober. In 1981, he heard the sound of drums and felt a stir in his soul. 'I realised there had been a void in me. I was returning to my culture,' he said. Ever since, his purpose in life had been to help young people discover their spiritual and cultural roots.

On the same day I visited MYC I met an Aboriginal outreach worker from an organisation that supported indigenous youth in the community. Just as Ray Minniecon had told me, 'I have come to see healing as a meaningless word for Aboriginal people, because we possess a wound that cannot be healed,' this Aboriginal man was also convinced that recovery was a path that could never be walked: 'The anger is always there. It's like a fire,' he told me, 'therefore the best that Aboriginals can do is to go down a path of accepting rather than mending because you can't put something back that wasn't there. The only thing that I have learnt is to acknowledge what happened to me and use it.'

The year 2021 saw a new reckoning for Canada when its cultural genocide received wide media coverage across the world.

In June that year 751 unmarked graves were discovered in a cemetery at a former residential school in the Prairie Province of Saskatchewan. It followed a similar discovery a few weeks earlier when a mass grave revealing the remains of 215 children had been dug up at a former residential school in British Columbia. I listened to a CBC report covering these two grim discoveries and heard Florence Sparvier, an eighty-year-old survivor of Saskatchewan's Marieval Indian Residential School, being interviewed. Her heart-breaking words mirrored the experience of so many: 'At that time if parents didn't want to allow their children to go to boarding school one of them had to go to jail,' she said. 'So, in order to keep the family together, we went to boarding school ... They pounded it into us ... When I say pounding, I mean pounding. Those nuns were very mean to us ... They were very condemning about our people. They told us our people, our parents and grandparents, didn't have a way to be spiritual because we were heathens ... We learned how to not like who we were.'[1]

With survivors like Florence Sparvier increasingly speaking out, 'sorry' has become a charged word in Canada. The Protestant churches were first to issue significant apologies at a national level, but it wasn't until after the residential story made headline news that in July 2022 Pope Francis travelled to Canada for what he called a 'penitential pilgrimage' in order to finally atone for the church's role in Canada's residential schools. His apology and plea for forgiveness was important because many indigenous people interviewed by the Truth and Reconciliation Commission of Canada between 2008 and 2015 had insisted that an apology from Pope Francis was essential in order for them to address their difficult journey of healing. The Truth and Reconciliation Commission was set up to reveal the history and impact of more than a century of forced residential schooling for indigenous children. Unfortunately, most of their recommendations intended to bring healing to the nation remain to this day uncompleted.

The horrific discovery of so many bodies on the sites of these two former residential schools reopened wounds that had never fully healed and inspired many in the peace and reconciliation movement to call once again on non-Aboriginal Canadians to address their past and not relegate what had happened to being an indigenous issue. Activists appealed to Canadians to guard against becoming the type of ancestor who would be held up in shame for what they did not do to set things right. And while the long overdue papal apology was broadly welcomed, many pointed out it would mean little without restitution and criticised the Pope for not having explicitly referred to the Catholic Church as bearing responsibility for the child sexual abuse.

Back in 2008 the Canadian government did at least try to make amends to the survivors of the residential schools by making a Statement of Apology in front of an audience of indigenous delegates. At one point in the speech Prime Minister Stephen Harper took his apology in an entirely different direction when he actually asked for forgiveness: 'The government of Canada sincerely apologises and asks the forgiveness of the Aboriginal peoples of this country for failing them so profoundly.'

Although some interpreted Harper's apology as a blatant attempt to obscure ongoing socio-economic injustices, the initial responses from Aboriginal leaders were largely positive and the request for forgiveness taken in good faith. However, Mary Simon, president of the Inuit Tapiriit Kanatami, informed the Senate on the day after the public apology that 'As individuals, we will all make our own choice in that regard. As leader of the organisation representing the Inuit of Canada, I believe that real and lasting forgiveness must be earned. It will only be forthcoming when it is clear that government is willing to act.'[2] Others made the point that there was also no actual mechanism put in place for the residential school survivors to offer forgiveness should they have wished to do so. This begs the question: did the government's request for forgiveness place yet another burden on survivors, or was the request actually empowering for Aboriginals for the simple reason that they could withhold it?[3]

Nowadays it is argued by many indigenous people that despite the highly publicised coverage of these national apologies, the majority of non-indigenous Canadians and Australians still do not possess any real insight into the extent of the devastation that white settlers and their descendants inflicted on Aboriginal people. Over time sincerity has been deemed insufficient to warrant acceptance of the apology, therefore relegating the broader aim of forgiveness to the footnotes.

This is why when Ray Minniecon talked of possessing 'a wound that cannot be healed' and the outreach youth worker in Winnipeg told me, 'you can't put something back that wasn't there', it becomes clear how complex ideas around healing have become for fractured and dispossessed communities. And, if the notion of healing is so complicated, where does forgiveness lie within it? The only useful framing for forgiveness I can find in this context is to pick up on Derrida's ideas again, which suggest that when nothing can be repaired and where there is no will for reconciliation and all apologies have proved inadequate, then forgiveness may just possibly be the only course of action left to achieve any form of sustainable restoration.

Indeed, in Canada there has been a forgiveness movement rumbling away in the background. Two years after Prime Minister Stephen Harper issued his apology, nearly 4,000 people, both Aboriginal and non-Aboriginal, gathered in Ottawa's Civic Centre to participate in the National Forgiven Summit. Here a coalition of First Nations, Métis and Inuit responded as individuals to the Prime Minister's apology. For some of those present, the summit was the culmination of five months travelling around Canada in what had been both a spiritual and literal 'journey of freedom', intended to prepare Canada's indigenous people to release forgiveness in response to Harper's apology. This was very much a faith-driven initiative, from mainly evangelical Christian communities, and was spearheaded by residential school survivor Chief Kenny Blacksmith, who proclaimed in a press release, 'For too long [the lack of] forgiveness and [the] bitterness have been a prison locking a vision that gives life and hope to our people. It's time to let go of a negative past.'

At the Ottawa summit, Chief Blacksmith stressed that forgiveness was not political or economic but rather it was spiritual, and it was for each person individually to make that choice. He read aloud the lengthy 'Charter of Forgiveness and Freedom', which declared forgiveness for many offences. This was followed by twenty-four elders, who had survived the residential schools, signing the Charter which was then presented to the Minister for Indian and Northern Affairs while Harper appeared by video link. Then Chief Blacksmith made the following bold declaration: 'Canada is a healed nation, more healed today than before because of what we were able to sign this morning. Mr Prime Minister, we forgive you!'[4]

This grassroots initiative has not been without its critics, as is often the case when forgiveness is introduced into a political context. Some said the summit achieved nothing politically because no genuine reconciliation followed, while others said that the offering of forgiveness simply served to let the church and government off the hook. And yet, inevitably, some people did benefit and find healing through forgiveness. For these individuals, forgiveness was described as a salvation, the only way they could finally break the cycle of pain and embrace a future with possibility. Dale Smith, for instance, began walking from Pinehouse Lake in northern Saskatchewan in March 2010 in order to undertake what he called his personal journey to forgiveness, which would finish at the summit, almost 3,000 kilometres away. Smith had grown up with a father who abused alcohol and who was unable to connect with his children due to spending a traumatic childhood at a boarding school where he was sexually and physically abused. Smith's story illustrates how the personal is political because as he walked his 'journey of freedom' he did so in the name of forgiving his father at the same time as forgiving all those in the church and the government responsible for this generational harm.

While there are certainly individual Aboriginal Canadians and Australians who have forgiven agencies for gross injustices so as to overturn personal pain, as a people there is no space for a national conversation on forgiveness when so much is still unreformed and unresolved. The same can be said for African Americans in the United States where there has been no racial justice for slavery or all the other injustices stemming from racism. In Tulsa, Oklahoma, where in 1921 a thriving Black community was razed to the ground and 300 Black people killed by an angry mob of white men, it took a hundred years for the Mayor of Tulsa to offer an apology. Mayor G. T. Bynum posted on Facebook in honour of the centenary on 31 May 2021: 'While no municipal elected official in Tulsa today was alive in 1921, we are the stewards of the same government and an apology for those failures is ours to deliver. As the Mayor of Tulsa, I apologize for the city government's failure to protect our community in 1921 and to do right by the victims of the Race Massacre in its aftermath. The victims – men, women, young children – deserved better from their city, and I am sorry they didn't receive it.'

To build racial harmony in a post-Trump era, President Joe Biden also became the first sitting American president to visit the site of the massacre, recognising that a national disaster finally needed a national response. Critics noticed, however, that he dodged questions about whether there should be a formal presidential apology, suggesting this was to avoid a rush for reparations from victims' families. Nevertheless, Biden's words were tremendously healing for many. 'For much too long,' he declared, 'the history of what took place here was told in silence, cloaked in darkness. My fellow Americans, this was not a riot. This was a massacre, and among the worst in our history.' He was also the first American president to acknowledge what had happened was a race massacre. In the years following Tulsa, many official records were lost or destroyed and references to what had happened excluded from all school curriculums. Biden's words were heard by the three remaining survivors of the massacre (all in their tenth decade) and by descendants of those who were killed. When an event as huge as Tulsa is erased from history for nearly 100 years, statements like those emanating from both a president and a mayor may not bring the satisfaction of justice, but they do finally bring acknowledgement or apology, which as Dr Eileen Borris has said is the first step towards healing. Yet they are in the long term insufficient if reparations for survivors are not also addressed because reconciliation then becomes just a distant dream, and forgiveness either irrelevant or impossible.

Val Napoleon, one of Canada's most influential indigenous legal scholars, has also spoken about the need for robust gestures of redress. She states: 'If reconciliation for Aboriginal people in Canada is ever going to move beyond rhetoric, reconciliation discussion must include substantive societal and structural changes that deal with power imbalances, land and resources.' And Father Michael Lapsley, who often says that the day he arrived in South Africa he stopped being a human being and became a white man, has thought long and often about what forgiveness means in relation to the humanitarian nightmare that was apartheid. 'In situations of oppression like in South Africa,' he asks, 'what does it mean for white people to say to Black people, "Please forgive us for what we did, but excuse me we will keep the wealth and the land and the power for ourselves."?'

In 2014 I had the privilege of hearing Pumla Gobodo-Madikizela speak at a conference at the Orange Free State University in front of an audience of mostly young Black South Africans. She told us how for many years she had researched forgiveness in the context of gross human rights violations, particularly Nazi perpetrators. She had been astonished at how much emphasis there was on the outcomes of forgiveness and yet very little on the significance of apology and acknowledgement. She suggested that perhaps this was because Nazi perpetrators had been largely unrepentant – some going to the gallows saluting Hitler. It was this that had led her research to now focus less on the power of forgiveness and more on the power of apology, for which, she said, 'the moral bar was lower because apology does not ask a victim to give up resentment.'

Gobodo-Madikizela maintained that apology and acknow-ledgement were critical to healing for those suffering from the effects of gross human rights violations. This is because, she said, when people are wounded, they feel dehumanised. By offering acknowledgement and apology, therefore, the perpetrator recog-nises the victim's humanity and is able to re-humanise them. She also stressed the importance of the perpetrator recognising their own guilt and shame and lamented the fact that many who were called to appear before the Truth and Reconciliation Commission in South Africa simply recited the facts without any acknowledge-ment of their own guilt.

'I think this happens because people are uncomfortable with their own shame, so they are afraid of acknowledging what they did in the past,' she continued. 'This makes people hide away. But unless you stand in your shame and apologise you can't feel or express adequate remorse. The reason this is so critical is because showing remorse and recognising the pain of the person you have harmed is an evocation of empathy.' She concluded with this powerful state-ment: 'The paradox of remorse is that it opens up for the victim the possibility of forgiveness.' When she said this, I immediately thought of the bonfire ceremonies of Sierra Leone where forgiveness had emerged out of a declaration of apology as perpetrators accepted the stigma that arises from public blame. Standing in their shame, they had not been coerced by judge or jury but had willingly held themselves accountable in front of peers and victims who were not there to punish but to find healing for all.*

Apologising for something means giving the person who has been hurt respect, thereby resetting the relationship back to where it was. Conversely, witnessing someone experiencing shame or humiliation for the way they've behaved can help to relieve bruised feelings or rebuild broken trust. Michael McCullough, author of *Beyond Revenge*, has said, 'Apology is really important, because when I apologise to you for something I've done, you see me squirming. You see me uncomfortable. You see me trying to reassure you that I'm not going to harm you in the same way again. You see me giving you respect as a human being with feelings. And all of a sudden, I've turned on a lot of the slider switches that make forgiveness happen in your head.'[5]

Professor Molly Andrews, co-director of the Association of Narrative Research and Practice (formerly Centre for Narrative Research), has spent decades researching the impact of apology and forgiveness on former dissidents from the hard-line communist state of East Germany. Taking part in her longitudinal study were forty men and women who were part of East Germany's anti-state underground movement and key actors in the bloodless revolution of 1989, plus two employees of the Stasi – East Germany's notorious secret police. Most of her interviewees had been subjected to years of surveillance and worse, by the Stasi. Just as Dr Andrews

---

* In her excellent book, *In My Grandfather's Shadow*, Angela Findlay signposts some interesting analysis around shame. 'In *Learning from the Germans*, Susan Neiman describes the work of Bryan Stephenson, an African-American lawyer and founder of the Equal Justice Initiative which has saved hundreds of prisoners from death row. He believes what is missing in America is shame. While regret or remorse has been expressed by some of the descendants of slave-owners, there is no sense of disgrace on a national level. "Without shame, you don't actually correct. You don't do things differently. You don't acknowledge."'

began her research in 1992, the Stasi files were released as a symbolic act of reconciliation between victims and perpetrator so that citizens could discover exactly who had been spying on them and who had been responsible for the state corruption and violence. The very personal nature of East Germany's security system meant that for the first time many people were discovering that friends, neighbours and even members of their own family had been reporting on them. Almost all of Andrews' interviewees spoke of wanting accountability from the Stasi for the actions they had done. For most of them, forgiveness was not a possibility in the absence of taking this responsibility.

Dr Andrews' research into forgiveness is intriguing and extensive. What interests me particularly is that she never actually set out to examine forgiveness but from the beginning questions of forgiveness seeped into many conversations, particularly because the timing coincided with the opening of the Stasi files. In an early interview in 1992 she was surprised by the response she got from one of her interviewees. She was talking to political activist Katja Havemann, who had been part of the Women for Peace movement and had been married to Robert Havemann, one of the most well-known symbols of East German resistance. Dr Andrews explains: 'For the last two years of Robert Havemann's life they lived under house arrest outside Berlin. I asked her – I think naively now as I look at it – could you forgive the Stasi for what they did? And she told me that no, it actually works in quite a different way: "They can't forgive us [for] what they did to us ... We are the living guilty conscience. We're still alive. We experienced it all. We are also still witnesses ... We were naïve in extending too quickly our forgiveness. We had hoped that they would readily say – we were really wrong about this one." I was stunned. So surprised – it was one of those few moments when you really feel you've heard something very different, really against what you expected. I spent the next years thinking about this question and researching it.'[6]

Dr Andrews found that often a victim was eager to forgive but the trouble was that nine out of ten of the former Stasi who came forward actually didn't offer the gift of apology; instead they justified and explained away their involvement. This just rubbed salt into the wounds of the victims, particularly as almost all the former dissidents considered acknowledgement and apology as prerequisites for forgiveness. Dr Andrews works from the forgiveness process model put forward by Donald Shriver in *An Ethic for Enemies: Forgiveness in Politics.* Here Shriver proposes four requirements for a negotiated forgiveness, namely: the two parties must agree that a wrong has been committed; that forgiveness requires forbearance from revenge; that there must be empathy (as distinct from sympathy) for the enemy's humanity; and that this forgiveness should aim at the renewal of a human relationship (renewal infused with memory and not amnesia).

It is obvious from this model why forgiving was so often not possible for the former dissidents of East Germany. While they may have received acknowledgement from former Stasi agents, remorse was mostly lacking and many victims were troubled that there had been no consequences to the injustices. They came to see their perpetrators' acknowledgement therefore as having been given purely in exchange for some sort of absolution.

While for most in a political post-conflict context remorse and acknowledgement will be essential in order to reconcile with the harm done, this is not always the case. In among Dr Andrews' fascinating research interviews is the story of pastor Ruth Misselwitz, who suffered serious injustices at the hands of the East German state and decided after having seen her Stasi files to invite into her home the agent who had been 'responsible' for her. Like so many others, this former agent, who had been part of one of the most tyrannical and successful intelligence services in history, admitted to what he'd done but did not apologise. Misselwitz tells Dr Andrews how she responded to this blatant lack of remorse: 'For me it was a very liberating experience because I finally saw a face. I didn't need an apology from him. It was enough that he came. That was a very, very difficult step for him.'

She realised that this former agent was now living a sad life, without friends or family, whereas by contrast she had achieved a rich and meaningful life. Ruth Misselwitz clearly doesn't require her former tormenter to say sorry in order for her to move on in her life, but when Dr Andrews presses her on what she feels about forgiveness and reconciliation, the pastor dismisses the idea, saying they are 'such big words'. At the same time, she is quick to affirm that she doesn't have any feelings of revenge.

It's important to recognise that not all apologies require words. In 1970 West German Chancellor Willy Brandt travelled to Warsaw on a state visit to attend a commemoration of the Jewish victims of the Warsaw uprising of 1943. Filled with emotion, Brandt spontaneously dropped to his knees before the commemoration monument. This silent apology was viewed as a profound act of repentance. Later Brandt said, 'I did what people do when words fail them.'

Asking victims to extend forgiveness in the absence of adequate gestures of repentance or accountability, or to accept an apology that seems weak-willed or motivated by self-interest, just encourages a continuation of the injustice. Perhaps the difficulty with public apologies is that that they are public. There is also a huge difference between saying sorry and 'doing' sorry, in the sense that public apologies can often be little more than an attempt to avoid reputational damage, an avoidance of guilt, or a bid for absolution. They are part of a blame culture where it is difficult to admit to making mistakes and which in turn just encourages corruption and cover-ups.

Genuine public apologies are rare, requiring a combination of accountability, sensitivity, selflessness and self-awareness, which must be followed by restorative actions. The same can be said of private apologies. As a friend said recently about something she couldn't forgive, 'I want accountability and not apology. I've received too many "sorry"s in my life. It's so empty unless it comes from someone who hasn't been shamed into saying it. I'm looking for action.'

Since apologies are very often also an admission of guilt or of institutional corruption, it is little wonder that the leaders of our administrations and institutions so rarely go in for the kind of apology that constitutes public shaming followed by restorative action. Some have asked whether the act of apology has indeed become misemployed. *Guardian* columnist Marina Hyde wrote this shortly after the English football players missed their penalties at the Euro 2020 match at the same time as Boris Johnson's government was being heavily criticised for its management of the Covid-19 crisis: 'There is something completely antithetical to modern political culture in it all. It is, on every level, absurd that it should feel socially necessary for footballers barely out of their teens to pen missives to the nation apologising for missing a penalty, but not for a government to even acknowledge vast and lethal mistakes, much less say sorry for them.'[7]

You only have to take a look at Britain's NHS,[8] or any other health system in the world for that matter, to see how medical staff fail to apologise for their failures. Advised by legal teams not to accept responsibility for medical error (for fear of crippling compensation bills), this is what happens when a system is incapable of showing remorse. There is also little opportunity for forgiveness when apology is so lacking, when to ask for forgiveness would just create further harm, and when self-forgiveness for medical staff can only be achieved through accepting responsibility.

In the UK, patients who have received a poor service of care or a harmful procedure outcome rarely want to go down the litigation route when mistakes are made but some will do so because it is the only way to get formal disclosure. Admitting guilt can of course be risky and the road to accountability protracted, hurtful and exhausting, so it is little wonder that many who have been harmed must hold resentment for years. As Joanne Hughes, the mother of a child who died due to medical error, has said, 'People are not to blame, actions are. If the medical staff had said they were sorry and told me what they had learned we would all have found healing.' I am convinced that if medical staff were only able to start talking about medical harm then the healthcare systems that we all use would be so much safer. In our blame culture, truth-telling without prosecution would be a radical way forward.[9]

A heartfelt 'I'm sorry' holds enormous power because it has the potential to enable someone who has been hurt to either square the score or let go of the ties. Andy Smith and his brother Matt were abused after being placed into the care system between 1990 and 1998. Over the years, as they tried to hold the authorities to account, their demands for an apology fell on deaf ears, until in October 2021 Andy announced on his Twitter feed: 'This weekend a social worker who made the decision to place us with our abusive carers got in touch to say sorry – she said she had been "haunted" by the decision. This lady is the ONLY person to have ever said sorry. We will meet her and give her a hug – forgiveness is key.' Here a single individual is somehow able to bring as much healing for two victims as an apology from an entire local authority. This is not an excuse for agencies and authorities to renounce their responsibility, but it does show that apologising is principally a personal process.

So often we hear of the anguish felt by victims of catastrophic failures when justice is no longer feasible. Steve McQueen's 2021 documentary *Uprising* explores the contribution racism played to one such failure by bringing to light the stories of thirteen young Black people who lost their lives in the 1981 New Cross house fire. In the film, Sandra Ruddock, whose young husband died in the fire, now a middle-aged woman, insists, 'All I wanted answers to was why, how and who and for someone to say they're sorry.'

The effectiveness of apologising, as with asking for forgiveness, lies perhaps in the possibility that it might be refused. In September 2021 the family of a care worker who died following the Manchester Arena bombing refused to accept an apology from the senior paramedic in charge on the night of the attack. The family blamed the ambulance service for having wasted precious time bringing 28-year-old John Atkinson to hospital in time to save his life and they said, 'We cannot accept this apology. Actions speak louder than words, and we wait to see what actions are taken to ensure this never happens again.'

Most of us will have received an apology at some time in our life which may have helped ease the discomfort caused by a surface graze or a deeper wound. Very often being sincerely apologised to will also prompt forgiveness, whether asked for or not. But, accepting an apology may come with conditions – 'Yes, I'll accept it, but you must change.' The inner work must be done because if you keep apologising and nothing changes (a little like if you keep forgiving and nothing changes) it becomes a pointless endeavour that may in the end do greater harm. Some apologies will never be accepted, in which case all you can do is acknowledge that nothing more can be done to repair the relationship and move on.

When one of my daughters wanted to connect more deeply with her Jewish roots aged sixteen, I became aware for the first time of the significance of the Jewish festival of Yom Kippur with its emphasis on forgiveness. Judaism requires you to repent and ask for forgiveness from anyone who you may have harmed, whether physically, financially, emotionally or socially. Jewish law is also very clear that forgiveness needs to be earned through a sincere endeavour to make reparation. Also, it suggests that the person granting forgiveness should be generous and gracious when offering it.

Jewish law says that you must ask up to three times and if after the third time forgiveness is still refused then, with some exceptions, you have done all that is required of you. This is really quite liberating because any blame for the lack of resolution becomes in part then the responsibility of the person who refuses to accept the apology. I like this because it demonstrates the dynamic energy that exists within forgiving, its ability to both alleviate the wrong-doer of shame and somehow move the story along.

If it is not possible to ask for forgiveness because the wronged person is inaccessible or no longer alive then the burden of regret is one that the offender must continue to carry. Rabbi Jonathan Wittenberg believes that just as important as the concept of forgiveness in Judaism is the Hebrew word *mechilah*, which means forgoing. 'In other words,' asserts Wittenberg, 'you don't forget and the pain is still there, but you no longer hold it against the person who has wronged you. You try to move on together.'

I am friendly with a neighbour whose behaviour has occasionally perplexed me. I had noticed that this sensitive and caring 45-year-old wasn't good at apologising and so I wasn't surprised when his sister told me this was a well-known personality trait of his as he had never apologised for anything as a child. I wondered if perhaps he couldn't face the feelings that came up for him when he had hurt someone or done something wrong. Perhaps it was too exposing and too embarrassing. Then when I thought more about this person's behaviour, I realised that even though he never *said* sorry, he had most definitely *done* sorry, and indeed in abundance through small random acts of kindness as well as grand gestures of generosity. This connects very much with what the late Reverend Ian Paisley, founder of Northern Ireland's Democratic Unionist Party (DUP), said when interviewed on BBC Radio 4 some years ago. He was asked how he could possibly sit in the Northern Ireland Assembly alongside Martin McGuinness, his life-long sworn enemy and a former leader within the Irish Republican Army, who had shown no remorse for various atrocities carried out by the IRA. His answer was simple and unequivocal. He told the BBC reporter, 'Repentance should be measured by how you live your life now.'

Sometimes an imagined apology can shift the story in a way that finds an ending in a new beginning. It can even provide solutions to those who are suffering when the culprit may be unwilling, unable or unavailable to make amends. *The Apology* is a beautiful and courageous example of an imagined confession written by V, formally known as Eve Ensler.* V has no time for forgiveness, which she sees as ignoring accountability, but her book is a hymn to the potency of apology and its capacity to resolve pain.

The sharp, hard-hitting prose written in her father's voice documents his appalling acts of physical and emotional cruelty over many years, including raping her at the age of five. Thirty-one years after his death and realising she has spent her entire life being her father's victim, V finally attempts to escape from the narrative by writing a blueprint for apology. At the start of the book the voice of her father makes this important commitment to his daughter: 'I will do my best neither to justify nor rationalise my actions. I will instead attempt to make an accounting of my actions and my intentions. The telling is not meant to elicit understanding or forgiveness. It is a confession in the deepest sense ... this is the moment when I give myself without reservation or justification, to this reckoning. I have asked myself, What is an apology. It is a humbling. It is an admission of wrongdoings, and a surrender. It is an act of intimacy and connection which requires great self-knowledge and insight.'

The Apology takes readers deep into V's heart by bringing to life the father she so despised – a process which is as much a

---

* Eve Ensler changed her name to V after writing *The Apology* as if finally to free herself from the final trace of her paternal identity.

spiritual cleansing as a means of exorcising demons. She describes this imagined confession as a 'letter from the other side' and an attempt 'to endow my father with the will and the words to cross the border and speak the language of apology so that I can finally be free.' At one point, V's father utters the words, 'Thank you, Eve, for summoning me, giving me this opportunity to reckon with my horrific acts.'

What is interesting here is that *The Apology* is not V's story; it is her father's story. And yet by V writing his story in the form of an apology, it not only acts to soothe her pain but ensures that his story becomes part of her recovery. As the cage of silence is broken and the terrible past revealed, a process of acknowledging and truth-telling unfolds. It feels reminiscent of what Gillian Slovo wrote about the Truth and Reconciliation Commission in relation to the importance of victims being witnessed. While Slovo's criticisms of the TRC are both valid and extensive, nevertheless she acknowledges that some of the victim participants did find a kind of closure as people were given a chance to tell what they had endured in public. She has written: 'As for the hearings themselves – these victims' hearings – well, they were shot through with accounts of what had happened to individuals and with lamentations of pain and suffering. People hadn't come to mobilise. They had come to tell their stories. They had come to mourn. To be heard. To put their truths on record.'[10]

V, therefore, by adopting the role of psychic sleuth, uses apology as an antidote to amnesia. As she researches her father's life story, she discovers that although as a child he had been excessively spoilt by his parents, he had also received no tenderness from them, which had meant he had nowhere to place his vulnerability. In the course of her investigation, she uncovers a level of understanding and compassion for her father which previously had been out of sight. In 2019 the stand-up comedian Marc Maron interviewed V for his weekly *WTF* podcast show;[11] here she explained that she had come to the following conclusion about her father's depraved behaviour in relation to how he had responded to her birth: 'My father had killed off his heart before I was born and then he reconnected with his heart. He felt this overwhelming tenderness for me and didn't know what to do with these feelings. That became sexual because he had to have it, possess it, seize it and take it. He couldn't tolerate his own tenderness.'

The book provides a model for the kind of reckoning that should make those responsible for gender-based violence quake in their boots. By putting her father under the microscope, V draws attention to the disturbing fact that abusers almost never apologise for the harm they cause. In the *WTF* podcast she insists, 'If men don't take responsibility for what they've done, women won't heal. They've got to apologise.'* In reflecting on her role as a writer she describes how she decided to frame her father's apology: 'I needed to know what the structure of apology looked like and I did this through thinking, *What do I need to be free?* And I thought, *I need my father to be vulnerable, humble. I need him to be equal and not above me* . . . Through apology you have to *re*member, *re*connect, *re*attach with what you've done in the past. It's also about accountability. It's *you* (my father) feeling what I felt like when you did what you did, so you open your heart to empathy and compassion, so you hurt the way I hurt.' The powerful sense of release at the end of the book comes from V, the victim, being freed from keeping her father as the monster he was. By being able to change the direction of her feelings, therefore, she can finally push her father out of her way.

---

* V's statement reminds me of these provoking words in Jack Kerouac's novel *On The Road*: 'My aunt said that the world would not find peace until men fell at their women's feet and asked for forgiveness.'

8

DEFEATING HATE

> 'I worry we are creating a world that's not
> interested in old-fashioned words like mercy
> or redemption.'[1]

DAVID BADDIEL

'A lot of the work I do is trying to get people to at least listen to each other ... so that peace can be found between people who are radically different,' said Bjørn Ihler. We were sitting drinking coffee in one of London's most popular coffee chains and I was thinking to myself, *Is this too early to be talking about forgiveness?* It was after all only a year since a terror attack on Norway's Utøya island very nearly claimed Bjørn's life.

Bjørn is a survivor, activist and internationally renowned expert in countering and preventing people from becoming radicalised into violent extremism. He is also someone who knows more than most about the horror of where hardened far-right beliefs can lead. On 22 July 2011, aged just twenty, Bjørn came face to face with Anders Behring Breivik on Utøya island. Brandishing his semi-automatic rifle, Breivik took aim, fired but missed, allowing Bjørn to escape by swimming to safety. On that day Norway's worst mass murderer shot and killed sixty-nine people on the island and injured 110 others. Most of the dead were students like Bjørn, attending a summer camp organised by the AUF, the youth division of the ruling Norwegian Labour Party. Earlier that day Breivik had carried out a bomb attack on government buildings in Oslo, killing eight people and injuring 209. What had fuelled Brevik's killing spree and crusader delusion was a fear that Europe would soon become subsumed by multiculturalism and feminism, a fear so paranoid as to morally justify mass slaughter.

As Bjørn told me in precise and painful detail what had happened on the island that day, I was acutely aware that the first anniversary of the attack had just passed. By now Bjørn had returned to Liverpool Institute for Performing Arts to continue his degree in theatre studies, while Breivik, following a two-month court case, had just received Norway's maximum prison sentence of twenty-one years.

At some point during our three-hour conversation, I repeated to Bjørn words from another of The Forgiveness Project storytellers, Khaled al-Berry. In 2005 when I met Khaled he was a BBC World Service journalist. However, in his previous existence he had belonged to the radical Egyptian Islamist movement Al-Gama'a al-Islamiyya. Reflecting back on an ideology which had led to him dreaming of martyrdom, Khaled told me that when he'd belonged to Al-Gama'a al-Islamiyya he had believed there was only one way to know truth – the divine way, the infallible way. Now, however, he saw the peril of this way of thinking and had come to believe that 'the most dangerous thing in life is to let people become convinced that truth has just one face.'*

---

* Similarly powerful is what former radical Jihadist Manwar Ali says in his TEDx Exeter talk: 'I continuously told others to accept the truth but I failed to give doubt its rightful place.'

These words are powerful to me because their relevance goes beyond extremist movements to any group or religious organisation, past or present, that promotes their way as the only way. By being right, as Robin Shohet said, you automatically make others wrong.

For Bjørn, the logic of Khaled's statement was exactly why he now felt compelled to fight radicalisation across the globe and work with youth to support them to challenge violent extremism in their local communities. Even before the Utøya island massacre he had known that storytelling was a powerful tool for bridging gaps between communities and ideologies, having worked with high-school students to tell their stories. He also recognised storytelling as a personal need in order to help him recover from the trauma of what he had witnessed. For this reason, he wrote down his experiences copiously – every memory meticulously committed to paper.

Going public with his story has been an important part of Bjørn's healing journey: 'I did my first interview in the week after the attack,' he said. 'Sharing it as widely as possible was a way of distributing the weight in many ways, making it not just my burden to carry. This might sound selfish, but at the same time it was also a way of sharing the responsibility of what happened because Breivik was part of our society. He was a white European man who was building his ideology on values that are prevalent in our Western society today.'

Since 2012 I've worked with Bjørn several times. Each time he has had something more to teach me. In the summer of 2019, we talked about the recent massacre in Christchurch, New Zealand, where a gunman had attacked two mosques, shooting and killing fifty-one people before being captured on his way to attacking a third mosque. He had also live-streamed the carnage and published his manifesto online. One of his heroes was Anders Breivik.

The Christchurch massacre was an act of terrorism that had

for me an unexpectedly disturbing personal twist. Shortly after I heard news of the attack my cousin texted me with an image of the gunman's ammunition, on which was scrawled the names of various historical European leaders who had fought against the Ottoman Empire, plus others like Breivik who had inspired his killing spree. Written there for all to see was the name Șerban Cantacuzino – a seventeenth-century Prince of Wallachia and an ancestor of mine who had planned a march on Constantinople to drive the Ottomans out of Europe. It was also the name of my father, who had died the previous year.

In what was in hindsight a slightly paranoid reaction, I expected a full onslaught of hate to come my way via social media – most especially because I was the founder of a charity called The Forgiveness Project. But in actuality nothing happened. It appeared no one took much notice of the historical symbols and influences of this fanatic, knowing perhaps that violent extremists always twist and weave historical figures to fit their own narrative.

But the fact that this happened led to a conversation with Bjørn about the ethics of naming terrorists in the media. I told him that I had written a Facebook post relating to the Christchurch massacre and had been criticised for mentioning the name of the far-right attacker. This person accused me of giving oxygen to terrorists, giving them the publicity that they wanted. I asked Bjørn whether he agreed with this or not.

'Publicity is not primarily what these terrorists are after,' he said. 'It is an element of what they are after, of course, and they want to spread their ideology as far as possible but, at the same time, I feel it is more important to have a discussion about who they are. They come from communities that are very similar to the community I come from, and I think, being honest about those things, means that we should also say their names.'

Bjørn's example for making this point was J. K. Rowling's Harry Potter stories. He explains:

It is a different kind of mythology, but Harry Potter is the only one who says the name of Lord Voldemort. I think learning from that is very important in that Lord Voldemort has less power over Harry because he will say his name whereas the rest of the community is afraid to. They are scared to confront this kind of real evil. Then, holding on to that in my own life I had to face Breivik, by seeing him in court. Personally, I feel I have to use his name otherwise I start going down the path of giving him this kind of mythological presence ... with not naming him he becomes again more of a monster than a human and that then gives us permission to ignore him ... Norwegians have tried to dehumanise Breivik and leading up to the trial there was public pressure to see him as insane. The assumption being that Utøya was caused by one single madman, almost like a natural disaster. I find people's efforts to de-humanise him really scary because that is what he tried to do to us.

In an article for the *South African Times* in 2006,[2] journalist Caroline Munro interviewed author and psychologist Pumla Gobodo-Madikizela about her influential interviews with Eugene de Kock, a man so hated during the apartheid era that he was nicknamed 'Prime Evil'. Munro asks her about how she came to see de Kock as a human being and whether she considers terms like 'prime evil' and 'monster' to be the products of people's fear. Gobodo-Madikizela answers that, undoubtedly, 'they dehumanise him and call him monster so that they can justify their hatred for him. Whereas if he were human we would somehow be implicating ourselves – dehumanising him expels him from society.'

Naturally I wanted to know where forgiveness lay for Bjørn in relation to Anders Breivik – a man who showed no mercy at the time of the attack and no remorse afterwards. He acknowledged that for him forgiveness was an enormously complicated concept and explained:

I choose to see forgiveness largely in the context of reconciliation, reckoning with what happened and then figuring out
how to build on from there. That has been my path. Yes, this
terrible thing happened and it is going to change who I am, but
it is now a part of my life and I need to come to terms with it.
That means not letting the tragedy guide me on to a destructive
path. In Norway the idea of forgiveness is closely tied to reconciliation but at the same time people tend to use forgiveness as
a way of saying, 'I accept what you did, I forgive you.' I do not
forgive Breivik in that sense and my level of reconciliation has
very little to do with Breivik. It has more to do with reconciling
with what happened and my personal journey within that. So,
forgiveness for me means I choose not to let this be a destructive
force. I refuse to carry the hatred and violence I saw that day.

We live in dangerous times. Policies of dehumanisation and
contempt for basic democratic norms are central to many governments and opposition parties around the world. As leaders distract
people with narratives of fear and anger, racists, Islamophobes and
anti-Semites everywhere have felt vindicated and mobilised. For
this reason, changing the pervading narrative of our time from a
hate-filled one to a broadly forgiving one seems more relevant and
essential than ever.

In the lead-up to the 2020 American election, BBC reporter
James Naughtie suggested that the incumbent President Donald
Trump was using his office to sow dissension, acting as if he
'enjoyed the idea of division as an engine of politics.' Creating
a divided 'us vs them' dynamic is a dangerous aspect of today's
politics, and unfortunately the voices proliferating polarisation
and xenophobia always seem louder and bolder than the voices
spreading empathy and tolerance. Perhaps this is because narratives
intended to fire up our righteous indignation are more defined in
their black-and-white rhetoric than the more nuanced restorative

narratives, which by their very nature are likely to be gentler in tone. Words matter, and the degradation of a reviled group has always been a dehumanisation tactic used by leaders and their armies to overcome the opposition. However, contempt for the outsider – people deemed as 'other' or 'foreign' – has become an everyday affair, spat out as much by public figures as the person sitting opposite you on the bus, and of course spread like a sickness all over social media.

In May 2020, against the backdrop of a raging Covid-19 pandemic, and with many countries still in lockdown, UN Secretary General António Guterres made an important public announcement. He declared, 'the pandemic continues to unleash a tsunami of hate and xenophobia, scapegoating and scare-mongering,' and he implored governments to act quickly 'to strengthen the immunity of our societies against the virus of hate.' His words were nothing more than a cry in the dark as, within a year, communities across the world were reporting spikes in hate crimes, with the pandemic unleashing racism towards Chinese and South East Asians in unprecedented numbers. Many believed President Donald Trump's inflammatory rhetoric, referring to Covid-19 as 'the China virus', was largely to blame. In the UK, police data suggested a rise of 300 per cent in hate crimes toward Chinese and East and South East Asians,[3] while in New Zealand, research by the New Zealand Human Rights Commission found that 54 per cent of Chinese respondents had experienced discrimination since the start of the pandemic.[4] In Australia the story was much the same, with the Asian Australian Alliance receiving an unprecedented 377 reports of Covid-19-related racism in just three months.[5]

With many countries in lockdown, domestic violence was also spiralling. In the United Kingdom, the charity Refuge saw an increase in calls to its national helpline of 61 per cent.[6] At the same time, in America the FBI reported a twelve-year high in hate crimes against racial minorities and marginalised groups, showing that 62 per cent of victims were targeted because of their race, ethnicity or ancestry, predominantly Black and Asian Americans.[7] In addition, a shocking report from the New York Police Department in 2021 showed that in one year in America's most populous city hate crimes increased by 139 per cent, and among Asian American and Pacific Islander communities the rise was an even more disturbing 400 per cent.[8]

Hate-filled language is the instrument of fear and paranoia, and anyone who spends time online will know how easily social media enables hateful speech to be communicated and spread. Largely unpoliced, the anonymity of the internet hands users all the power and none of the responsibility. Despite social media sites coming under increasing criticism for their lack of regulation, they continue to favour a person's right to free speech over the potential injury of their words. A high-profile example of this might be J. K. Rowling's famous Twitter feed, which saw lines firmly drawn between those who saw the internationally acclaimed author as a powerful advocate for feminism and a critical opponent of trans extremism, and those who saw her as peddling dangerous transphobic rhetoric that denigrated LGBTQ people and their rights. Against this backdrop, recent hate crimes data for 2019–20 in England and Wales revealed an escalating number of incidents targeting LGBTQ people, with sexual orientation hate crimes increasing by 19 per cent to 15,835 and transgender identity hate crimes by 16 per cent to 2,540.[9] Indeed, a police officer who came out as trans in 2021 was reported to have received an estimated 'two million hate comments', including on far-right and neo-Nazi message boards.[10]

Disabled people are also facing increasing abuse, with cyber disability hate crimes rising by 71 per cent. Hate is filling our schools too. An investigation in 2019 by the London radio station LBC found that hate crimes in schools and colleges had more than doubled in three years, with nearly three-quarters of these hate-related incidents described as being racist.[11] Additionally, with tensions in the Middle East escalating once again, reports of anti-Semitism in the UK reached their highest recorded level in 2021. The Community Security Trust (CST), a charity that monitors anti-Semitism, recorded 2,255 anti-Jewish hate incidents in the UK in 2021 including a surge of people shouting abuse from passing cars. One victim of this wave of growing intolerance towards Jews was Joseph Cohen, who in an unprovoked attack in central London was pushed and punched amid a stream of torrid anti-Semitic abuse. Later, when interviewed by the BBC, he warily conceded that 'most Jews that I know feel unsafe in a country we've lived in all our lives.'[12]

Hatred is found embedded within insults like 'vermin' or 'scum', words so often thrown out by the public at those considered unwelcome, even at medical and NHS staff seen as traitors to the anti-vax movement. Hate speech was laid bare in all its gory detail by Donald Trump before he was banished from Twitter, allowing the President of the United States of America to continually and noisily use labels like 'evil' and 'enemy' for the many individuals and institutions he disagreed with. Belittling and humiliation is a tactic used to shame one's opponents. If you don't like the question, one strategy is to demean and silence the questioner. This is what a Member of Parliament attempted to do in June 2020. As lockdown was loosened, and a number of Labour and Nationalist MPs didn't return to the House of Commons for shielding or safety reasons, instead of concluding this might be because of their age or their health, Conservative Henry Smith MP viciously accused his opponents on the other side of the House of being 'work-shy' and 'lazy'.

Brené Brown, who has spent the past two decades studying courage, vulnerability and empathy, believes that we use a language of insults and shame out of desperation. But, she says, 'shaming the enemy is like wanting to hurt someone by putting poison in the water supply – you're going to have to drink that water too.' She is referring, for example, to the way we call the police 'pigs', or politicians 'psychopaths' or use hashtags such as #fucktrump. Rather than meet hate with hate, we should spend time and energy holding those people accountable, argues the trenchant Dr Brown.

Sometimes people are attacked because of their class or even because of the way they speak. During the 2020 Olympics in Tokyo in the summer of 2021, British broadcaster and politician Lord Digby Jones tweeted nastily: 'Enough! I can't stand it anymore! Alex Scott spoils a good presentational job on the BBC Olympics Team with her very noticeable inability to pronounce her "g"s at the end of a word. Competitors are NOT taking part, Alex, in the fencin, rowin, boxin, kayakin, weightliftin & swimmin'. And in a similarly classist vein in 2019, and also on Twitter, the *Daily Telegraph* columnist Allison Pearson rounded on the then shadow education secretary Angela Rayner, calling her poor GCSE results 'scary' and implying that someone who hadn't achieved good examination grades at school had no authority or credibility to speak on matters of education. Both incidents, however, also demonstrated a better side of human nature – namely that hate can breed love as well as more hate, because very quickly the tables turned. Digby Jones's comments unleashed a battery of criticism – this time aimed at him, while to Allison Pearson's mean-spirited remarks many pointed out that perhaps, on the contrary, someone like Angela Rayner was exactly the kind of person most suited to know how an education system might be improved.

Tom Krattenmaker, writing in *USA Today* at a time when Trump was refusing to accept the legitimacy of the 2020 election result, called on the American people to adopt a no-hate commitment by remembering 'the humanity of the everyday people with whom we compete in the political arena.'[13] Urging readers to speak to the people they disagree with and interact with them in a way that lets them know they are not dirt to us, Krattenmaker went on to quote Biden's acceptance speech, when the President-Elect told Americans: '[we need to] see each other again, to listen to each other again.' It is significant too that as an antidote to the hate rhetoric that has soaked through America for so long Biden chose to share on several occasions his mother's teaching: *I am no better than anybody else. And I am no worse.* It was a moment of cautious hope, though most warned – as it turns out completely correctly – that these words would do nothing to soften America's hardened divisions.

On 12 July 2021 England woke up with a hangover and a heavy heart. Some 31 million people had tuned into the Euro 2020 final the previous evening to watch England's disappointing penalties defeat to Italy. However, the story that hit the headlines the next day was not about how the team had lost this much-anticipated match but rather about the horrific racial abuse that three of its players – Marcus Rashford, Jadon Sancho and Bukayo Saka – were now receiving. For many this was not a surprise. From the moment three Black players missed their penalties, it was blindingly obvious that a torrent of racist abuse would follow.

A little later that day the England team's empathic manager Gareth Southgate described the abuse that some of his players were receiving as 'unforgivable'. To the shattered Southgate, dealing with the aftermath of this bitter defeat, as well as countering the racist pile-on, I imagine the word 'unforgivable' was code for telling offenders they had crossed the line. Talking in terms of unforgiveness felt exactly the right response at this particularly painful time. While the abuse felt intensely personal, on another level it extended far beyond those it was intended for, spreading and multiplying through the insidious and systemic structures that breed racism. This in part is because racism aimed at people who are famous normalises and exacerbates the racist abuse aimed at those who are not.

On top of the online abuse, in the hours that followed England's defeat, Manchester's iconic mural of local hero and Manchester United player Marcus Rashford was defaced. The brighter side of the mural's vandalism was the massive stream of love that followed, sent by people all over the world as a counteroffensive to the racist hate. The thousands of tributes and heartfelt messages that were posted on social media or left beside the Manchester mural have now been archived by the Manchester Art Gallery to be used for anti-racism education. Thankfully such levels of support aren't unusual and examples of ordinary people coming to the defence of victims of hate crime can be found everywhere if you look hard enough. For example, as Covid-19 was first sweeping the UK, a group of men verbally abused and physically attacked university lecturer Peng Wang (a Chinese national) while he was out jogging.[14] His story soon inspired positive actions on social media and solidarity walks all over the country.

In a similar public response to the racist hate hurled at Marcus Rashford, another of the racially abused England players, nineteen-year-old Bukayo Saka, returned to his club Arsenal to be presented with hundreds of messages of support that had been sent in by fans. A picture shared widely in the media showed the young player standing in front of a wall of letters and drawings looking overwhelmed. 'I am speechless,' he is reported to have said.

Southgate talking about 'unforgiveness' is a good example of how in the middle of a heated and immediate struggle any notion of forgiving feels unseemly and even harmful, particularly in the context of sickening racist behaviour. But might forgiveness ever be on the table in this context?

Perhaps if one of the racist trolls were to discard their anonymity, see the error of their actions and freely offer a sincere, public apology to the footballers? In reality it is very difficult to personalise or humanise wrongdoing on a platform where its very raison d'être discourages any notion of repentance or apology, let alone forgiveness.

But at least one act of reconciliation on social media has taken place. British historian Mary Beard has received more than her fair share of online abuse, having been repeatedly subjected to chauvinism, rape threats and pornographic photoshopping. It's hard to discern what exactly her crime has been, as she mostly comes across as ultra-reasonable. Perhaps it is *only* that she is an older woman who dares to have an opinion. She has described a Twitter storm against her as 'like being beaten, being whipped and punched repeatedly. Sometimes you can manage that and sign off with a jolly quip – other times I feel I have been assaulted ... It is utterly enervating.'[15]

Despite such relentless and personal onslaughts, forgiveness is still very much on the table for Mary Beard. In an interview for *Radio Times* in 2018 the journalist Michael Hodges (alluding to Beard having once written about being raped as a student in Italy) asked if she now despairs of men. Her response was instructive. Beard acknowledged she would be willing to forgive men for many of their crimes if they would simply stop doing bad things. 'If the price for getting men to stop was an amnesty then I would take that, I would wave the magic wand and make it happen,' said Beard. However, she has also come unstuck when talking too freely about forgiveness for crimes considered unforgivable. Many people were outraged when she queried the 125-year jail sentence given to former USA Gymnastics doctor and sexual abuser Larry Nassar, because she said it prevented the possibility of 'redemption, forgiveness and making amends'. In the *Radio Times* article Beard elaborated on this particular Twitter storm, saying, '[In the debate] everybody thought redemption should be extended to some people. What interested me was where they drew the line. Some said not for child abusers, others not for terrorists. My logical position was "yes" for everybody, in theory. But it's easy to say everybody is capable of redemption. You then have to think, "How would I recognise it?"[16]

Although internet etiquette advises to ignore your trolls because engagement will only amplify their views and status, Mary Beard does not always turn a blind eye to the threats and insults hurled at her. You sense she prefers to take issue with what people say, not only to shine a light on bad behaviour but also as an attempt to have a polite debate, to widen the lens and get underneath someone's moral rage. Trolls will tear people apart for the smallest things, and what I love about Beard's response to all the hate levelled at her is her fundamental belief that humans need to be heard before they will listen. It is for this reason that when a twenty-year-old university student called her 'a filthy old slut' and taunted, 'I bet your vagina is disgusting', she retweeted his comment for all her followers to see. This fearsome demonstration of public shaming then led – I must say extremely unusually – to the student getting in touch with Beard and apologising. The dialogue was then taken offline when the two met in person for lunch. Later, in a powerful signal of forgiveness, Beard provided him with a character reference for job interviews, not wanting their online interactions to have damaged his career chances. Several other trolls have likewise apologised to Mary Beard, including one who has subsequently come to her support whenever she is attacked on social media.

We live in contradictory and conflicting times. Culture wars have spawned tribalism, hardening positions into ideology over-reach, giving free rein to intolerance and leaving little room for apology and redemption. For some, cancel culture (although the terms 'consequence' or 'call-out culture' might be preferred) is an exhilarating new form of mass democracy in which mis-demeanours can be quickly and effectively held to account and those responsible punished by being stripped of status. For others, by refusing to give a platform to views deemed dangerous or distasteful, cancel culture is a threat to free speech and therefore puts at risk the very fabric of our democracy. Some debates have become so pernicious that people do not dare speak out for fear of being ridiculed or attacked. In a world so full of outrage, faux hashtags and toxic truth, it is increasingly hard to find a middle path for those yearning for nuance and proportionality. Culture writer and novelist Kat Rosenfield speculated on a BBC documentary hosted by David Baddiel that cancel culture also cancels out conversation by allowing us 'to indulge the desire to savage someone but never with the possibility of forgiveness because we have no stake in this, it's nothing to us, it's just like a spectator sport.'[17]

The experience of American couple Linda and Peter Biehl was frequently mentioned to me in the early days of The Forgiveness Project. Their story had received a huge amount of coverage both in the United States and in South Africa, not only because in 1993 their daughter Amy had been murdered by four youths in a Black township near Cape Town, but also because here were two parents who had forgiven. Moreover, in the years following the Truth and Reconciliation Commission, they had invited two of their daughter's killers to work for the Amy Biehl Foundation Trust, the organisation they had founded in their daughter's name. It is a bitter irony that Amy, who had come to Cape Town as a Fulbright scholar to work on South Africa's transition to democracy, was killed on the edge of Guguletu township two years after apartheid legislation had been formally dismantled. When in 1998 the four young men convicted of her murder were granted amnesty after serving just five years in prison, it was a decision supported by Amy's parents.

I first got to hear Linda's story in 2003 while in Cape Town collecting forgiveness stories for *The F Word* exhibition. It was then ten years after Amy's murder and as a way of commemorating the anniversary the Foundation was planning a number of awareness-raising events. I felt immensely sad for Linda because not only was she here in South Africa to mark ten years since her daughter's death, but she had come alone. In the previous year, Peter had died of colon cancer at the age of fifty-nine.

I had planned to meet with Linda to interview her, and then afterwards to talk alone with Easy Nofemela and Ntobeko Peni, the two men working for the foundation. However, in the event, Ntobeko didn't want to speak to me. It turned out that a documentary aired the previous night on one of South Africa's most popular TV channels had told Amy's story and referred once again to both men as 'killers'. Still struggling to come to terms with what they had done, it was a label they had worked hard to shed and one which they believed no longer described their identity or their motivation. Both were now spending much of their time working with youth in the townships, in violence-prevention programmes. While Ntobeko hastily wandered off, returning later only for the photograph, I managed to persuade Easy to agree to have a cold drink with me in the café on the street below where we spoke for ten minutes before he hurried away too.

A year after Easy and Ntobeko were released from prison, they had sent a message to Peter and Linda saying they would like to meet them. They were running a youth club in Guguletu at the time, not far from where the attack had taken place, and they were keen to show Amy's parents their work. 'This was a big challenge. I'd grown up being taught never to trust a white person, and I didn't know what to make of them,' Easy confessed. 'I had been a member of the Azanian People's Liberation Army, the armed wing of the Pan Africanist Congress, and our slogan was "one settler, one bullet". So, the first time I saw Linda and Peter on TV I hated them. I thought this was the strategy of the whites, to come to South Africa to call for capital punishment. But they didn't even mention wanting to hang us. I was very confused. They seemed to understand that the youth of the townships had carried this crisis – this fight for liberation – on their shoulders. Not till I met Linda and Peter did I understand that white people are human too.'

As Easy described the TRC's process and how his amnesty was granted, he started to relax. 'At first I didn't want to go to the TRC to give my testimony,' he went on. 'I thought it was a sell-out, but then I read in the press that Linda and Peter had said that it was not up to them to forgive, it was up to the people in South Africa to learn to forgive each other. So, I decided to go and tell our story and show remorse. Amnesty wasn't my motivation. I just wanted to ask for forgiveness. I wanted to say in front of Linda and Peter, face to face, "I am sorry, can you forgive me?" I wanted to be free in my mind and body. I am not a killer, I have never thought of myself as such, but I will never belong to a political organisation again because such organisations dictate your thoughts and actions. I now passionately believe that things will only change through dialogue.'

What Easy described to me was yet another example of how the gift of forgiveness can have unforeseen consequences in terms of setting things right. When a victim offers forgiveness to an offender it has the potential to not only release the victim but revive the morale and spirit of the offender, which in turn can influence others. In July 2021, a professor from Queen's University in Ontario specialising in terrorism, radicalisation and diaspora politics posted an interesting Twitter thread in response to news that far-right extremist Matthew Heimbach's 'renunciation' of white nationalism had been short-lived, as Heimbach had recently relaunched his old hate group amid a flurry of hostile threats.[18] For many it was a huge shock because a couple of years earlier Heimbach had declared himself changed and become affiliated with *Light upon Light*, an online portal which platforms former extremists and describes itself as creating a 'space free of hate'. Now, however, as it became clear that Heimbach's repentance had most likely been a sham, many of those working to counter violent extremism buried their heads in their hands convinced that Heimbach's false conversion would only cause trouble in their field. Professor Amarnath Amarasingam warned on Twitter that there would be 'a lot of dunking on former extremists, using Heimbach as some sort of example for why formers are liars, shouldn't be trusted and so on.' The professor had some timely advice, however, for all of us. He said: 'They need support, care, and eventual forgiveness and acceptance. People like Heimbach, whatever his motives, do a lot of harm to how societies perceive formers and make it very difficult for people to move on. If our goal in this is *actually* deradicalization and reintegration, then forgiveness must be part of our toolbox. Otherwise, you are in the wrong space.'

Former white supremacist Arno Michaelis has told his story countless times, mostly for conferences, NGOs and schools. He is a towering warrior of a man; a long-time Buddhist who at the age of twenty-five swapped white power fury for global peace advocacy. His forearms are covered in tattoos and his deep bass of a voice a signal of authority. The first time I met Arno was in 2011 when we were both invited to a conference in Dublin organised by Google Ideas, who were launching their Against Violent Extremism Network. In an ultra-chic hotel on the outskirts of Dublin, the conference brought together former extremists, and some survivors, from all over the globe. Delegates from the neo-Nazi youths of Milwaukee to the radical Islamists of Tower Hamlets set out to address issues of propagation and prevention, asking fundamental questions such as: how do you reach people who are intent on harming others because of the colour of their skin or the nature of their beliefs?

A few years later I met up with Arno again, this time in London, where he had been invited to the East London Mosque in Tower Hamlets as part of national Islamophobia Awareness Month to speak about his involvement with white supremacist groups. Of particular interest to those in the room was how he had got out of the movement and what he was now doing to further understanding and peace.

I knew already that Arno had been a founding member of one of the largest racist skinhead organisations in the world, the Northern Hammerskins, as well as a lead singer for the race-metal band Centurion, which had sold over 20,000 CDs to racists and neo-Nazis around the world, but here in the East London Mosque I got to hear much more about his background. He had grown up in Milwaukee, Wisconsin, in an alcoholic household where emotional violence was the norm. Starting out as the bully on the school bus, by the time he was in middle school he had graduated to committing serious acts of vandalism. As a teenager the punk rock scene soon became the ultimate outlet for his aggression and when he encountered the racist skinhead movement, at last he felt he'd found a purpose – namely to save the white race from extinction.

'And so I embraced this "magnificent" cause and truly believed white people were under threat of genocide at the hands of some shadowy Jewish conspiracy,' he explained to a room full of Muslim worshippers and educationists, who appeared neither shocked nor surprised. 'It made total sense to me, probably because nothing else in my world was making sense. I assumed an identity where all that mattered was the colour of my skin.' He described one Thanksgiving dinner as a teenager when he had been vehemently and drunkenly spouting off his views when his mother interrupted him to say, 'Well, Mr Nazi, did you know that you're one-sixteenth Indian?' Her comment shut Arno right up but later that night he went back to his own house and continued to drink beer out of glass bottles, until he broke one and slit his wrist. 'That's how convinced I was that my racial identity was all I had,' he said.

Arno went on to explain how violence soon became a self-fulfilling prophecy. 'I wallowed in violence as a means of self-destruction and stimulation. Using white power ideology as justification and profuse alcohol abuse as a spiritual anaesthetic, I practiced violence until it seemed natural, becoming very proficient in aggression. With my bare hands, I beat other human beings to the point of hospitalisation over the colour of their skin or their sexuality, or simply just for the adrenaline rush. I radiated hostility, especially towards anyone with a darker complexion than mine, and I had a swastika tattooed on the middle finger of my right hand.'

Arno's turning point came soon after becoming a single parent at the age of twenty-four. Witnessing friends die or end up in prison, and fearing that street violence might take him away from his precious daughter, he began to distance himself from the movement. And, of course, the moment he did this the movement began to have less grip over him. As a result, he experienced a kind of aesthetic liberation, rejecting the cultural references approved by the white power movement and allowing himself to listen to whatever music he wanted and watch whatever television programme he chose.

Soon he became immersed in the rave scene and, while still indulging in 'irresponsible behaviour', he discovered there was a lot of forgiveness in the rave community. 'I was embraced and accepted by people who formerly I would have attacked on sight, and that was a very powerful thing for me. But it took me a long time to work through my feelings of guilt and remorse for the harm I'd caused. I wouldn't be here today if it hadn't been for those brave individuals who showed me kindness, and in some cases forgave me on the spot. Such acts of kindness and forgiveness have the capacity to change people like me. That's why I believe that forgiveness is a sublime example of humanity that I explore at every opportunity, because it was the unconditional forgiveness I was given by people who I once claimed to hate that demonstrated the way from there to here.'

Arno then referred to an incident that had taken place in a

McDonald's restaurant in Milwaukee just as he was beginning to question the whole premise and purpose of his racist life. It was to be one of a series of epiphanies that contributed to his spectacular change of heart. 'There was this one time I was in McDonald's getting a burger when I was greeted by a Black lady at the cash register with a smile as warm and unconditional as the sun. When she noticed the swastika tattoo on my finger, she just looked me in the eye and said: "You're a better person than that. I know that's not who you really are."' Feeling powerless against such compassion, Arno then fled from her steady smile and authentic presence, never to return to that branch of McDonald's ever again.

To say that the event at the mosque went down a storm is not an exaggeration. It was as if those present had been waiting to hear a story like Arno's to give them hope that Islamophobia could be diluted and transformed. Later that evening, once everyone had gone home, we ate a meal in a nearby curry house with one of the mosque leaders. Here Arno gave us a fascinating insider's perspective into the structure of a racist mind. Describing the precarious nature of extremist thinking, he said that the views he had once held – which at the time had felt solid and completely watertight – were, he later realised, as 'fragile as a house of cards'. Therefore, he had needed to protect their fragility with the armour of certainty. 'So, you see, I was carrying around this armour with me all the time, until I realised I didn't need to wear it anymore,' he said. 'That was incredible because it took me to a whole new level of connecting with my fellow human beings. Being suddenly vulnerable, I could now connect with others' vulnerability.' Abandoning his racist identity ultimately meant not only relinquishing his sense of belonging to a group but also giving up all national and cultural righteousness. 'Instead,' Arno said, 'I learnt once and for all to be present with fear, uncertainty and failure.'

Two years later, in May 2017, The Forgiveness Project collaborated with the Frank Zeidler Center in Milwaukee to create a

Circles of Compassion: The Power of Forgiveness dialogue. I had flown in from New York to introduce the topic for this public discussion, but the main attraction of the evening were the two storytellers who had been invited to share their personal testimonies, after which participants would then join a guided conversation in small listening circles led by Zeidler facilitators. Arno arrived from his home down the road in the northern suburbs of Milwaukee to speak at the event, and alongside him this time was his close friend and ally Pardeep Kaleka. Pardeep was well known in the city, and many had come to hear him talk about community healing in the aftermath of his father's racist murder. In 2012 neo-Nazi Wade Michael Page had stormed the Sikh Temple in the suburb of Oak Creek, killing six people and wounding four others before turning the gun on himself. Despite Milwaukee being one of the most racially divided cities in America, a tremendous show of solidarity from both Sikhs and non-Sikhs alike had eventually emerged as the collective pain metamorphosed into a delicate balance of outrage and hope.

It was the first time I had met Pardeep and heard the pair speak together, and like most in the room I was struck by the moral courage of their united front and heartened by the warmth of a friendship between two men from such different and conflicting backgrounds. Pardeep spoke with a calm resolve, explaining how immediately after the massacre (which he had only avoided because his daughter had been late for the Temple that morning) he had entered a long period of mourning and deep reflection, wondering how this tragedy could have happened to the father he was devoted to and to his peace-loving Sikh community which had previously experienced so little trouble. He also spoke of feeling a visceral anger for what had happened.

On another occasion when we were alone, Pardeep went further into his story, explaining how his rage in the early days had been aimed not only at the gunman but at the emergency services who had taken so long to respond. 'I felt rage, anger, frustration,' he said. 'I felt like our community was not a priority. I thought about how long it took law enforcement to get into the Temple itself and wondered, if it had been another population would they have treated it differently? Would people have gotten in sooner? There were people who bled out there!'

I had always assumed it was Arno who had been the one to initially reach out to Pardeep, perhaps because Wade Michael Page had belonged to the Northern Hammerskins, the same white supremacist group that Arno had co-founded. But, in actual fact, it was Pardeep who had reached out to Arno. Because his father's killer had taken his own life, Pardeep had questions which he longed to have answered, and having read about Arno's international reputation and the work he was doing in countering violent extremism, he sent him an email asking to meet. 'The questions which were burning inside me were: Why did the shooter do what he did? Why were we targeted? And, maybe the other one, that wasn't so intentional at the time: what can we do about it as we go forward?'

And so it was that just three months after the massacre Pardeep and Arno met up in a Thai restaurant on the east side of Milwaukee where they talked for nearly five hours. Apparently, realising the significance of this encounter, the staff kept the restaurant open until late that night. Initially Pardeep had been sceptical, not really believing racists could change, but their conversation soon showed him otherwise. 'You know what the comforting part was?' explained Pardeep. 'I had a small injury to my eye where my eyelid was lacerated, and I couldn't blink. Arno asked me about that injury and that took me aback a bit because here's a person that I am looking for answers from and he opens up with genuine concern.'

At this first meeting Arno spoke at length to Pardeep about the self-destructive nature of hate, and the painful consequences of having identified with the white supremacist ideology. 'This is where our relationship started,' Pardeep recalled, 'from this level of concern, empathy and understanding and even a kind of relationship building through the mutual klutziness that we both had. At first, we talked about everything except the incident, but we did finally get to the place where we talked about that too. And one of the comforting things that Arno told me was that "hurt people hurt people". That's something that I was able to hold on to. And it's something that we could go forward with.'

Every Sikh in the country was affected by events in Wisconsin on that summer's day in 2012. It was one of the first religiously motivated terror attacks in America and naturally many Sikhs in Oak Creek, afraid for their safety, initially became more closed and inward-looking. Pardeep, however, decided to take the opposite path, deliberately choosing to let go of his rage and try to become more open. 'I decided to respond to this tragedy with compassion,' he said, explaining that there is a saying in Sikhism, *Charhdi Kala,* which he took to mean 'we move forward in relentless optimism'. This had become his guiding mantra. 'I believed that on 5 August 2012 there was a purpose to what happened,' he said. 'Someone came to our temple trying to divide us, saying that we didn't belong and that we weren't wanted in his country. With *Charhdi Kala* the purpose of our response is to reach out, to get to know our neighbours, and say this will not happen again.'

In the intervening years the Sikh community in Oak Creek has indeed come together to work in peace with their neighbours. Pardeep and Arno have co-founded an organisation called Serve2Unite, which encourages children of all ethnicities to come together to cherish each other as human beings and to assume the identity of peacemakers. Pardeep and Arno have also co-authored a memoir called *The Gift of Our Wounds* which is subtitled *A Sikh and a Former Skinhead Find Forgiveness After Hate.* 'We've become as close as brothers,' Pardeep acknowledged, 'and we're here to wage peace together – to honour my father and all the lives lost in the wake of violence.'

Like Arno, Pardeep is a strong believer in the efficacy of forgiveness. 'I think forgiveness is very natural. I think that when we don't forgive, that's not natural. For me, forgiveness is freedom and sometimes that is self-forgiveness, which is also freedom. And communal forgiveness is freedom. Institutional forgiveness is freedom. But if you think about America right now ... I don't know anybody that can say that they truly feel free and live the existence that they want to live. Racism, also, is causing us to not be free. And that's when anger, frustration, rage and hatred cause you to become insular and to exist in the trauma. So, we are not really free and if we're not free we can't enjoy how beautiful another person is.'

For Pardeep, forgiveness also means taking responsibility for a society we have helped to create. I remember being very struck once by the words of Andrea LeBlanc shortly after the shootings of twenty young children and six adults in Sandy Hook Elementary School in Connecticut in 2012. Andrea, a member of September Eleventh Families for Peaceful Tomorrows, became involved in peace work after her husband was killed when United Airlines Flight 175 became the second plane to crash into the World Trade Center. In an attempt to reframe how we think about evil acts and in response to the Sandy Hook tragedy, Andrea wrote in an email to fellow peace activists: 'There are no words that will assuage the victims' families' grief ... the wounds will remain.' Then she added, 'we need to understand that the gunman and his family are victims too. Perhaps victims of the society we have responsibility for.' This is not a comfortable message for people to hear. It is easier to blame politicians but much harder to imagine that we ourselves are partly culpable for some of the world's worst atrocities. Yet, it is a message repeated often by other members of September Eleventh Families for Peaceful Tomorrows, for instance

Phyllis and Orlando Rodriguez, whose son, Greg, was employed by Cantor Fitzgerald in the World Trade Center and who was also killed in the terror attacks. I once asked Phyllis whether she could possibly feel any empathy towards Zacarias Moussaoui, who at the time had just been charged with conspiracy in connection with the 2001 attacks. Her response was: 'If empathy means seeing him as a fallible human being who's capable of evil *and* capable of good – yes, then sure I have empathy for this man, because I believe, under the right circumstances, I'm also capable of evil.'

Arno and Pardeep's work, like that of Andrea and the Rodriguezes, and indeed like so many who have told their stories through The Forgiveness Project, is revolutionary. It's revolutionary because their refusal to demonise those who demonise others isn't some bland act of compassion but a deeply held conviction that the only way of preventing another act of violent extremism is to consign ideas of revenge and retaliation to the moral dustheap of history. Their work is focused now entirely on helping to prevent hurt people from causing hurt to others. In words that echo those of both Bjørn Ihler and Kemal Pervanić, Pardeep told me: 'I think that as a society we can't understand our own complicity in creating a rejection culture and therefore I think we have a responsibility as a society not to wash our hands of the race haters of the world. If we say, "Well, those guys are just evil, they are just monsters," we will never make any progress.'

Sometimes people hate each other, and go to concerted efforts even to kill each other, not because they come from a different ethnic group, religion or ideology, but simply because of where they live or what school they attend. In a sense this is no different to the loyalties placed in rival football teams, except that supporting a football team doesn't usually result in killing your opposition. The drug-fuelled violence perpetrated by gangs exists in every city of the world, as well as increasingly in smaller rural and coastal towns. Communities are silenced by fear as gangs settle scores and reward acts of violence among their members with ratings – a concept known as 'street capital', leading to sickening acts of brutality to protect turf. In some areas simply walking down the wrong road or entering a different neighbourhood can be a suicidal act.

In America's urban street wars, two of the largest and most violent associations of street gangs are the Bloods and Crips, whose rivalry began in Los Angeles in the 1970s. Both gangs have since spread throughout the United States, with an enmity that remains fierce and bloody to this day. In terms of demographic there is little to distinguish members of these two gangs except for a colour code – with the Bloods identified by the colour red and the Crips by the colour blue.

Aqeela Sherrills was raised in this war zone in the run-down housing projects of the Watts neighbourhood of Los Angeles and joined the Crips at a very young age. When in 2005, on a scorching summer afternoon, I went to meet him in Southern Los Angeles, this fearlessly empathetic former gang leader started off by telling me about the enduring rivalries of gangs. 'But we didn't call ourselves gangs; society did,' he explained. 'We were a bunch of kids who had been wounded. Gangs were our surrogate families because so many of us had lost our nuclear families. Our enemy lived on the other side of the tracks in Watts, and Markham Junior High School stood in the middle: a gladiator school dividing the two communities, creating a violent culture and shaping our perspective. As a young person I lived life on the edge and made a lot of bad decisions; robbing, stealing and beating people.'

Eventually, to escape the violence, Aqeela left the Watts area and went to college where he fell in love with a woman. But life in a gang had left him both insecure and immature, and it wasn't long before jealousy raged. 'I didn't believe she could love me,' he said, 'and so I perpetrated the ultimate betrayal. I slept with another girl, contracted an STD and I passed it on to her.'

Aqeela continued to tell me how his betrayal had proved to be a pivotal moment in his life. Harbouring shame and guilt, and after a long drug-induced reflection, he decided to tell his girlfriend what he had done. 'And so I did the first noble thing in my life and told her the truth,' he said. 'She asked how I could have done this and so I thought about it, and I said, "Maybe because of what happened to me as a kid." And then for the first time I shared this secret with her about how I had been molested in my own home. Doing so set me on fire. I didn't have the language or courage to confront the abuse in my own household and now I started feeling rage about this victimisation. In my search for answers I read Malcolm X and James Baldwin. Soon rage gave way to an epiphany. I saw the link between the violence in my house and the violence in the hood. And I thought, *What can I do to try to prevent the killings in my neighbourhood?*'[19]

In 1988, having by now returned to the Watts neighbourhood, Aqeela began galvanising others with his desire to bring peace to urban war zones. Soon he was even talking to the enemy. His message was a simple one: 'No matter which side of the tracks you live on, we all come from similar backgrounds and are all dealing with the same problems.' By 1992 community leaders had signed a peace treaty between the Crips and the Bloods. Aqeela remembered the elation of that year, as children played in parks again and the number of gang homicides dropped by 44 per cent. Ten years of ever-decreasing violence in the city followed as Aqeela laboured in the frontline of the peace movement.

On the afternoon that I met with Aqeela a friend of his was by his side – fellow peace advocate Calvin Hodges. Both men had transcended gang culture but when they were young they would have been trying to kill each another. Calvin, the younger man, had an identical profile to Aqeela, except that the gang he had left behind was the Bloods. 'There was no communication between the Bloods and the Crips, even though we were the same,' he explained. 'Like many of my friends I had no father and joined the gang in order to belong. I've been shot, stabbed, slammed on the sidewalk and have served time in jail, too.'

When Aqeela talked about his years of building peace within the gang community, Calvin joined in telling me that he had been involved too. 'The 1992 peace treaty changed things,' he said. 'I was doing security when all the gangs came together. That's when I first met Aqeela. He was one of the lights committed to change. The peace treaty gave me hope because I never thought peace was possible. For the first time you could go off limits and cross the tracks; there was even crossbreeding between the Reds and the Blues. Healing comes when you can sit down and laugh with someone. The more you communicate the more difficult it is to commit violence.'

Then Calvin warned me that peace was much more difficult than war because it was always easy to kill, but infinitely harder to stop the killing. And of course, in the aftermath of violence you are having to deal with the damaged emotions of its legacy.

Calvin Hodges is one of the few storytellers from The Forgiveness Project whom I've lost touch with over the years. In writing this book I thought to Google his name to see if I could find out where he was now. I knew that Aqeela had founded the Reverence Project – an initiative working with survivors of crime aimed at shifting the current social-philosophical culture of shame and violence to a more loving culture of compassion and forgiveness. In the meantime, I knew nothing of Calvin's whereabouts.

My search on the internet revealed only two relevant items, both of them upsetting in different ways. The first was an article in streetgangs.com from 2010,[20] five years after I met Calvin when he was thirty-five years old. The headline read 'Gang worker wounded in his body but not in heart.' It appears that while doing the dangerous work of a gang outreach interventionist, operating alongside the police and other community organisations, he had been attacked. In trying to help a youth leave the gang he had been targeted, shot three times and left partly paralysed and in a wheelchair. Interviewed for the online publication at the Watts public housing complex where he grew up, Calvin is reported as saying that he is not angry at the men who shot him but angry at the mindset that made them the way they are.

The second link I found on my internet search was from Getty Images, which displayed a picture of Calvin in his wheelchair under a title reading, 'Calvin Hodges, a respected gang intervention worker, was counselling a youth in the Watts area late last year when he was shot seven times in a drive-by shooting. He survived, though he was severely injured and partially paralyzed.' It's a spare, unflinching photograph taken by Robert Gauthier from the *Los Angeles Times*. Calvin is sitting in his wheelchair facing out to the left of the frame somewhat dwarfed by the immense mottled sky above him, and the sharply white walls of a windowless house behind. In an image that captures his humanity as well as his predicament, the sunlight casts his shadow on the wall and his eyes are closed. In a column to the left, alongside the page, the rights to use a large-size image of this photograph are advertised at £370.

9

FACING THE ENEMY

'Because crime hurts, justice should heal.'

JOHN BRAITHWAITE

A few years after I founded The Forgiveness Project, I chaired a panel discussion about forgiveness and countering violent extremism. Alongside me were two people who'd had experience of terrorism. One was a father whose son had been killed in an international terrorist assault, the other was Patrick Magee – the man responsible for planting the Brighton bomb, who in 1998 had been released from prison under the Good Friday Agreement after serving fourteen years.

I had met Patrick many times, usually alongside Jo Berry, whose politician father had been killed in the Brighton bomb, and both had contributed their shared narrative to The Forgiveness Project's exhibition and taken part in a number of our events.

The panel discussion was due to start at 7 p.m. but by 6.55 p.m. the father of the child who had been killed still hadn't arrived and I had no way of contacting him. In the end his chair remained empty throughout the discussion and somehow Patrick and I managed to carry the conversation along without him. The next day I received a message from the father apologising for his unexplained absence and telling me that he had been all ready to set off for the event when the enormity of what he was about to do had hit him. He simply couldn't face sitting on a chair next to Patrick Magee, a man responsible for a terrorist attack in which innocent people, just like his child, had been killed. I'd felt stressed and a little annoyed when he hadn't shown up for the event the night before, but now I totally understood. Of course he couldn't face sitting on a platform next to Patrick Magee. Why on earth did I ever think that he could? Meeting in person someone who has harmed you, or someone who has harmed others just like you, is in reality so much more difficult than it might appear to be in the days and weeks leading up to it.

This wasn't the only occasion that Patrick's public appearance caused a backlash. Another similar incident took place at The Forgiveness Project's inaugural annual lecture in 2010, delivered by Archbishop Desmond Tutu and entitled 'Is Violence Ever Justified?' As was customary with any event held by The Forgiveness Project, the keynote speaker was joined on stage by people with lived experience, and on this occasion Patrick Magee and Jo Berry sat alongside Desmond Tutu. The great nave in St John's Smith Square church, situated just a mile from the Houses of Parliament, was tightly packed with an extremely eager audience of over 700 people. Most were there to hear Desmond Tutu's lecture, but some had come specifically to hear the stories of those with intimate and personal experience of violence.

At some point in the middle of the event a woman whose family had been killed in a genocide took exception to something Patrick said and walked out. Patrick remembers the incident as well: 'It was traumatising for her. There have been other times when I've been speaking alongside Jo, and perhaps in response to questions from the room, I can feel myself putting that political hat firmly on my head because I feel I have to respond politically to specific questions about the struggle and the power imbalance. It can be a very difficult thing for people who have been traumatised and still have memories of loss to listen to. There have been times in my dialogue with Jo where we couldn't continue because of this. It has been hurtful for her and that is something we always have to bear in mind and yet we continue to talk. We go away and think about these things and then meet again to continue.'

After the lecture, audience feedback revealed that people found the event intriguing, inspiring and, at times, uncomfortable. Some reported profound moments of understanding. Richard McCann, for instance, whose mother was murdered by serial killer Peter Sutcliffe, had come all the way from his home in Leeds and later told me that what Desmond Tutu had said had been a life-changing experience for him. 'It blew me away. It was a revelatory moment,' he said. 'I actually chased after Tutu when he walked off stage and managed to catch up with him. I told him what he said had helped me forgive the man who murdered my mother. I have always known I could never turn back the clock but hearing Desmond Tutu's words showed me I had the capacity to change the situation by changing how I felt about what had occurred.'

The discomfort felt by some audience members arose, I suspect, from a tension that is always present in conversations about forgiveness between people who have been harmed and people who have harmed others. While these are often profoundly healing spaces, they can also create an atmosphere which is raw and tense.

This inaugural Annual Lecture produced one critic in particular. A woman contacted me a few days later saying that while she had loved Desmond Tutu's lecture, she could have done without the other speakers, particularly Patrick Magee. 'I resented them taking time in which "the Arch" could have been speaking,' she wrote. She went on to say she had found what Patrick had to say hard to fit into the mould of the other Forgiveness Project's stories because, she suggested, 'Jo is the person doing the forgiving and for me Patrick came across as self-serving and self-centred. I felt uncomfortable.'

I remember at the time feeling stung by these criticisms, but recently, as I read the email again over ten years later, I found myself more interested than defensive, not least because Jo in fact rarely talks in terms of forgiving Patrick. Her story is a journey of understanding, of trying to move beyond the power dynamics of forgiveness. In the years following that lecture I came to see that while most people attending our events have found them a life-affirming experience, a few do become angry and resistant. Jo and Patrick's story sums up the gritty, difficult, grey area of a dynamic that occasionally confuses people, leaving them, as my critic said, feeling uncomfortable.

Since 2000 when Jo and Patrick first met privately, they have appeared together in public more than 300 times. Jo always speaks from the heart about how her father's death has inspired a lifetime of peace building. Patrick's motivation is solely to try to widen people's understanding of the conflict in terms of context and intent – something he believes to be both necessary and vital in pursuit of understanding and the hope of reconciliation. One of the more controversial occasions was an event organised by the All-Party Parliamentary Group on Conflict Issues in partnership with The Forgiveness Project, which was held at the House of Commons to mark the twenty-fifth anniversary of the Brighton bomb. Chaired by the Liberal Democrat MP Simon Hughes, this was a conversation with Jo and Patrick in front of an audience of parliamentarians and invited members of the public, all singularly aware of the symbolism of the location.

Many Members of Parliament welcomed this display of reconciliation, but there were some MPs and peers who condemned the very idea of inviting the man who had planted the Brighton bomb into the heart of an institution that he had once tried to destroy.

None were more angry than Norman Tebbit, whose wife had been paralysed in the attack and who maintained that despite Patrick Magee having received eight life sentences for the bombing, he had got off lightly when released early through the Good Friday Agreement.

It was the question of remorse that had triggered Tebbit's fury because to his critics Magee appeared to justify his actions and to be largely unrepentant. Headlines over the years, such as 'Brighton Bomber: I would do it again', portrayed a man who was at best deluded and at worst dangerous. Patrick has always had a problem with this premise, insisting that 'it's perfectly possible to regret something deeply, every day of your life, and yet still stand over your actions at the time. At the end of the day it's about legitimacy and about who is allowed to use force.'

Tebbit's main criticism of the House of Commons event was that Patrick Magee had been lauded and employed by organisations like The Forgiveness Project. In May 2007, in a stinging attack on the 'Brighton bomber' and the BBC (which had invited Tebbit – unsuccessfully – to take part in Radio 4's *The Reunion* programme alongside Jo and Patrick), Tebbit wrote to the *Daily Telegraph* saying: 'Now it seems we are to be encouraged not merely to accept Mr Magee as a respectable human but to admire him and – most sickeningly of all – to like him.' Some years later, in an article published in the *Financial Times*, Tebbit declared that this amounted to a type of appeasement which was symptomatic of the weakness and lack of resolve of modern British society. To the question of whether he would ever like to meet Patrick Magee and his accomplice, he replied, 'Yes, I would like to bump into them. If I was driving a heavy truck.'

Before the House of Commons event, I wrote to Norman Tebbit as a matter of courtesy to warn him that Patrick would be speaking in Parliament. I said I knew this was likely to stir up painful memories for both him and his wife, and I explained that the reason for putting on such an event was to understand better what drives people to violence and how communities can reconcile with the painful aftermath. I tried to convey that Lord Tebbit's views were as important as any of the other victims of the bombing. I meant this, as I hate the idea that The Forgiveness Project is asking the world to fall into a daze of forgiveness. In response, I received a brief but fierce letter back, stating, 'Your project excuses, rewards and encourages murder.'

I certainly would not suggest that Tebbit should have felt or behaved any differently. His experience as a victim of the Brighton bomb is as valid and as true as anyone else's. I am also as appalled as he is that some people over the years have suggested that he should forgive his attackers: as I learnt from the former UVF paramilitary Alistair Little, expecting victims to forgive only victimises them further. Any attempt to understand extreme violence must never explain away the behaviour of killers; the tension lies in the fact that any explanation should set context but never become an evasion or consolation. When I asked Patrick if he understood why Tebbit might feel so much hatred towards him, he replied, 'Of course! Norman Tebbit's crusade against me is totally understandable – his wife is in a wheelchair. Why should he have an obligation to forgive? If I was in his position and someone had hurt my relative, I don't know if I could forgive.'

I have never wanted to present these forgiveness narratives as easy or glib and my intention has always been to explore not preach, to uncover rather than smooth over. I want people who are still working things through – who don't necessarily have tidy stories or eloquent answers – to be given a platform. Presenting complicated narratives is important because we need complexity, ambiguity and even contradictions and disturbing paradoxes to widen our lens on life. My hope is that people who are exposed to these stories will be able to zoom out from the individual personal narratives to look at the bigger picture and ask different and difficult questions. Yet the dilemma for those of us creating a platform for 'formers' such as Patrick is how far do we go in pursuing a debate around understanding and forgiveness at the risk of offending those who have been most hurt?

Hearing the perspective of 'the enemy' is part of the tension that moves the story along, and this kind of dialogue, which brings together a victim and perpetrator, can help to repair the harm done by humanising violence. That is not to say to make violence more palatable, but rather to help us recognise under what circumstances ordinary people will hurt their fellow citizens, and what can be done to prevent it. Patrick's message is complicated because although he has frequently spoken out against violence and is a strong advocate for Northern Ireland's peace process, he is reluctant to renounce the use of violence altogether as a political tool, telling me once, 'I could never say to future generations anywhere in the world, who felt themselves oppressed, "Take it, just lie down and take it."'

One reason that some people feel hostile when listening to Patrick is because they want to fit a neat ending into his narrative. Most will much prefer a pacifist approach with a 'mea culpa' finale because it is much less challenging to hear someone say, 'I was wrong, I should never have done this,' than to hear them say, 'I had no other choice, we were combatants fighting a war.'

For this reason, the atmosphere is always charged when Jo and Patrick take part in a public exchange. There is nothing in the slightest bit rehearsed about their conversation and no two events are ever the same. Despite an atmosphere of reconciliation, difficult questions are always raised and Sir Anthony Berry's memory casts a long shadow, perhaps because as Patrick has said, 'No matter what we can achieve as two human beings meeting after a terrible event, the loss remains and forgiveness can't embrace that loss.'

For Jo, having had dialogue with Patrick over many years on different platforms across the world, she has got used to him shifting positions between defensive justification and sincere regret. As Patrick himself writes in his memoir *Where Grieving Begins*: 'It is hard to conceive of a more difficult dialogue.'[1] His response, Jo fully appreciates, will usually be dependent on whether he perceives the audience to be hostile or welcoming.

The social psychologist Jonathan Haidt has said: 'If you really want to change someone's mind on a moral or political matter, you'll need to see things from that person's angle as well as your own. And if you do truly see it the other person's way – deeply and intuitively – you might even find your own mind opening in response. Empathy is an antidote to righteousness, although it's very difficult to empathize across a moral divide.' Patrick Magee has certainly claimed this position in the years of being in dialogue with Jo Berry, having reached an understanding of the legitimacy of different positions. 'Just like the loyalists and the security forces, we believed right was on our side,' he writes in his memoir, conceding that since then he has come to 'accept and extend that same understanding to the people we were facing.'

Patrick's position is not dissimilar to that taken by some of the Palestinians I've met through Combatants for Peace (an initiative committed to non-violent action made up of former Palestinian combatants and former Israeli soldiers), whereby they do not regret having used violence in the past against the Israeli occupation, but at the same time insist that now the emphasis must be on finding peaceful solutions. One man, who had attempted to blow up an Israeli police station, told me, 'We were freedom fighters seeking independence from our occupiers,' and a young woman who had tried to stab an Israeli check point soldier explained, 'When I was fifteen I believed suicide bombing was a means of resistance but now I believe violence breeds violence and there's no choice for me other than to find another way.' Both these former fighters – like Patrick – believed they were defending their people whose territory was occupied and for this reason they had no other choice but to take violent action. This is not dissimilar to the stance taken by Nelson Mandela, who in 1985 responded to President Botha's address to the House of Assembly by attributing acts of violence by black South Africans as the responsibility of the apartheid regime, proclaiming that had there been democracy there would be no need for violence. Looking back at the history of South Africa, people generally understand this now.

Why do people like Patrick Magee, as well as others who have committed acts of violence, agree to hold public dialogues with those they have hurt? I've always thought it would be much easier to keep quiet, so as not to be continually labelled as the person who did this terrible thing, or have your story relayed and dissected repeatedly in the public domain? Perhaps they place their story in the spotlight out of a need to be understood, or a wish to make amends; or, in the spirit of restorative justice, perhaps out of a willingness to address questions that need answering? Whatever the reasons, I truly believe that this kind of dialogue can hold enormous potential in offering potent examples of restoration and reconciliation.

Patrick Magee shed some light on his motives for going public when he explained to me once that if he could walk away from it all he would. 'But', he said, 'if you have hurt someone on a personal level it's about repairing the harm or trying at least. It might also, at some level, encourage others to meet with people they have great difficulty dealing with.' Much of his unique relationship with Jo Berry is documented in his 2021 memoir, which is also the culmination of his struggle to make sense of the past and an effort to build a bridge to a common understanding.

The fact that Patrick asked Jo to write the foreword to his memoir bears testimony to the enormous respect he holds for her. In the opening pages of the book, she writes, 'Pat has been a teacher for me, sometimes very challenging and also very transformational ... I salute his courage to have become vulnerable, to feel the cost of what he has done and to write about it in this book … He chooses to meet me despite what I represent – I am no easy option instead a difficult mirror and a reminder of the choices he made. He trusts me and together I believe we show what is possible.'[2]

What happens when someone who has been harmed or injured reaches out to the person who has hurt them, but that person refuses to recognise their pain? This is precisely what happened to Marian Partington.

In 1973 Marian's sister, Lucy, disappeared on her way home. For twenty years no one could explain the reason for this mystifying and uncharacteristic disappearance until bodies were discovered in the cellar of 25 Cromwell Street in Gloucester. Soon it was confirmed that Lucy had been one of multiple victims of the notorious serial killers Fred and Rosemary West. Ten years after the shocking discovery of Lucy's remains, Marian wrote a letter to Rosemary West, who was by now serving a whole-life tariff at HMP Low Newton in County Durham for the murder of ten women and girls, including Lucy. It is a remarkably compassionate letter which acknowledges the sexual violence Rosemary West suffered as a young girl. It also describes Marian's inner work of forgiveness and conveys some of the wisdom that Buddhism has taught her over the years. The letter ends on a note of extraordinary generosity:

> I know that you have known a lot of fear. You said that you felt that you had been always looking over your shoulder, all your life. I feel fear in my belly. Sometimes I feel heavy and black. When I looked at the mountains yesterday, I saw my heart. Some of it is still frozen like the snow on the peaks, some of it has melted into the lake at the bottom of the valley. Sometimes it catches the sun and shines. I am sending you these words in the hope that they may help you in some way. Please know that I

do not feel any hostility towards you, just sadness, a deep sadness that all this has happened, and that your heart could not feel a truth that I wish you could know. Our lives are connected and I am sending you the springing of the branch as a token of hope.[3]

It is impossible to know how Rosemary West might have reacted had she opened the letter and read it. Instead, eight weeks after sending it, Marian received an official prison reply in the post in which it was requested that she should 'please cease all correspondence' because Ms West did not 'wish to receive any further letters'.

It was a stinging riposte and one which you might expect to inflame feelings of anger and frustration in Marian. However, because most of her adult life had been dedicated to navigating a way through the agony of traumatic loss, she had wisely known after first writing the letter in 2004 (while on a Buddhist Chan retreat in Switzerland) not to send it then. In her memoir *If You Sit Very Still* she explains: 'In 2008, four years later, I posted the letter to Rosemary West. It seemed like the right time to do it. I had waited until I did not expect or need to have a reply.'

That is all Marian writes about Rosemary West's response to her letter. There is no sense of disappointment and therefore perhaps no words needed to explain more. The letter was written as part of transforming unfathomable cruelty into a message of hope; it was written to give voice to a humanity born out of sorrow, and as such the lack of response therefore becomes irrelevant, part of the old and now relinquished story.

In 1978, when Margot Van Sluytman was sixteen years old, her father was murdered during an armed robbery at the Hudson Bay store in Toronto where he had been working in the menswear department. Eight years earlier Theodore Van Sluytman had brought his family from Guyana to Toronto in order to raise his children in safety. The very last time that Margot was to look into the face of her father was three days after the shooting when she visited the funeral parlour along with her mother, brother and two sisters to say their final goodbyes. Appalled to see him lying there dead in the casket, she bent to kiss him on the forehead, whispering the words, 'Dad, I promise you that your life will not be for nothing.' At that time, she had no idea what this vow meant.

Three men were charged with the shooting - one of them Glen Flett, who was twenty-seven at the time. The murder shattered the family in every conceivable way. Within three months of her father's death, feeling bereft and suffocated by grief, Margot moved out of the family home knowing she needed to be alone in order to mourn and feel the pain. The pain, however, wouldn't go away, and two years later, aged eighteen, she tried to kill herself by overdosing on pills. It was only when her mother pleaded, 'I've lost Daddy, I can't lose you too' that she vowed she would never try to take her own life again. During the next few years she suffered from depression and eating disorders.

'I would walk around feeling like half a person, completely lost. Somehow, I managed to get an Honours degree in English and Philosophy and although I didn't believe in much, I did believe in love and so when I fell in love with someone we got married and started a family. The marriage didn't last but my two daughters gave me a reason to stay alive. Yet still my life felt full of existential angst. An author I knew once said to me, "You're not the only one who feels pain, Margot." But I was trapped in my hurt, and any injustice filled me with vitriol.'

In the end it was poetry that saved Margot, with words becoming 'an ally', offering solace and a way to address painful and complex things. Margot even managed to carve out an ideal job for herself using poetry as a form of healing to help others navigate their grief. In the succeeding years she ran courses, published several books and became an accomplished poet.

Over the decades Margot's grief has changed tenor and shape, transforming like a kind of alchemy from overwhelming despair into a tenacious crusade to create a more connected world. One important way she has done this is by promoting and reframing the idea of Sawbonna to fit in with a victim-led restorative justice model which even Canada's Department of Justice has shown interest in adopting. Sawbonna, or *Sawubona*, is a Zulu greeting which recognises the healing power of seeing and being seen; it is an invitation for a deep kind of witnessing that invites us to communicate and explore the possibilities of helping each other. For Margot, Sawbonna is an opportunity to break beyond the rigid justice system and exist in a shared humanity no matter what we have done.[4] In a recent interview, she explained: 'I believe people do not have to forgive and love each other, because that may not be possible. Sawbonna *is* possible. It says we're staying the course; we're in shared humanity. We don't have to be best friends, but we're not looking to harm each other. We're looking to have conversation.'[5]

Everything Margot puts her mind to is done with fierce intensity, whether it's teaching students creative writing, giving lectures on transforming the justice system, or developing virtual healing spaces under the name of Theodore's Place, which one day she hopes will also be a 'bricks and mortar' initiative for victims' therapeutic healing. The loss of her father continues to inform her work, done out of deep admiration for the man whose 'vital energy for life and for living continues to infuse my life with passion, purpose, and joy.'

The first time one of her father's killers physically appeared in Margot's life was three months before she met him face to face. She had noticed her publishing press had received a donation in the name of Glen Flett sent by Flett's wife. Margot explains:

> It turned out that Glen Flett [who had transformed his life in prison and been released after fourteen years of incarceration] had attended an event aiming to bring victims and perpetrators

together, where a woman had asked if he had ever thought about contacting the family of his victim. When he replied 'yes', she went away to research what I was doing and then showed him my publishing press work. So, I replied to Glen's wife to thank her for the donation and ask if her husband would consider giving me an apology. She emailed straight back saying, 'He has been waiting a long time to do this.' From then on Glen and I started to exchange emails. They were emails filled with humanity. His words really helped to heal me, but after a while the words weren't enough, and I knew I needed to look into his eyes. So, three months later I met the man who killed my father. After introducing myself, we both started to sob and just hugged each other. It was extremely powerful. We did lots of talking and lots of crying – it was as if we knew each other.

When I first met Margot in a crowded café in London in 2013, she told me this story with much excitement. At the time jetlag had made her rather hyper and edgy, while I was tired and a little downbeat, but even so I was grateful for the sheer force of her free spirit and raw honesty.

After Margot had told me about her father, and about meeting Glen, and then about the enormous significance she placed on her work around Sawbonna, we discussed her uneasy relationship with forgiveness. She had initially loathed the very notion of forgiving her father's killer, even though her mother had embraced it almost immediately. Indeed three days after the shooting, a journalist had come to the door of the family home to talk to her mother. 'Do you ever think you'll be able to forgive the men who killed your husband?' the journalist had asked, and without hesitating her mother had said, 'Yes, I forgive so that I can live.' At the time Margot recognised absolutely that her mother couldn't afford not to forgive, and yet she felt very differently herself, developing over the years a kind of aversion to the very idea of forgiveness, especially as it was so often presented as a prescription for recovery from trauma. 'To tell someone who is in pain to forgive is brutal,' she said, holding my gaze as if throwing down the gauntlet.

She then explained that while she still held this view, her thinking about forgiveness had started to change due to her relationship with Glen Flett, but also because of something that had happened when she gave a public talk. An audience member had told her about having chosen to forgive the perpetrator of a heinous crime and then shared how it had brought her great peace of mind. The story made Margot wonder if perhaps she had been too narrow-minded when contemplating forgiveness. 'The moment I began to even consider forgiveness, my whole body started to feel different, more complete and more at peace,' she told me. 'For me forgiveness is a fluid process which means healing. Before I embarked on this path half of me was a void and full of nothingness, whereas now I have a friendship with the man who killed my father and that has helped put meaning back into my life.'

The second time I met Margot was also in London. This time I heard how she and Glen had given a number of talks together and how she continued to support him in his journey and his life. She was very keen for me to come to Canada to meet and interview Glen in order to place his lived experience alongside hers and thus make her story complete. I noticed she had developed a very real sense of gratitude towards him, perhaps because his redemption gave her experience a deeper significance and brought her closer to finding peace.

I never did get to interview Glen Flett, because the third time I met Margot again in London, where she had come to share her story for The Forgiveness Project at a mental health secure unit in Croydon, they were no longer speaking. Something had happened that I have seen happen before when victims of serious crime choose to start a dialogue with the person who has hurt them most. Disappointment sets in, expectations are not met, ill-conceived words pierce old wounds – and very often these interactions become a source of additional and aggravated grief. In Margot's case she had gone along to give a public talk with Glen but he decided he would do it alone. By the time I got to share the platform with Margot in Croydon it was clear that her thoughts had continued to evolve and now she was once again far more comfortable addressing the dangers of forgiveness rather than its benefits.

These days Margot's views on forgiveness are born from a very real sense of injustice about what she sees as the flawed assumption that unless a victim forgives and chooses to side with the offender, they do not care about human rights, or indeed about searching for a shared humanity. This, Margot believes, is 'limited, limiting and wrong'. She is also keen to bring balance to a debate which she sees as steeped in a binary and judgemental tone.

Margot's insights into the limitations of forgiveness are partly formed by what she sees as the often unspoken expectation that victims who meet their offenders through restorative justice should then forgive. Many victims I've met who have experienced restorative justice describe a feeling of forgiveness, or something closely related to it, despite the fact that they embarked on restorative justice never expecting to offer forgiveness or feel empathy for the offender. It appears that seeing your perpetrator reveal genuine signs of fear and regret humanises them and therefore can quickly elicit feelings of compassion. Compassion operates in and through social relationships and that is why it's not surprising to me that restorative justice can and often does culminate in a final demonstration of forgiveness.

When I started collecting stories of reconciliation and forgiveness, I didn't know what the term restorative justice meant. It wasn't until I started meeting people from Canada, America and Australia who were proponents of restorative approaches that I was first introduced to this alternative theory of justice. Both restorative justice and healing circles are a way of addressing harm, arising from the traditions of indigenous peoples who sought to solve problems of crime and punishment by bringing people together in constructive conversation.

Ever since then, through my work with The Forgiveness Project, I have been trying to unravel what happens when people from opposite ends of the justice spectrum come together and are given the opportunity to hear each other's stories. Restorative justice involves communication between the offender and the victim, which can be conducted in a number of ways; often through a face-to-face meeting, but also it may be done through written communication or through messages passed via a mediator or facilitator. Sometimes it can be a combination of all three. Tim Newell, a former prisoner governor and long-standing advocate of restorative justice, sums up the underlying philosophy perfectly. He writes: 'Restorative Justice views crime primarily as injury (rather than law-breaking) and the purpose of justice as healing (rather than as punishment alone). It emphasises the accountability of offenders to make amends for their actions and focuses on providing assistance and services to victims. Its objective is the successful re-integration of both victim and offender as productive members of safe communities.'[6]

Several years ago, I was asked to speak at a restorative justice conference in Belfast during which a leading pioneer in the field asked the audience of delegates what they thought was the most important word connected to restorative justice. People started guessing words like 'apology', 'honesty', 'truth', but nobody guessed correctly. The answer, said the speaker, was 'forgiveness'. I felt oddly chuffed, but in the intervening years I've come to disagree with this, in part because of what I've learnt from the many scholars and practitioners I've been exposed to. I've come to see that while forgiveness may well be an outcome of restorative justice, it should never be an objective. Victims enter the process to ask the question 'why me?'

and to be able to tell the story of how the crime has affected them. Offenders want to make amends and explain why they committed the crime in the first place. John Braithwaite, a criminologist who has been active in the social movement for restorative justice for five decades, once said, 'Forgiveness is a gift. It loses its power as a gift if you make it a duty.'

V described an apology as an 'act of intimacy and connection'. She could just as easily have been talking about the process of restorative justice. I've listened to many people's experiences of restorative justice from the point of view of both victims and offenders, and all these stories have demonstrated to me the power of apology in private settings. Whether the apology presents in the form of repentance, or simply taking responsibility for the harm done, often a bond emerges through the connection of two people joined through a deep injury or crime.

In the UK various studies and trials[7] have shown restorative justice to be one of the most effective ways of reducing reoffending and yet it has never been widely adopted, partly because of the cost but also because it is frequently viewed as being soft on crime. Because restorative justice is rarely an alternative to punitive justice and because I've heard many offenders say that meeting their victim was tougher than any prison sentence, I know that restorative justice is not the soft option.

It was Canadian-born Anne Marie Hagan who first provided me with me the most eloquent description of the power of restorative justice when she described what happened when she came face to face with her father's killer. For decades she said she had been campaigning to prevent this severely mentally ill man from being released from prison, believing the longer he was locked away in jail the greater the value of her father's life. But when Anne Marie was offered restorative justice, instead of dismissing it she realised she was curious to meet the man who for so long had occupied so much space in her head.

Her description of the meeting shows restorative justice to be a pathway to understanding another's pain and a means to finding a shared humanity through cognitive empathy. 'In that face-to-face meeting, which lasted one hour and forty minutes, sixteen years and ten months of misery was just wiped away,' she said. 'As he started to cry and said, "I'm to blame, I'm to blame," I couldn't take it anymore. I rushed around the table and hugged him, telling him that I forgave him. I remember saying to him, "Blame is too strong a word, blame is too strong a word." I could never have imagined that in doing so, I would set myself free. Finally, I was able to let go of all the pain and torment that had held me captive, realising that I had been my own jailer. My life changed from that day as I began to see the world through new eyes. I felt joy again, the numbness was gone.'

Sometimes restorative justice produces results you could never foresee. For example, when Linda Biehl and her husband, Peter, got to meet two of the youths who had beaten and stabbed to death their daughter, not only did they offer Easy and Ntobeko work, but several years later, when I asked Linda how she felt being so closely associated with them, she said with astonishing generosity, 'Actually, I've grown fond of these young men. They're like my own kids. It may sound strange, but I tend to think there's a little bit of Amy's spirit in them.'

In 1981, in the woods near her school in Vancouver, thirteen-year-old Carmen Aguirre was sexually assaulted by serial rapist John Horace Oughton. Thirty-three years later, Carmen, now a writer and theatre artist, travelled to meet him in the medium-security prison in Alberta where he was being held. By coming face to face with her attacker she was hoping to even out the power imbalance. By her side was a woman called Laura, another of Oughton's victims who also wanted to look the man who raped her in the eyes. This restorative justice meeting is meticulously described in Aguirre's deeply intimate memoir, *Mexican Hooker #1*.

Describing the lead-up to the meeting, she writes: 'Everyone has asked us why we want to meet him. I tell them what Laura, one of the wisest, most articulate people I've known, says. "Because I'd like to meet the man I've been in a relationship with for my entire life".'[8]

She explains how the meeting is tense and unpredictable because Oughton begins by saying he has no memory of the rapes. Eventually, he acknowledges that while remorse is hard to find for something you can't remember, he is learning to have compassion for his victims. This is enough to satisfy Aguirre and prompts her to say something that to most people will seem incomprehensible. She thanks Oughton with the words: 'John, I have spent many years pondering why you did what you did to me. And I know why. It was to teach me compassion. Even in the moment, during the actual attack, I could feel your pain. I could feel it. And so I want to thank you.' Perhaps these words begin to make sense if you consider this radical act of kindness as the fulcrum of her healing; an enormously effective antidote to hatred that brings symmetry back to her life. Forgiveness is not mentioned here but we're in the same territory, with compassion becoming the only way of transcending the violence of rape.

In 2014 Paul Kohler was savagely attacked when four masked men forced their way into his home demanding 'where's the money?' Paul realised they must have somehow come to the wrong address and that this was a case of mistaken identity, but the assailants didn't listen to his protestations and immediately began laying into him with their fists. Meanwhile in the upstairs bedroom two of the men found his wife, Samantha, and made her lie down, using her own jumper as a hood. Thankfully, their daughter and her boyfriend were at the top of the house and, hearing the commotion below, quietly secured their door and called the emergency services. Within eight minutes the police had arrived and very likely saved Paul's life, who by now had a fractured eye socket, broken nose and was suffering an extensive loss of blood.

When I met Paul at his house in south-west London where the incident had taken place, he told me how two of the gang had been caught on the night of the attack and the other two only apprehended after the media used a graphic image of his bruised face. While Paul was grateful for the coverage, he also noticed how the story was manipulated. 'Unfortunately, some elements in the media and in politics misused the story; for instance, it was used to feed the flames of anti-immigrant, anti-EU feeling. I was portrayed as an English hero defending his castle against foreign invaders. I wasn't happy with that.'

The case went to trial and the men received lengthy prison sentences, but Paul felt he still had many questions left unanswered. As a result, the charity Why Me? offered to facilitate restorative justice for the family with one of the assailants – as the others were not considered suitable to go through such a process.

Paul explained the family's different motives for wanting to meet their attacker: 'I went into this meeting wanting to know why they'd attacked me. My wife wanted to tell him how angry she felt, and my daughter wanted to find out if this man was going to mend his ways. In the end, during the course of a two-hour meeting, it emerged that only my daughter's question was of importance. I was never going to find out why they'd chosen me. I'm sure they had got the wrong house enforcing a drug debt. My wife discovered that actually he knew already exactly how she felt because of the way she'd looked at him during the attack as he made her hide her face. However, my daughter's question mattered because after he apologised to us we felt we had to discover in this meeting whether the apology was genuine or superficial. Our only means of testing his sincerity was by asking him about what he was doing to change his life. And when he told us how he was trying to mend his ways (by studying and working constructively within the prison) we felt it was genuine.'

For Paul's daughter, meeting the attacker rehumanised him and stopped him being a monster in her eyes. 'It was,' said Paul, 'a very important part in her recovery.' He's still not sure what effect the process had on him, but he knows his wife didn't like it. Even though Why Me? had stressed that restorative justice was not about forgiving the offender, nevertheless Samantha felt she had somehow been too forgiving of him. It took her a long while to reconcile with having been nicer to him than she wanted to be. For Paul, on the other hand, forgiving the perpetrator was an important stage on his journey.

'For me forgiveness felt quite natural, perhaps so that I could reconcile with what had happened. Some people came up to me afterwards and said how religious I must be to have forgiven such evil. As a 'God-fearing agnostic' this always made me smile as I think of forgiveness as part of the human condition rather than something inherently religious. Forgiving the perpetrator is really dealing with your internal issues and ensuring you are no longer embittered by the experience. So, forgiveness paradoxically is almost a selfish act whereby you reconcile internally with the trauma. The consequence of that is of course that you also forgive the perpetrator.'

Dr Mark Umbreit, founding director of the Center for Restorative Justice & Peacemaking at the University of Minnesota's School of Social Work, is an internationally recognised practitioner and scholar with more than forty years of experience as a mediator, peacemaker, author, teacher and researcher. When I was visiting Minneapolis in October 2013, I was delighted when he agreed to meet me at the lakeshore café in the beautiful Como Park. He told me how the victims' movement in America had originally feared restorative justice because they felt it diminished the harm that had been suffered. Because Umbreit's work at the time depended largely on building bridges with restorative justice sceptics and criminal justice organisations, for many years he intentionally avoided tackling the subject of forgiveness. Yet, he said, from the very first time he witnessed a victim–offender mediation, he was aware of the energy changing in the room that left a space for forgiveness. As a result, it was a matter of time before he came to the conclusion that there was very often more energy of forgiveness in a restorative justice facilitated meeting than there was in a mosque, a church or a synagogue.

Mark Umbreit also told me about the research he had recently undertaken with Dr Marilyn Armour, a University Distinguished Teaching Professor at the University of Texas, and founder and former director of the Institute for Restorative Justice and Restorative Dialogue. He spoke about the 'paradox of forgiveness', by which he meant that in a restorative justice setting, the more you talk about forgiveness or encourage it, the less safe people will feel. On the other hand, the more you create safe conditions, the more likely it is that forgiveness will occur.

Later that month I also got to meet the impressive Dr Armour in Austin, Texas. 'So much is in the body language. So much is done non-verbally,' she said. 'We keep insisting on an explicit concept of forgiveness but that is fraught both religiously and politically. It's too clouded. We need to redefine forgiveness. I'm interested when you see it in the body language, the facial expressions. But if you say, "Do you forgive me?", people back off.'

While the public generally have a very positive response to ideas around restorative justice, if you put forgiveness into the frame then the response becomes more hostile. Elizabeth and Fernando Jimenez were delighted to share their story in the *Mirror* newspaper in August 2021[9] because they were eager for the world to know about the possibility of redemption for the young man who killed their daughter through dangerous driving. They were also keen to talk about the healing power of forgiveness. As Fernando puts it, 'At first it was very difficult to forgive Nick until I realised it was not about forgiving the man but about forgiving his stupidity.'

Their story is unusual because they didn't just forgive the man who caused their daughter's death; they actually brought him into their home, visited him in prison, treated him like a son and continue to be a major support in his life today. Once the article in the *Mirror* was published, some of the readers' comments reflected the customary level of incredulity that I have come to expect when victims of crime speak about forgiveness. For instance, one person wrote, 'Sadly, there are many do-gooders in this world, that have hope and trust in others, but end up being taken advantage of by criminals and they or innocent others are victimized through their naivety.' Another commented, 'He would be invited in to the family home!!! But his new home would be in a hole in the garden the same day . . .'

While the public may be ready to support restorative justice as a way of reducing crime, it is not ready to consider forgiveness as a way of reducing psychological pain, and especially not if that for-giveness is handed over to the offender with an abundance of love and generosity, as in the case of Elizabeth and Fernando Jimenez. Kay Pranis is a national leader in restorative justice in America, spe-cialising in peacemaking circles. She told me how for a long time she had avoided using the word forgiveness until she started working with Native Americans. 'Then I couldn't avoid it any longer,' she said, 'because they would say that every time you don't forgive you put another pack of salt on your back.' Although Pranis maintains that victims have every right not to forgive or reconcile with their wrongdoer, she believes that society has a duty to forgive, in the sense of accepting an offender back into the neighbourhood once they've been released from prison. 'It is the community's responsi-bility to reconcile with the one who has harmed because if they do not, they set up the next victimisation,' she said.

In the United Kingdom too you might assume that offenders have earned society's forgiveness once they have served their sen-tence. However, with an increasingly righteous public, instead of moving towards models of restoration and rehabilitation, we just seem to be creating further marginalisation for those already living on the edge. Societal blame and a hostile public mood to offending make it difficult for people with criminal records to be restored to fully participating members of our society from where they can begin to repair the rupture that criminal offending creates. Not all members of the public are hostile, however. James Timpson, chief executive of the family firm Timpson's, employs more people with a criminal record than any other company in the UK (at least 10 per cent). Perhaps it is a sign that society is more forgiving of offenders than we think when he insists, 'We have more customers who come and shop with us because of what we do, rather than who try and avoid us because of what we do.'[10]

It's worth remembering that one of the more arresting ideas to emerge from evolutionary psychology is that forgiveness – just like vengeance – has evolved as a tactic to decrease the risk of future harm in the face of past injury.[11] Our justice system is a punitive one rooted in blame and retribution. It is also extremely expensive and fails in one of its key objectives – to reduce crime. It may be a radical hypothesis, but imagine a more humane society, where the state's forgiveness – if it were to work properly – might change an offender's motivation as well as their attitude towards their victim, which in turn would reduce crime, minimise costs, and most importantly break the never-ceasing cycle of vengeance.

10

OUT OF THE STRAITJACKET

"I wondered if that was how forgiveness
budded; not with the fanfare of epiphany, but
with pain gathering its things, packing up, and
slipping away unannounced in the middle of
the night.'

KHALED HOSSEINI, *The Kite Runner*

In October 2013, on a rainy morning near Central Park, I met
Reverend Cathy Harrington, who had travelled from Wisconsin to
New York City especially to meet me on the ninth anniversary of
her daughter Leslie's murder. At the time of our meeting Cathy was
doing victim outreach work and living in Michigan as a minister in
the Unitarian Universalist Church, a faith tradition that upholds the
inherent worth and dignity of every human being.* I hadn't realised it
was the anniversary of Leslie's death until Cathy told me that morning
and it moved me that on such a momentous day, and in the spirit of

---

* Unitarian Universalism is characterised by a 'free and responsible search for
truth and meaning'. Worshippers are not necessarily Christians, though some
remain Christ-centred in their spirituality.

healing, this mother of a murdered child had come to Manhattan to share her story with an organisation called The Forgiveness Project.

As disturbing as our conversation was that morning, there were also flashes of understanding and hope as Cathy told me about what happened to her daughter in the summer of 2004, and how her moral and spiritual life had been shaped from the legacy of that pain. 'When you lose a child it's like a nuclear bomb has dropped. Your world becomes a barren landscape where nothing grows anymore,' she said. 'It's as if all your landmarks are gone and you don't know where you are anymore. It's taken me a very long time to find my way.'

After graduating in 2004, Leslie had come to live with her mother near Berkeley in California, where Cathy was finishing seminary college. Later that summer when Cathy was called to a church in Michigan, Leslie stayed on in the Napa Valley, moving in with two girlfriends.

'I heard the news from my sister,' Cathy said. 'On 1 November she rang to tell me she'd heard on TV there'd been a murder in a house in Dorset Street where the girls lived. I wouldn't believe it at first but then I rang the Napa Police and when they said, "We've been waiting for you to call, Mrs Harrington," my heart completely dropped. It turned out that having handed out candy on Halloween night the girls had gone to bed. But someone had broken into the house and stabbed both Leslie and her friend, Adriane. Fortunately, the other girl, whose bedroom was downstairs, was unharmed. The attack on Leslie was so ferocious that the police believed the murderer must have known her. It took another year to discover that the killer was in fact a boyfriend of Adriane's best friend called Eric Copple. Copple was working in a civil engineering company and had no prior criminal record and had never even met Leslie.'

As Cathy put down the phone to the police she sat in silent shock, immobilised by the intensity of unbearable grief. In a heartbeat her life had changed forever. 'What do you do when you hear news like that?' she asked, explaining how her advisor in the seminary school had then called and told her to buy an air ticket and fly out to California to be with her. 'So, I did, and she stayed by my side and protected me during those first terrible weeks. I needed it. The media intrusion was horrible. Murder is entertainment and I realised very quickly that dead people and the bereaved have no rights. The coverage of Leslie's story was sensational, vulgar and diminished her in every way.'

At Leslie's funeral, Cathy's two sons took her aside to beg their mother not to oppose the death penalty for their sister's killer. She was confused and didn't know what to do because while her faith called her to reject any form of state-sanctioned killing, she wasn't willing to put the life of Leslie's killer above her relationship with her sons. Their request preoccupied her for weeks until she came up with the idea to contact the one person who might be able to help her navigate such a painful dilemma – Sister Helen Prejean, the Catholic nun and prominent campaigner against the death penalty whose book had inspired the film *Dead Man Walking*.

Cathy went on to tell me how Sister Helen's advice had nourished her.

She told me that it made sense my sons would want the ultimate punishment for the murder of their sister. But she also told me that when the disciples needed to make meaning out of Jesus's death they produced the Gospels, and she invited me to write Leslie's gospel. So, I started to think about my daughter's legacy. And I immediately thought about how full of love she had been and how many friends surrounded her. Sister Helen also talked about the mother of a murderer in *Dead Man Walking* who'd had to leave town because people were so viciously abusing her. She said, 'Jesus asks us to stretch, Cathy. There are two arms of the cross; one side is for the victims and their loved ones and the other side of the cross holds, in the same light of love and hope, the murderer and his family.' For the first time I felt a measure of compassion for Eric's mother, and I could feel my heart open, suddenly aware that it had been clenched tightly like a fist. Looking back, I must have been thinking that a broken heart had to be bound tightly like a tourniquet. What Sister Helen told me poked a hole in my darkness because for a moment when I thought of Eric's mother, I realised that there was something worse than being the mother of a murdered child.

This image of Christ stretching out his arms on the cross to reach and embrace both the wronged and wrongdoer reminded me of something I'd heard from Mary Johnson, whose story I touched on in Chapter 2 when considering premature forgiveness. Like Cathy, Mary has profound faith and some years after her son, Laramiun Byrd, was murdered she was prompted to meet with his killer, Oshea Israel. This only came about after a dramatic change of heart which Mary was neither expecting nor looking for. One day, after many years of being torn by grief and anger, trying and failing to forgive, Mary heard a poem recited about the commonality of pain called 'Two Mothers'. The poem told of a fictional conversation between Mary, the mother of Jesus, and the mother of Judas Iscariot, the disciple who betrayed him. 'Suddenly I had this vision of creating an organization to support not only the mothers of murdered children but also the mothers of children who had taken a life,' she says. 'I knew then that I would never be able to deal with these mothers if I hadn't really forgiven Oshea.' Consequently, Mary arranged to meet with Oshea in the prison where he was serving his sentence and during their two-hour conversation she tells of an intense experience of forgiveness, both literal and divine. 'I felt something rising from the soles of my feet and leaving me,' she says. 'From that day on I haven't felt any hatred, animosity or anger. It was over.' Perhaps it is little wonder that Mary now refers to Oshea as her spiritual son – a sign as much of mercy as of grace.

In New York, Cathy appeared comforted thinking of Sister Helen Prejean and continued to tell me about how the court case had unfolded. 'We made it clear to the prosecution that we didn't want to endure a public trial and if they could work out a plea agreement then we would prefer it. Since Eric Copple had admitted to both killings that's what happened and by the time of the sentencing hearing in 2007 my sons no longer felt they wanted the death penalty. Once it was all over and the media left the court, my friend whispered, "Cathy, do you want to meet Eric's mother?" I was absolutely terrified but when I saw her coming towards me, I knew I needed to. She was trembling – more terrified than me. I was stunned by how similar we looked, and I thought, "Oh my God. I'm her!" Then we just embraced and there was such relief and compassion in that embrace.'

After the sentencing hearing the family were able to breathe again. Copple received a sentence of life without parole and waived his right to appeal. He had avoided the death penalty and in a newspaper report of that time, Cathy is reported saying that it was the 'most compassionate outcome for the terrible and unspeakable thing that has happened. This stops the cycle of violence.'

After the sentencing Cathy was left with the aspiration that Sister Helen Prejean had gifted her – to create Leslie's gospel. And so, as an attempt to make sense of the enormity of her loss, she spent time experiencing street retreats with San Francisco's poor and living among the dispossessed of Nicaragua. 'I found comfort here,' she said. 'If there was one place where I could find grace it was in the streets. The Nicaraguans have a saying that you make your way by walking. And that's what I did – I just put one step in front of the other.'

Well into our conversation I asked Cathy how she felt about forgiveness, realising this might be a subject hard to access. But because of her many years' experience of Unitarian Universalist Ministry I was interested to know whether it was something she hoped one day to achieve. She told me:

> Two years after Leslie died, I read in the news about how the Amish had forgiven the shootings at their school, I said to my grief counsellor, "Damn the Amish! I don't believe or trust it." I couldn't forgive so how could they! My grief counsellor replied, "Their faith calls them to walk towards forgiveness." And I found that helpful. Remarkably, Jesus was capable of forgiving his murderers as he suffered on the cross. As a Unitarian Universalist Christian minister, I seek to follow the teachings and the example of Jesus but forgiving the murderer of my daughter and for the loss of my never-to-be-born grandchildren – babies that my arms ache to hold – still seems inconceivable to me. Honestly, I'm terrified of facing the murderer of my child one day, and I don't know if I will have the courage and the grace to ever forgive but it is my hope and prayer.

A week after I met Cathy, I happened to cross paths with Sister Helen Prejean, who was speaking at the Roman Catholic Basilica of St Mary in downtown Minneapolis. Here in a church which describes itself as 'a place of refuge for the poor', the example of grace came up again. Sister Helen was describing the first time she met a man on death row. Having never come face to face with a murderer before, she didn't know what kind of monster to expect. 'But then I looked into his face and saw his humanness. It was a moment of grace,' she said. She told the audience: 'Sometimes we have to have our hearts broken to get to a new place where we can reconfigure everything in our lives.' I thought of Cathy.

The writer Laurence Gonzales has spent years studying how people survive the worst kind of disasters, from plane crashes to concentration camps. He identifies grace as key to survival, as a voyage of transformation that brings clarity and focus in traumatic circumstances.[1] For some, to encounter grace invokes an intense spiritual experience that has the capacity to heal and comfort.

Since Cathy and I met in New York, her life continues to be shaped by the legacy of her daughter's death as she dedicates herself to a new ministry serving congregations, first in Chattanooga in Tennessee where she became a volunteer police chaplain, and now in Asheville, North Carolina. Recently she told me she had connected with Fr Michael Lapsley's Healing of Memories workshops in America which has been 'tremendously important in my own healing process and the healing of countless others'. She has also experienced moments of grace which at times have had the power to alleviate her sorrow: 'There has been a gradual adjustment over the years as my eyes have slowly adapted to the dark. I found that when I reached towards the heavens from the hollow emptiness of my sorrow, I found grace. Grace was here waiting for me, quenching my sorrow, a trusted companion on the lonely journey. All I can do is keep on walking in that direction.'

The Forgiveness Project has no religious affiliation, but we share many restorative narratives which explore the relationship between faith and forgiveness. In the early days, because I was wary of the theological absolutism lens through which forgiveness was so often viewed, and because I was keen to avoid overtly spiritual overtones, I would always describe the organisation as 'grittily secular'. I stuck to this rigidly for a while until Marian Partington pointed out to me that she didn't think it was true. She was referring to the fact that almost every story collected by The Forgiveness Project had a profoundly spiritual dimension. When I thought more about it, I realised that if you take spirituality to mean greater consciousness and connectivity – whether to a higher power, the natural world, oneself or humanity – then she was absolutely right. Theologian and satirist Mike Yaconelli summed up exquisitely this blending between mystery and actuality when he said: 'Spirituality is not a formula; it is not a test. It is a relationship. Spirituality is not about competency; it is about intimacy. Spirituality is not about perfection; it is about connection. The way of the spiritual life begins where we are now in the mess of our lives.'[2]

I love this description of spirituality as it perfectly describes how connection can stretch one's life into wonderfully new alignments. And since forgiving someone can open up a whole new geography of the spirit, then at its very core you might argue it is a spiritual phenomenon. Indeed, even the self-avowed atheist Letlapa Mphahlele describes being forgiven by Ginn Fourie, the mother of one of his victims, as a spiritual experience rather than a religious one. 'I am an atheist, Ginn is a Christian, and I have learnt to appreciate the fact that forgiveness has little if anything to do with one's faith beliefs or the absence of them,' he says.

My concern around linking forgiveness to religious or spiritual belief systems has always been one of exclusivity. I have worried that stories which position someone's faith as the driving force of their ability to forgive may alienate those who do not have a faith by being seen to promote forgiveness as something only achieved by the mentally strong or the spiritually superior. I've never wanted people to think that they can only forgive if they have the support of a god or because their religion instructs them to. So often forgiveness is placed in the straitjacket of religion, which seems limiting. As Marian Partington once said, 'The trouble with forgiveness is that it is barnacled by aeons of piety.'

In the thick of strong cultural headwinds and at a time when arguments around ideology and identity are siloing people into narrow factions, wisdom can surely be found in the world's faith traditions. The following passages contain some brief and extremely broad-brushstroke explanations of how each of the major religions views forgiveness, although I realise this can never do justice to the nuance and complexity of these teachings and will be hopelessly incomplete.[3]

In Judaism (as discussed in Chapter 7) it is not God in the first instance you ask forgiveness from but the person who has been offended, and if the offender does not apologise there is no religious obligation to grant forgiveness. The victim may be asked up to three times and if they continue to refuse then you must turn to God and ask for His forgiveness. Survivors cannot grant forgiveness in the place of the victim, for instance in the case of murder. However, while survivors can't forgive on behalf of the dead they can help the perpetrators on their path of reflection and they can be forgiving of the pain that they themselves are carrying. Judaism also has a ritual for asking for forgiveness of the dead.

In Christianity forgiveness is a deliberate act of love, which draws on the mercy and grace of God. It is therefore something in which inter-personal and divine human relationships are both at play at the same time. Some Christians believe unconditional forgiveness is absolutely required and non-negotiable because in Matthew's gospel Jesus commands his followers: 'If you forgive those who sin against you, your heavenly Father will forgive you. But if you refuse to forgive others, your Father will not forgive your sins.'[4] Moreover this is seen not just as a one-off but something that should be repeated as necessary, the Biblical 'seventy times seven times'.[5] On the other hand, to be able to receive forgiveness from God a Christian should experience sorrow for what they have done and change their ways, that is 'repent'; and there is a lively debate among Christians as to whether the obligation to forgive extends to the people who are staunchly unrepentant.

The act of forgiveness is one of the highest spiritual acts within the religion of Islam. The Qur'an teaches that Allah is the source of all forgiveness, but also that forgiveness requires the repentance of those who are being forgiven. Depending on the offence, forgiveness can come direct from Allah or from the person who received the wrong. However, forgiveness from God must meet the criteria of sincerity and has three requirements: that the wrongdoer recognises the offence itself and admits it before God; that the wrongdoer makes a commitment to God not to repeat the offence; and that the wrongdoer asks forgiveness from God. If the offence was committed against another person, then a fourth condition is required, namely doing whatever needs to be done to rectify the offence and asking pardon of the offended party.

In the Buddhist belief system, where there is no concept of a God with power to punish or forgive, forgiveness for self and others is seen as a practice for individuals to prevent harmful thoughts from taking a grip. Buddhism recognises that feelings of hatred and ill-will can have a lasting effect on the psyche because if you can't forgive you will keep cementing an identity around the pain. Forgiveness in Buddhism is more often explained as generating compassion or loving kindness towards others. The belief in karma also means that if someone has been hurt they don't need to get even because the offender will automatically receive karmic retribution.

In Hinduism, atonement, forgiveness and penance are the best means to self-purification. The Hindu spiritual scripture, Bhagavad Gita, clearly states that forgiveness arises from God alone. Sinful karma is purified, and believers are fully exonerated through God's forgiveness.

Sikhism considers forgiveness as the remedy to anger. You forgive an offender when aroused by compassion. The act of forgiveness is not the work of human agency but a divine gift in order to protect against pride which would otherwise hinder a person's spiritual progress.

While I have tried to secularise and de-mystify forgiveness, nevertheless several of the stories shared by The Forgiveness Project are rooted in a deep faith where a solid belief system is able to convert division and hate into unity and togetherness. The story of Azim Khamisa, whose twenty-year-old son, Tariq, was murdered in 1995 while out delivering pizzas, is one such example. Azim came to my attention when I was looking for stories of faith-inspired forgiveness. I had heard how Azim had forgiven his son's killer and founded a not-for-profit organisation called the Tariq Khamisa Foundation in his son's name. The foundation is dedicated to preventing youth violence and over the years has reached millions of youth across every state in America and beyond. In crowded school halls, and on conference platforms, Azim frequently talks to young people about the story of his son. He also talks about his son's killer, Tony Hicks, who 'had the face of a child but the mind of a killer.' Joining a street gang when he was eleven, at the age of fourteen Hicks shot Tariq dead in a totally unprovoked attack to prove himself to the gang leaders.

I have met Azim several times and heard him speak at schools, to policy-makers, at conferences and on courses. He is softly spoken with a gentle and assured way about him, and there is no question that his sincerity is born out of suffering.

As a Sufi Muslim, Azim says it was his spiritual life that saved him:

When I got the phone call saying that Tariq was dead, I was in my kitchen. I lost strength in both of my legs and as I collapsed to the floor, I hit my head against the refrigerator and curled up into a ball. It was like a nuclear bomb went off in my heart. The pain was so excruciating that I remember leaving my body. There was no solace to be found in my mind and so, as a Sufi, I turned to my faith. I believe in God and I believe I left my body and went into a loving embrace of God. I don't recall how long I was gone but I remember being held in this embrace and then when the explosion subsided God sent me back into my body. For the next few weeks, I survived through prayer and was quickly given the blessing of forgiveness. In my faith, on the fortieth day after a death you are encouraged to channel your grief into good compassionate deeds: deeds which provide high-octane fuel for the soul's forward journey. Forty days is not a long time to grieve for a child, but one of my motivations for starting the Tariq Khamisa Foundation was to create spiritual currency for my son, as well as to give myself a sense of purpose.

Azim puts his resilience down to his faith. He describes being alone with his best friend shortly after Tariq's murder when his friend said, 'Whoever these kids are who killed Tariq I hope that they fry in hell.' He expected Azim to agree with him, but Azim just looked at him and shook his head. 'I don't feel that way,' he said. 'I see that there are victims at both ends of the gun.' His friend looked astonished: 'If somebody took my son's life not only would I want the killer but the whole clan to suffer,' he said. When I asked Azim where he had found his strength, he said, 'I have learnt that sometimes in the aftermath of deep trauma and tragedy there is a spark of clarity. It didn't come from my intellect. I don't think us mortals are capable of that. It didn't come from my loving heart. It was a download from a higher power.'

Soon after the killing, Azim reached out to Ples Felix, Tony Hick's grandfather and legal guardian. Ever since then the two men have stood together on a stage telling their shared narrative as friends and collaborators. Ples, an African American and practising Christian, and Azim, a devout Sufi Muslim who grew up in Kenya, have been bound together by heartbreak as well as by an unwavering commitment to the principles of non-violence, compassion and forgiveness. 'Who is the enemy?' asks Azim every time he speaks to an audience. 'The fourteen-year-old who killed my son or societal forces that forced Tony to join a gang?'

The work Azim does to 'save' violent young people is all about transformation, or what he calls change at a *soulular* level – a term he coined to express deep, sustainable inner change. Wary of the politics and dogma of organised religion, he prefers to talk about spirituality and is convinced that encouraging young people to respect and embrace different wisdom traditions can give them an inner resource that will sustain them through hard times. It's what he calls our 'internal navigation system' – a spiritual life that, if tapped into, can allow for profound shifts to take place.

What marks Azim's story out is not only his pull towards forgiveness but also the fact that he holds himself in part responsible for the damage wreaked by Tony Hicks. That's not to say that he considers himself personally to blame, but rather that as a member of society he believes he is not separate from the sins perpetrated by members of that society. As he says: 'I felt as an American citizen that I must take my share of the responsibility for the bullet that took my son's life because it was fired by an American child and I am a first-generation American citizen. I see the enemy as societal forces that make many young men, especially young men of colour, fall through the cracks and then choose lives of crime, gangs, drugs and weapons. Tony was radicalised, much like we see in terrorism. Tariq was a victim of Tony, but Tony was a victim of American society – and society is a mirror image of each and every one of us.'

In this respect Azim shares the same broad perspective as Andrea LeBlanc, whose husband was killed when the second plane hit the World Trade Center in 2001, and Pardeep Kaleka, whose father was murdered in the Oak Creek Sikh Temple shooting in 2012 (their stories were mentioned in Chapter 8). This worldview is also echoed in *The Brothers Karamazov*, where Dostoevsky writes in the voice of the Elder Zosima, 'we are responsible for everything and everyone.' The notion of common responsibility arising from common culpability gives powerful impetus to a healing that comes from recognising a shared humanity with all, victim as well as perpetrator.

Azim has spoken and written copiously on the subject of forgiveness: his belief in its transformative power is watertight and unambiguous. He first met Hicks in prison a few years after Tariq's murder, and looking back he believes it to have been a moment of profound catharsis for both of them. 'I remember meditating several thousand hours to get the courage to do this and I recognised that for me to complete my journey of forgiveness, I eventually had to come eyeball to eyeball with Tony. I asked Ples to go with me. I also told him, "I would like you to introduce me to Tony but then I need some alone time with him because you are his grandfather and I have some tough questions for him, and he will be defensive." Ples was very gracious, and he left us alone for an hour and a half while Tony and I talked man to man. I could tell that my forgiveness had shifted him because he was well-mannered. He was articulate. He was remorseful, plus I knew he was not going to repeat that behaviour.'

The last time I spoke with Azim was in 2020 while recording an episode of *The F Word Podcast*. Here he told me that Hicks had now been released from prison after serving twenty-five years and was getting involved in the work of the Tariq Khamisa Foundation. Soon Azim hoped Hicks would be speaking in schools too – because what could be more persuasive than having him tell young people the consequences of violent crime, and what could be a more powerful symbol of forgiveness than seeing Azim stand next to the person who had killed his son?

Azim talked as much about compassion as he did forgiveness. 'I think the precursor of forgiveness is compassion,' he said. 'And the precursor of compassion is empathy, and a precursor of empathy is to get to know the person because you can't have empathy with somebody you don't know. I know everything there is to know about Tony, his entire life history, and sometimes I wonder if I had grown up like him, having such a tough life in South Central Los Angeles, would I have made the same choices as he did. There is a great quote from Gandhi, "Hate the sin, love the sinner." I think at some level we have all harmed. We are all fallible. We are all humans and to have that level of empathy I think one really needs to understand the other person.'

Azim then said something which I have since held tight to because it explained so well how some people have the capacity to forgive in the most devastating of circumstances. He told me, much in the spirit of Sister Helen Prejean, that 'a broken heart is an open heart', explaining that if you can open your heart in the midst of pain then gentle transformation will begin to manifest. 'We are very quick in our society to judge and close our hearts, but you cannot get to forgiveness and compassion with a closed heart.' He told me he worked hard to leave his heart open and by way of explaining his process paraphrased one of his favourite sayings from the Sufi mystic poet Rumi: 'God will break your heart over and over and over and over and over and over again until it stays open.'*

There are others whose stories I have shared who, like Azim, have been protected by their faith, and through ritual, prayer and worship have reached a place free of bitterness and hatred. After escaping an abusive marriage, Ruchi Singh left Australia and returned to her parents' house in India. Initially her reasons to forgive her violent husband were entirely pragmatic as she was determined not to become cruel and hurtful like him. She also knew that holding on to hate might cause her to sink into depression. She explains: 'One way of staying internally clean has been by never calling him abusive names. I have even blessed him. It's not easy, but it's helped me free myself. Forgiveness doesn't mean saying I'm OK with what he did; it means I can continue with my life in a more peaceful frame of mind.'

But to strengthen this resolve to forgive she also knew she had to work on her interior world by taking forgiveness to a deeper level. 'It took three months of intense meditation, conscious breathing

* In early 2022 I received an email from Azim which said: 'Tony and I are now speaking together to students – we just last week spoke to 350 students. And he is volunteering for the Tariq Khamisa Foundation while working as a plumber. I am very proud of who he has become even after being subjected to a negative environment since age fourteen. We have saved Tony but more importantly he will save many young souls. This is the authentic power of forgiveness.'

and chanting mantras to forgive,' she says. 'I couldn't just think myself into forgiving. I had to take action. And my action was my spiritual practice. I had to clean out the muddy water by feeling my way through all the ugly emotions until finally these negative feelings began to dissipate.'

Jean Paul Samputu is a musician and a survivor of the Rwandan genocide. When I first talked to Jean Paul about his experiences it was 2012 and we were in Kigali. It was the last day of a conference organised by the Guerrand-Hermès Foundation for Peace which had been focused on 'Healing the Wounds of History' and sought to address the roots of violence in this small African country. When Jean Paul described how he had been able to escape when most of his family had not, the story was by now all too familiar, having heard numerous extremely distressing testimonies from survivors over the past few days. Even the country's Roman Catholic Church had been complicit in crimes against humanity. Jean Paul shared the outrage of many survivors when he learned that churches had been a major site for massacres, and many Christians had participated in the slaughter.

He described how events had unfolded for him: 'When the government started teaching Hutus how to hate, my father warned me to leave the country as I was a well-known Tutsi musician and therefore an obvious target. At first my parents didn't realise that they were also in danger because in the Butare south we lived side by side with our Hutu neighbours and my father would say, "I trust them, they are my friends." Even when I begged him to leave, he said, "I'm eighty-six years old, I want to die here."'

Jean Paul escaped on foot, walking through the forest until he reached Burundi, but news spread quickly that Hutus were killing Tutsis and soon he learnt that his parents, three brothers and a sister had all been massacred. It transpired later that his father had been killed by a neighbour, Jean Paul's close friend, Vincent.

Jean Paul told of the devastation of hearing not only that his

family had been murdered but that one of his oldest friends had
taken a machete to his father. 'The shock was so great that I started
drinking and taking drugs to forget. I wanted to take revenge. I
wanted to kill Vincent. But I couldn't find him, and so I started
killing myself. It took nine years for me to deal with my anger, my
bitterness and my desire for revenge. As I moved between Rwanda
and Canada, where my wife and disabled daughter lived, anger
and bitterness took hold to the point that I could no longer sing
or show up on stage. By now I was an addict and an alcoholic.'

He went on to explain how God had saved him from destroy-
ing himself. 'All the time some of my friends were praying for me
because they knew I was going to die,' he said.

Then, one day, this miracle happened. In the midst of all this
hell, I suddenly felt a strange peace in my heart. Faith helped
me to stop drinking. I had tried many things – drugs, witch
doctors – but none of it worked. So, I took a Bible and I went
to a prayer-mountain, and spent three months away from everyone just to discover God's healing. During this retreat I heard
a voice telling me that even if you become a Christian it's not
enough, you need to forgive the man who killed your father
because you cannot love again if you still have hatred in your
heart. And that voice was telling me forgiveness is for you, not
for the offender. Of course, it took time to accept that message,
but in the end I had no choice and one day I said 'YES! I'm
ready to forgive.' On that day I suddenly felt totally free. I felt
a power that I cannot describe.

A few years later Jean Paul reconciled with Vincent and was able
to tell him to his face that he had forgiven him. In what was to
be a very healing transaction, Vincent then told Jean Paul where
his father was buried. It also helped enormously when Vincent
explained to him the law of genocide. The law of genocide stated

that you must kill your closest friend first because if you don't then they will kill you. 'Hearing this I began to understand that genocide can make a monster of any of us,' said Jean Paul.

After cultivating his forgiving heart, his life began to fall back into place. 'In time the songs flowed again; thousands of them. And in 2003 I won a Kora Award – the most prestigious music award in sub-Saharan Africa. It helped me to go to America with my music where I started to tell everyone about this most unpopular of weapons – forgiveness. It's unpopular because it's a hard topic and a difficult process. Some people don't want to teach it to their children, even in the church, because they look in the mirror, and they cannot preach what they cannot do.'

For some the requirement to forgive that is associated with Christianity can become a dreadful torment. Sister Dianna Ortiz was an American Roman Catholic nun working with the indigenous community of Guatemala when in 1989 she was abducted, tortured and raped by the Guatemalan military. Reading the details of what happened to Ortiz, who died of cancer in 2021 aged sixty-two, is one of the most sickening descriptions of torture that I have ever come across.[6] In the ensuing years after her release, she fought for justice in both American and Guatemalan courts, claiming that she had 'filed suit against the Guatemalan security forces instead of forgiving my torturers'.[7] Later she founded the Torture Abolition and Survivors Support Coalition International and wrote her memoir, *The Blindfold's Eyes: My Journey from Torture to Truth*. What caught my attention when reading her story is that right up to her death Sister Ortiz said she continued to struggle with the Christian ideal of forgiveness, and on one occasion told National Public Radio, 'I leave that in God's hands ... The fact that I'm a Catholic nun and I'm not able to forgive, that makes me feel all the more guilty. I'm not sure what it means to forgive.'[8]

*

Framing forgiveness through the prism of Christianity rather than science and psychology can sometimes cause offence. Fr Michael Lapsley has witnessed how some clergy unwittingly weaponise forgiveness. These ministers and pastors have good intentions, he says, but are actually often increasing a person's burden by saying they 'should' forgive when all they want 'is a loving embrace and for their pain to be heard.' He frequently asks members of the clergy if they have found forgiveness easy in their life, and when they consistently tell him that no, they have never found it easy, Fr Michael asks them why then they never preach about the difficulty of forgiveness. 'The lived experience of religious people belies sometimes the sermons they preach and some who I have worked with have said they never ever preached about forgiveness the same way once we had that conversation.' Fr Michael also makes another important point. 'Sometimes when I do preach about forgiveness in a sermon and say it is costly, painful and difficult, at the church door people often come up to me and say, "I am so thankful that you said that because it means there is nothing wrong with me."'

Bjørn Ihler, who survived Norway's Utøya island massacre and whose story I shared in Chapter 8, told me that when Archbishop Desmond Tutu urged Norwegians to forgive the worst criminal in the nation's recent history, it didn't go down well. Talking at a press conference at the Oslo Nobel Peace Centre three years after the attack, Tutu was responding to a question about the appropriateness of forgiving Anders Breivik when he said that forgiveness would certainly be his position. 'I think this would be God's position too,' he said. 'God hates no one. We are all God's children and there are those of us who become bad children but we're still children, we still belong to the family.'

Bjørn has concluded from the 'massive outrage' these comments caused that forgiveness is perceived differently in Norway compared to other parts of the world and therefore it is often misunderstood. The reaction of his fellow citizens frustrated him, because, he said,

'I'm sure Desmond Tutu didn't mean forgive in the sense of excuse or giving someone a free pass to repeat the offence. I think his views are closer to mine, about accepting and being able to move on while still recognising the pain. This type of forgiveness is about finding some wisdom that we can take out of what has happened to ensure that violence doesn't repeat itself. Desmond Tutu was an archbishop within the religious community whereas Norway is a very secular country; and the religious relationship with forgiveness is very different from the secular relationship with forgiveness. Norwegians are more comfortable with notions of reconciliation and peacebuilding than forgiveness.'

Faith can be used to urge believers to forgive. In 2006, when milk-truck driver Charles Roberts stormed a one-room Amish schoolhouse in Nickel Mines, Pennsylvania, and shot five girls dead before taking his own life, the tragedy made headlines across the world. While the story was initially reported with horror and shock, soon the focus changed to asking how was it possible that the Nickel Mines Amish were not calling for retribution? Indeed, within a few hours of the shooting, members of the community, including those who had lost children in the attack, were expressing forgiveness for the killer and his family.

Perhaps people shouldn't have been surprised by the Amish's response because for the 342,000 members of this Christian denomination it is sinful to withhold forgiveness. However, this type of total forgiveness, when church members must rigorously obey religious imperatives to forgive, can in itself become rigid and *unforgiving*. And the whole thing becomes particularly murky when you consider that some Amish have seemed willing to forgive members of their own church who have been exposed as sex offenders.

Amish leaders can be suspicious of law enforcement, choosing to manage disagreements on their own. At its best this may resemble a form of restorative or community justice but there is also a danger that if a religious group has the power to discipline and forgive abusers, these abusers will be let loose into the community again. It's also the case that sometimes Amish victims are viewed by their community as just as guilty as their abusers, expected to share responsibility and quickly forgive. In 2020, *Cosmopolitan* magazine and Type Investigations identified fifty-two official cases of Amish child sexual assault in seven states over the past two decades.[9] The article claims that the #MeToo movement has made it a little easier for Amish women to report abuse, but in a religion steeped in a patriarchal and isolated lifestyle, and with their justice system prioritising repentance and forgiveness over actual punishment or rehabilitation, church leaders have covered up child sexual abuse, discouraging and intimidating victims from going to the authorities in favour of dealing with abuse internally.

Susan Waters is a survivor of childhood sexual abuse. She is a poet, the mother of three adult children and lives in the Midlands, United Kingdom. For a long time, her story appeared on The Forgiveness Project website under a pseudonym, alongside a photograph which didn't identify her. This is a story which pits a person's religious faith against an inflexible theological view of forgiveness. Initially Susan reached out to me after The Forgiveness Project was featured on a Sunday morning TV programme. I drove north to meet her with ex-UVF paramilitary Alistair Little, who at the time was often in London helping me find a pathway through the dense undergrowth of forgiveness. We met Susan in her family home where she made us cups of tea and told us her story. Leaving later that afternoon, I felt immense gratitude to her for sharing an experience that illustrated the messy, contentious, difficult and yet transformative nature of forgiveness.

Susan started out by talking about her childhood:

My brother, Robert, was a gentle boy before the darkness came. He was ten and I was seven when our relationship altered

irrevocably. We had started lessons at Richmond Swimming
Baths. My brother Robert's instructor, Bob C, was a loud,
attractive personality. He took Robert out for treats and before
long invited himself to our home to offer us both a day out in
London. Childhood ended that day. Bob C's particular evil was
to set one child against another, turning Robert against me: he
presented himself as the generous care giver (*I don't want to hurt
you*) and Robert his small henchman issuing rehearsed threats
(*I will break your legs if you tell*). I thought of myself as a thing to
be offered up. Bob C was the instigator, but my brother continued to abuse me into adolescence. Home was not a safe place
to be. How could I tell our parents about their gross error of
trusting Bob C or what happened when they went to work? I
was anxious about getting my brother into trouble and terrified
about what might happen if I disclosed. It was very confusing.

A year later, on a swimming club trip, Susan witnessed Bob C
molesting a girl sitting next to him. From then on, she vowed not
to speak with the swimming instructor ever again, but her mother
took this to be an act of rudeness and, despite Susan's protestations,
her brother continued to be taken out by Bob C. This went on
until one day a policeman knocked at the door of the family home.
Bob C's predatory net had finally unravelled when he was caught
abusing a boy. In his confession Bob C named Susan's brother as
another victim. 'I remember Robert went with our father to the
police station to make a statement; a frightening and embarrassing
situation for them to face. They returned, stone-faced, not saying a
thing to Mother when she came home from her work as a Health
Visitor. She only found out later by reading the local newspaper.
There wasn't the language to communicate as a family back in
1970; our relationships fractured under a toxic silence. It was easier
for all of us to bury the trauma beneath a thick sheet of ice and
pretend everything was normal.'

Susan grew up in a Christian household and her faith remained important to her into adulthood. She had been taught the Lord's Prayer, *forgive us as we forgive others*, and worried that God would stop loving her if she couldn't forgive. The pressure to forgive locked her in silence and made her feel unsafe. It was only when she became a mother herself and discovered what it really meant to love and be loved that the secret could no longer be contained. 'The crisis arrived when I was bathing my seven-year-old daughter and I recognised the loss of innocence at that age,' she said. 'For a while I quietly tried to find some answers in Christian literature, but these were all perfect stories of reconciliation. What I was looking for was permission to end the relationship with my brother and I could not find this wisdom in Church teachings.'

A few years later, in a rare visit from her brother, the façade finally cracked. Her youngest child became tearful at his uncle's teasing and Susan lost control, angrily shouting at Robert to leave her house and not return. When her mother later called to ask why he was no longer welcome, she disclosed the truth about the past, knowing her confession would split the family apart. 'Overwhelmed by shame, I suffered a complete mental collapse,' Susan said.

It was only when her mother died ten years later that, as sole executor of her mother's will, Susan was legally obliged to find and contact her estranged brother again. But not before she went for trauma counselling, leaving her shoes at the door to stop herself from running out. However it was here that she remembered something important: 'Working through the rage, I recalled something Robert had said long before in one frank conversation. "If there is one thing I could change about my sorry little life," he said, "it would have been to protect you from Bob C." There was both remorse and fear in the tremor of his voice.'

The siblings conducted the business of the will via email, which proved to be an empowering experience for Susan because this time she was the one in charge. It seemed that Robert's interest was solely financial, as he neither asked about their mother nor about how Susan was coping. Provoked by his lack of interest, she firmly raised the matter of their damaged past, requesting a small part of his bequest to cover counselling costs as an act of restoration. 'This was given without further comment or apology.'

Despite the turmoil of everything that had happened, Susan never abandoned her belief in the existence of a higher power and a greater goodness. Personal healing came through Buddhist wisdom that when it feels impossible to forgive, you are allowed to forgive yourself for that. Facing the things that need forgiveness with honesty is a process. On better days Susan could safely love her brother at a distance, remembering the gentle boy he once was. And so, the final thing she wrote to her brother, knowing it would be their last conversation, were sincere words offering forgiveness. 'In this resolution I found liberation for myself,' she explained, recalling that Desmond Tutu had counselled to forgive others, not because they deserve forgiveness, but because *you* deserve peace.

Some years after I first met Susan, she got in touch again after both her parents had died to ask if she could change her story on The Forgiveness Project website and now identify herself by using her real name. It transpired that her brother, who had been living with his family abroad, had been battling his own demons, and after sinking into alcoholism had eventually committed suicide. 'Some have said he got his comeuppance,' she wrote, 'but I sense rather the pain of an angry and lonely death.' There had been some profound resolution for Susan too, revealed in a mystical revelation that came unexpectedly. 'Early one morning, comfort came to me in a warm and loving presence whom I believe was my brother; I now can rest in the peace of that moment,' she said.

Forgiveness for Bob C has been more difficult to find. Susan thought he must have died as many years had passed and she researched local newspapers to discover the facts about his arrest. Always believing he had received a prison sentence, she was disgusted to discover that in fact he had only received a mere £50 fine with a caution for good behaviour. 'But then,' she said, 'as I searched the Census just to ensure Bob C was indeed dead, a wave of compassion took me by surprise when I read his birth record. I saw the man, not as a looming figure, but as a baby. What happened to you, I wondered, to make you the person I knew?'

I have often wondered whether there might be an intrinsic difference in the quality of the act of forgiving experienced by people with a strong religious faith and those who have no faith at all. If there is, it has nothing to do with the potency of the experience but rather with the fact that people who believe in a power outside of themselves can hand over some of the heavy lifting and seem to occupy, therefore, a space of enduring conviction where forgiveness becomes the most essential and durable aspect of their healing. I'm reminded of three parents of murdered children, all of whom have forgiven and whose faith has formed the framework to their healing. Wilma Derksen forgave the unknown killer of her daughter, Candace, despite vocal criticism from many in her community; Mary Johnson felt a rush of energy pass through her body immediately after first meeting the man who killed her son and never felt bitterness or anger again; and Azim Khamisa relentlessly used prayer to sustain him in the hours after learning of his son's death.

And then there is Mary Foley, who for several years worked with The Forgiveness Project sharing her story in front of groups of men in prison as part of our RESTORE programme. Mary's daughter Charlotte was fifteen when she was murdered at a house party in east London by another teenager, eighteen-year-old Beatriz, who later received a life sentence for this completely unprovoked attack. In the years after the killing, Mary started to write to Beatriz, and it was these letters that Mary would read to the prisoners, as an example of a restorative act in her quest to find peace amid the misery. I once asked Mary whether she thought her forgiveness was different from the forgiveness of someone who did not believe in God.

'I don't think so,' she said. 'I have known many people who don't have a faith in God or in anything who have had bad things happen to them as children and they choose to forgive and move on in their life.' She thought hard and then went on to explain what she believed the difference was. 'They manage to suppress the trauma, ignore it and move on. But that pain is still there, the trauma is still there. The fact that I have got a faith doesn't make me any better than anybody else but the difference is that the pain and the trauma that I experienced with Charlotte is not there. It's been taken away.'

Could Mary have felt that in this complete erasure of the trauma, she had been given a helping hand from God? 'Oh yes, I was,' she said, 'because I don't go back and have regrets. I haven't got that pain. I haven't got that trauma of reliving it constantly. There's a possibility that some people without faith can do that but how they do that, I don't know.'

I have reflected a lot on how Mary describes her trauma as having been completely wiped away, and I wonder if this is linked to her feeling no sense of shame for what happened. So often it is the shame associated with unresolved trauma that keeps intrusive and engrained pain very much alive. This may not make logical sense because if a deep hurt is inflicted on you, why should you be the one feeling shame? But the fact is that victims of crime so often do. Those who have been burgled blame themselves for leaving their homes vulnerable just as those who have lost children to murder are often weighed down by guilt for not having been able to save them. There is something that is deeply resolved in Mary's experience – a woman who has found peace through trusting in prayer. Perhaps because, as the British prison psychiatrist Dr Bob Johnson said, 'The antidote to trauma is trust.'

11

THE MECHANICS OF FORGIVING

'I imagine one of the reasons people cling to their
hates so stubbornly is because they sense, once hate
is gone, they will be forced to deal with pain.'

JAMES BALDWIN

Over the many years that I've spent unpicking and excavating
forgiveness, trying to zero in on the bare bones of this complex
psychological construct, I've always hoped to discover what *exactly*
it means to forgive, to be able to crystallise the concept into something tangible – a single definitive explanation so that everyone
might better understand it. Of course, the more I've investigated
and searched for substance, the less clarity I've found. Forgiveness
is an exasperating, slippery subject for the simple reason that it
means so many different things to different people: no one can
quite agree on the meaning of this skill, gift, attribute, practice,
state of mind – or however you choose to categorise forgiveness.

Because of this, my motivation has always been to use real stories as both a source and a barometer. I have been resistant to offer
people guidance around how to forgive other than to point them

towards the experiences of others who have done it. However, I am also intrigued by what it takes to forgive and why some people choose it while others do not; why some people embrace it spontaneously while others may only grasp at it as a last-ditch survival response.* In my search for answers, I worked with psychologist Dr Masi Noor to create The Forgiveness Toolbox, whereby Masi analysed the stories and together we worked out some of the key components of what it took to forgive. Since then, by further simplifying this initial analysis, I have come to believe that there are five, perhaps six, main ingredients to establishing a forgiving attitude.[†]

CURIOSITY

Firstly, an inquiring mind seems essential. Having curiosity indicates recognition that you don't have everything figured out; you don't have the full story. Being curious is more than being interested. Sometimes it means looking for what's not evident, for

---

* What makes some people more forgiving than others? One paper (Marianne Steiner, Mathias Allemand, and Michael McCullough in the April 2012 issue of *Personality and Social Psychology Bulletin*) focuses on personality factors. Dividing people into two main personality types: agreeableness (people who try to get on with others) and neuroticism (people who feel stress, fear, sadness, anxiety) the authors found that those prone to agreeableness were more likely to forgive others and self. Studies also suggest that because older adults experience fewer negative interactions with other people than younger adults, and because of their greater life experience, older adults don't get as upset about these negative interactions and are more forgiving.

[†] I have often been asked whether women are more forgiving than men. From listening to people's experiences of forgiveness I'd always assumed that gender didn't actually play a part until I came across a fascinating meta–analysis conducted in 2008[1] which found a small but potentially significant gender difference suggesting that women do indeed tend to forgive more than men. With men scoring higher on measures of vengeance, for women it is the desire to maintain relationships that encourages them to forgive rather than to seek justice. Dispositional qualities such as empathy, and women's orientation toward an ethic of care, also play a role; as does religion since studies consistently show women tend to be more religious than men.

words unspoken and for what's being left out. Talking about his community's response to the shootings at the Sikh Temple in Oak Creek, Wisconsin, Pardeep Kaleka recognised the power of being curious: 'We understood the how of what had happened but not the why. Until you understand the why you can't make meaning and until you make meaning you cannot heal,' he said.

PERCEPTION CHANGE

Curiosity in turn leads to the second ingredient of forgiveness – the ability to shift perspective.* If black-and-white reasoning serves to solidify intolerance and if righteous anger just keeps us stuck in an 'I'm right, you're wrong' position, then forgivers tend to be far-reaching thinkers able to adopt an open-minded, flexible point of view. When Maria Jimenez was killed in a road accident caused by her friend Nick's 'catastrophically dangerous driving', her mother's reaction on first hearing the news was an early indication of forgiveness. Certainly, Elizabeth Jimenez's world collapsed around her, but she also found herself instinctively and urgently looking for answers beyond her reactive thinking: 'In those first few moments I remember thinking, *If the person behind the wheel had been my own son, or my husband, or myself even, how would I want the world to react?* That was my first thought and it saved me.'

Both these first two qualities – the inclination to be curious and the ability to see the world through a wider lens – bear out Dr Kathleen Lawler-Row's research, which revealed that forgiving people possess a wide-angle view on the world and have fewer fixed expectations of how life or others should be. Similarly,

---

* A recent study suggests that teaching children to understand other people's perspectives could make it easier for them to learn how to forgive other people. The study also found that teaching children to make sincere apologies can help them receive forgiveness from others. https://www.sciencedaily.com/releases/2021/12/211208110307.htm

psychotherapist Robin Shohet sees perception change as the key element of forgiveness because it makes everything fall into place. I heard him say at a conference once: 'Forgiveness is left-field. You're either stuck in revenge or you turn 180 degrees the other way. An awakening happens after a period of disruption, after a crisis, a moment of hurt or failure and at this point a complete change of perception can happen. A true act of forgiveness is not about taking the moral high ground, but it's when you see the world in a different way.'

Shohet likes to tell people about a powerful forgiveness technique he used to make peace with his stepson, whom he was angry with for many years. 'The feeling was mutual,' he says, 'and we would both complain to my wife about what the other had done.' Determined to sort out a relationship which seemed intractable, Shohet embraced the ancient Hawaiian practice of Ho'oponopono. Hawaii is one of the most isolated places in the world and its indigenous people, knowing that they could not run away from one another, have developed a rich history in learning to mend relationships through prayer, discussion, confession, repentance, mutual restitution and forgiveness. The process rests on four simple steps which can either be practised with someone else, in groups to promote healing justice, or spoken privately like a mantra. It involves saying four affirmations repeatedly: 'I am sorry', 'Please forgive me', 'Thank you', 'I love you'.

'I would do this walking down the street (with some resistance) for a few weeks,' says Shohet, 'and then one day as I was returning from a boat-trip I heard myself say, "It's over." What I meant is that I had had a sudden dramatic change of perception. My grievances with my stepson were in the past. I didn't forgive him or not forgive him, but I saw what had happened between us was not the truth of our relationship. I had been so attached to the need to prove I was right, and *this* was the problem, not him. Nothing external had changed, but from then on because I viewed the whole situation differently, I had a complete change of heart.'

FINDING EMPATHY

The third ingredient of forgiveness concerns developing compassion and empathy, which means being able to stand in someone else's shoes no matter how ill-fitting those shoes might be. Empathy also indicates that, at some intrinsic level, we are all part of a shared humanity, and as such are inextricably linked with our fellow human beings, even our enemies. To forgive in this respect involves a refusal to demonise or dehumanise others. It is so often an unexpected moment of empathy that shifts the dynamic of a relationship away from hate. Bassam Aramin's story illustrates the integral role empathy plays when you forgive others. Bassam is a Palestinian member of The Parents Circle – a group of bereaved Israeli and Palestinian families. He is also a former combatant who grew up in the West Bank and who, as a young man, was sentenced to seven years in prison. He often tells of how during his time in prison he was shown a film about the Holocaust. He wanted to watch this film because he was sure he'd enjoy seeing Jews being killed. However, when he realised just how many helpless people had been slaughtered at the hands of the Nazis, he found himself suddenly and unexpectedly breaking into tears. It was, he said, the first time he felt empathy for his enemy. 'I tried to hide my tears from the other prisoners who wouldn't have understood why I was crying about the pain of my oppressors.'

LETTING GO OF RESENTMENT

The fourth ingredient of forgiveness relates to relinquishing resentment. When you realise that bitterness or hatred is a heavy load to carry, then letting go of it becomes an act of self-compassion. It may require giving up a hard-won sense of power, including the power of being morally superior or the position of being right. It requires you to have the capacity to accept that life is morally complicated, that people will not behave as you expect them to and that everyone is more than the worst thing they have ever done.

Sammy Rangel, a former violent gang member turned peace activist, was abused by his mother and uncle as a child. As a result, he spent most of his early years in mental institutions, foster homes and detention homes. By the age of eleven, he was consumed by violence and before long had joined the largest Latino street gang. At seventeen, Sammy received his first prison sentence for stealing a car in Chicago. As an adult he spent long periods behind bars until finally an intense drug rehabilitation programme helped him to put his life back together again. For Sammy, forgiveness was a critical part of his healing, and when he left prison, he was determined to find forgiveness – not only from his son and daughter but also for his mother. 'I had created myths as to why I couldn't forgive my mother – the myth that she must accept my forgiveness, that she didn't deserve it, and most of all that what she had done was unforgivable. I realised now I needed to let go of these myths because as long as I tried to collect what my mother owed me I would never move forward in my life. And so, in the end, forgiveness released me from the hate that was consuming me.'

MAKING MEANING

If there is a fifth element to complete this puzzle of forgiveness, it's around the process of meaning-making. As human beings we tend to alleviate suffering through a mixture of avoidance and endurance – but many people are capable of enduring great pain if they believe it to be purposeful. For some of us the ability to assign meaning to terrible experiences may be the very thing that forges our identity and makes us into the person we are. The process of finding new meaning out of past experiences is a way of creating a new under-standing out of the 'why' of what happened. Finding meaning is the ability to move from the narrative of an offence as hurt feelings to the narrative of an offence as an experience of significance. This is about taking the pain and making it part of who you are, because, as Aqeela Sherrills put it, 'Where the wounds are the gift lies.'

Writer Andrew Solomon has spent his career telling stories about the hardships of others and described the essence of meaning-making in his outstanding 2014 TED Talk. In it he describes what it takes to find meaning in adversity: 'You need to take the traumas and make them part of who you've come to be. And you need to fold the worst events of your life into a narrative of triumph, evincing a better self in response to things that hurt.'[2] Here he is specifically referring to the bullying he received as a child, how when he was in second grade a boy called Bobby Finkel had a birthday party to which he invited everyone in the class except for Solomon. As a young gay man, he then describes how he persistently felt ostracised and marginalised. Only after discovering his identity at Gay Pride many years later did he eventually find happiness by marrying his partner and having children. He sums up so well the gold to be extracted from finding meaning in pain, with the important realisation that he was in fact 'indebted even to Bobby Finkel because all those earlier experiences were what had propelled me to this moment, and I was finally unconditionally grateful for a life I'd once have done anything to change.' He concludes: 'There is always someone who wants to confiscate our humanity and there are always stories that restore it.'

Another helpful description of finding meaning comes from Fr Michael Lapsley, who often makes the point that although the bomb blast took so much from him, he was still able to retain a great deal of his old life, and even gained some things too. 'I would say I am a better human being because of the journey that I have travelled. The bomb helped me realise that actually perfection is not the human story; the human story is imperfection, incompleteness, and that actually we need one another to be fully human.' And Rami Elhanan, whose teenage daughter was killed by a suicide bomber in Tel Aviv, believes creating meaning out of what happened has established a lasting connection with his daughter. 'Telling my story gave my life meaning and purpose and got me out of bed in the morning. I have the feeling my daughter is standing behind my back and pushing me forward,' he says.

SELF-REFLECTION

If the building bricks to forging a forgiving mindset are curiosity, perception change, finding compassion, letting go of resentment and making meaning, then it's important to add just one more layer, because nothing can fundamentally change without the capacity for self-reflection. All of the people whose stories I've collected have embarked on often long and difficult journeys of self-discovery leading to transformation. This is important, because if we don't understand ourselves, we are more likely to become deluded and therefore create damage. How deeply we meet ourselves depends on how deeply we are able to meet others.

One of the greatest acts of defiance is to tell your story and remember. A young female victim of sexual assault once told me, 'Telling my story saved me from it.' When Rami says, 'Telling my story gave my life meaning,' he is voicing something I've heard articulated many times. Storytelling is a multifaceted exchange of ideas and in the case of telling true stories it is a way of sharing a personal experience which can create meaning out of painful events for the storyteller as well as provide insight for those hearing the story.

In the 1980s, psychology professor James Pennebaker discovered that writing about your feelings could significantly improve not just your mental health but also your physical health. There is robust evidence to suggest that keeping emotions closed and locked away may ultimately make you sick. In a number of studies, Pennebaker found that writing down thoughts and emotions, and disclosing things that were difficult and painful, led to feelings of relief. He also found that committing words to paper was a way of labelling these feelings and putting them into a coherent story. This was important because when people were able to construct a story from their experiences, they could then walk through it more easily.

Richard McCann, whose mother was killed by the serial killer Peter Sutcliffe, told me: 'Writing my story was like shedding a skin. I confronted the past and talked about taboo subjects. It liberated me.' Anne-Marie Cockburn, whose fifteen-year-old daughter, Martha, died after being given half a gram of pure crystallised MDMA, started writing her memoir the day after Martha's death and often talks about writing being her 'fourth emergency service'. For Margot Van Sluytman it was poetry that saved her, providing what was to become 'a lifelong conversation on the page'.[3]

The actress, director and scriptwriter Michaela Coel, who has received widespread international praise for the fictionalised drama of her sexual assault in the twelve-part HBO-BBC series *I May Destroy You*, also recognised the power of liberating a story of trauma, observing that, 'Like any other experience I've found traumatic it's been therapeutic to write about it and twist the narrative of pain into one of hope and even humour.'[4]

If telling your story of pain is therapeutic, it can also help nurture seeds of compassion. In chapter 9 I referred to the story of Carmen Aguirre, who was attacked by a serial rapist in the woods near her school in Vancouver in 1981 at the age of thirteen. Part of how she channelled love back into her heart was by being able to transform her experience into a performance. In an interview in the *Guardian* newspaper in 2016, she explains: 'I wrote a number of plays, including one about the attack called *The Trigger*. Victims who'd never gone to the parole hearings came when it premiered and waited to speak to me after the show. I played the rapist and the main victim.' The play ends with a monologue from 'Carmen' imagining her rapist having a sudden rush of feelings where 'remorse, compassion, sadness, grief, anguish, devastation and bone-crushing pain come up like a flood. And his heart explodes.'[5] By imagining her rapist having compassion, Aguirre's own compassion is fuelled for a man whom she believes must have been tortured to do what he did. Writing and performing the play made her curious to meet her attacker, which she finally did as part of a restorative justice programme in the prison where he was serving a long sentence.

Working creatively with a story of pain can be redemptive. It can also open the eyes of people who read it, see it or hear it. Gill Hicks lost both her legs in the London transport bombings of 2005 and has moved away from speaking her story in front of audiences to expressing it through paintings and designing prints on fabrics so that her art becomes part of a 'restorative conversation'. This new medium has created a very different tone and frequency to the story, as well as giving Gill greater peace of mind after having been trolled for choosing peace over revenge. In particular, she has been drawn to making scarves because using a scarf as a tourniquet to stop the blood flow saved her life on the morning of the attack. 'I need the art to be on a scarf because I need people to wear these things to start conversations,' she said. Many of the designs are monochrome, the weave forming a repetitive black-and-white pattern. I asked Gill if that was intentional. 'Absolutely intentional,' she declared. 'That was literally taken from me thinking about the bombers' black-and-white mindset and how a lot of us live in that way of "us and them". I was just so eager to try and find a way of [asking], where is the grey, where is that in-between?'

Another helpful way I've found to map these forgiveness journeys is to think of healing processes in relation to a diagram called the Trauma Healing Map, or the Circle of Reconciliation. I first discovered this model of trauma healing online[6] and have since adapted it for my work, as indeed have others working in the field of recovery. The map was originally developed by a Russian psychologist and conflict resolution expert, Olga Botcharova, who lived and worked in Bosnia-Herzegovina during the Bosnian War. Interestingly, in her first articulation of the process, she called the map 'Seven Steps Toward Forgiveness', but the word forgiveness seems to have been dropped by all those who have borrowed the model since.[7] The Trauma Healing Map opened my eyes because it so accurately and persuasively mirrors the pathways to recovery that so many of those I've spoken to have taken. Trauma healing involves recognising and reconciling with the impact of lingering trauma and paralysing fear, although equally the map may be useful when trying to rid ourselves of micro resentments and grievances, the sort that show up through-out our lives, often becoming so familiar that we barely notice them. On the map, the inner circle looks towards a natural and instinctive revenge journey. It also represents an addictive cycle out of which it is sometimes hard to break free, while the outer circle follows a path towards acceptance and reconciliation. The map is not supposed to indicate a linear progression from A to B but rather add scaffolding to a healing process in which people are likely to bounce around the circles, moving between the inner and outer realms.

THE TRAUMA HEALING MAP

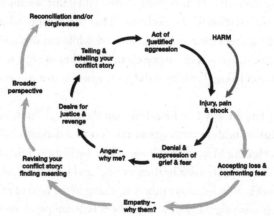

Injury, Pain and Shock

The pain starts at the point of a rupture where a shock or injury takes place. This might be a sudden act of violence such as a loved one's violent death, or an unexpected and unwelcome loss such as a partner walking out. At this point something happens to harm us, we are thrown off course because our world is punctured and our sense of self shattered.

Denial and Suppression of Grief and Fear

One coping strategy that can bring comfort following a shock or traumatic loss is to retreat into denial or silence. We heard this from both Lis Cashin and Susan Waters, whose families couldn't process the sudden trauma inflicted on them and so withdrew into silence. Similarly, Kelly Connor, who accidently ran over and killed an elderly woman on a pedestrian crossing, has talked about how her mother's way of dealing with the tragedy was to lay down the edict that they must never talk about it again. As Kelly said, 'For nearly two decades I didn't speak about the accident at all. At one point I was so convinced I didn't have the right to continue living, I tried to commit suicide.'

In 2016 Rosie Ayliffe's twenty-year-old daughter Mia was murdered while backpacking in Australia during her gap year. Mia had just moved into a hostel in Queensland to take a job on a sugarcane farm when she was fatally stabbed by French national Smail Ayad. Another young backpacker, Tom Jackson, died later of wounds sustained while trying to protect her. This is how Rosie describes what happened after hearing the news of her daughter's murder: 'I felt nothing. It was like I disassociated from my emotions, as if I were a bad actor in a movie I didn't want any part of . . . In the months after the murder I found my grief had a physical impact on my body. I went from being an active person who took care of my physical and mental states to being literally crippled by grief: the effects of PTSD took their toll, manifesting in joint pain, exhaustion and tension.'

ANGER – WHY ME?

Staying within the inner circle, anger is also a potent and useful survival mechanism. Nina Simone always said that it was anger that had sustained her by nurturing both her energy and creativity. The difficulty comes when our pain at injustice causes enduring anger or overwhelming self-pity because this will eventually deplete us and may lead to cycles of self-destructive behaviour. Geoff Thompson, whose life changed forever the day an adult in authority abused him, says, 'All I remember was waking up the next day with the darkest depression squatting deep inside my breast. For a long time, I didn't tell anyone.' His depression soon turned to anger as he used violence to suppress his feelings.

Ray Minniecon, the campaigner for Australia's Stolen Generations, said something once that interested me about anger. He said that while he could manage, control and understand right-eous anger because it was part of human nature, he had concluded that when anger turns to bitterness here lies the problem. 'I've experienced that kind of bitterness and it buckles and twists you up, causing you to lash out. I have to be careful when this happens not to fall into that trap. I've fallen into it before, and it takes a long time to get back on my feet again ... You have to be very conscious of your inner compass and the inner realities of where you are to avoid it.'

Trauma can be managed, too, by blaming others. At the age of five, Salimata Badji-Knight was told by the women of her village in Senegal that she was being taken on a picnic, but in fact they were taking her into the woods so that they could hold her down and perform female genital mutilation on her. 'For a long time, I blamed all the women in my community who had united to do this to me, and I blamed all the men for standing by and allowing it to happen. I blamed my mother because she condoned it, and my father because he had never been there to stop it.'

DESIRE FOR JUSTICE AND REVENGE

Denial and anger can lead to obsessive revenge fantasies and endless rumination about what happened and how to get even. Revenge can feel good too and can certainly bring short-term benefits. It can empower people, heighten feelings of self-worth and mask uncomfortable feelings such as shame or grief. James Baldwin believed that 'one of the reasons people cling to their hates so stubbornly is because they sense, once hate is gone, they will be forced to deal with their pain.' Like all negative feelings, which can for a while be strengthening, the desire to avenge can become compulsive, binding a person both to the harm as well as to the harmer.

I'll never forget Margaret McKinney's words when I interviewed her in Belfast early on in my quest for forgiveness stories and she described how she had felt in the years immediately after her 22-year-old son Brian was abducted and murdered by the IRA in 1978. 'If I'd known who Brian's killers were, I would have gone out and killed their children. I wanted them to know how it felt,' she said. I've rarely heard such a true and unsettling articulation of what revenge feels like and there is no doubt that for a while thoughts of murder calmed Margaret's broken heart.

TELLING AND RETELLING THE STORY

Telling and retelling the grievance story is what people do when they're hurt. It's a way of shoring up support and intensifying the call for justice. Rebecca DeMauro's eleven-year-old daughter, Andria, was murdered in Arkansas in 1999 by a relative called Karl Roberts. 'There is no way to explain the loss of a child, other than to say that dying by slow torture would be better. I have never experienced such great pain emotionally or physically,' she says, describing the capsizing grief that overwhelmed her.

Initially when Karl Roberts was given the death penalty for first-degree capital murder it seemed to pacify her rage, but soon he began to consume her thoughts again as she looked for every opportunity to voice her hatred of him. 'I wanted to blow his brains out. I wanted him to suffer long and slow. I even gave him a nickname, "Spawn of Satan", and prayed to God that he was being raped and tortured in prison,' she said. In order to keep her story alive, she clung to other parents of murdered children, joined writing classes to write similar stories of revenge, and played computer games so she could create an avatar of Karl Roberts to torture.

ACT OF 'JUSTIFIED' AGGRESSION

Taking revenge can feel sweet if you've harboured deep pain inside of you. Witnessing the Israeli military kill Palestinian children was Bassam Aramin's reason for trying to blow up an Israeli military convoy with a grenade at the age of sixteen. Having suffered years of violence at the hands of the Israeli army, he eventually retaliated. 'I developed a deep need for revenge,' he said. 'I became part of a group whose mission was to get rid of the catastrophe that had come to our town. We called ourselves freedom fighters, but the outside world called us terrorists.'

Without some profound inner shift which will send people on a different trajectory, the pain of trauma may well continue, with a combination of isolation and suffering keeping a traumatised person locked into the inner circle. Key to healing and recovery, therefore, is the ability to soften all the above stress reactions into something that resembles self-compassion. As Stephen Levine (the author and teacher best known for his work on death and dying) wrote in *Unattended Sorrow*, 'Healing, then, becomes not the absence of pain but the increased ability to meet pain with mercy instead of loathing.'[8]

The shift required in order to bring symmetry back into one's life often occurs because people feel exhausted and hopeless as they remain stuck in the inner circle, caught between the power of payback and the powerlessness of acute pain. Critical to trauma healing is acceptance of the enormity of loss and the ability to confront fear. This may result in being able to express grief, feel the pain and mourn fully.

ACCEPTING LOSS AND CONFRONTING FEAR

American comedian and *Late Show* host Stephen Colbert gives a moving description of this kind of grieving. In 2015 Colbert gave an interview to *GQ* magazine in which he told of how his father and two older brothers had been killed in a plane crash when he was ten years old.[9] Following the crash, with his surviving older siblings already having left home, Colbert found himself living alone with his mother, struggling to come to terms with their devastating loss. He saw his mother demonstrate strength in the face of fear, her joy irremediably intertwined with her sorrow, and this in time led to his own acceptance and even gratitude for a tragedy that had shaped his life. In the interview he talks about how he uses this joy in his comedy, and how having come from the darkest place he learnt from his mother to stare into the headlights of grief rather than run away from them. 'By her example I am not bitter,' he told *GQ*. 'She was not. Broken, yes. Bitter, no. It was a very healthy reciprocal acceptance of suffering. Which does not mean to be defeated by suffering. Acceptance is not defeat. Acceptance is just awareness.' Playwright and activist V once said, 'bullets are hardened tears', and when interviewed by Marc Maron on his *WTF* podcast in 2019 she reminded him of her words. They were discussing her recent memoir, *The Apology*, and the legacy of her father's brutality when V spoke of the enormous value she had placed on her ability to shed tears. Otherwise, she asked, 'Where does all the sorrow, shame, tenderness go? It goes into violence. When I grew up, I'd weep all the time. What would have happened with my rage if I hadn't been able to weep? That rage would have turned into violence.' This is something I've heard repeated a number of times when people have described the ways they had found to transform abuse into wisdom or pain into compassion. Camilla Carr, for example, who was held hostage in Chechnya in 1997 and repeatedly raped by one of her captors, described to me how, after she was released, she managed to deal with the encroaching residue of trauma. 'First you have to deal with anger, then with tears, and only once you reach the tears are you on the road to finding peace of mind,' she said with quiet certitude.

EMPATHY – WHY THEM?

To be able to dig deep to find empathy or compassion for someone who has hurt you is, as we've seen, a part of the process of forgiving. Also critical to reconciling with trauma is re-humanising the enemy. Salimata Badgi-Knight talks about empathy as understanding, in relation to coming to terms with what had happened to her in the woods when she was five years old. 'It was only when I became a Buddhist and stopped viewing myself as a victim', she says, 'that I stopped feeling unworthy. Out of rage came compassion, and the realisation that this was not my mother's fault, nor the fault of the women who had done this to me. They were simply blinded by tradition.'

REVISING THE CONFLICT STORY – FINDING MEANING

Feeling and expressing compassion will inevitably revise the conflict story, which may be necessary in order to move from a position of 'why me?' to 'why them?' This is where the importance of finding meaning shows up again. Neurologist, psychiatrist, philosopher and survivor of Nazi death camps Viktor Frankl often talked of the importance of finding meaning from the ashes of his life, stating in his 1946 memoir, *Man's Search for Meaning*, that the trauma survivor, in order to cope with misery, needs to 'find some purpose and meaning in the suffering,' not through 'a tensionless state but rather the striving and struggling for a worthwhile goal, a freely chosen task.'

Dr Masi Noor has also stated that one way to overcome the trap of beating yourself up for harm done to, or by, you is to 'utilise your tragedy and to share the lessons of what you've gone through. Personal stories shed light and become transformative – not just individually or personally but way beyond at a societal level too.'

For bereaved parents who have lost children to violent deaths, even a funeral can provide meaning. Margaret McKinney had to wait twenty-one years before the IRA admitted to her son's murder and revealed the exact location of his grave across the border in County Monaghan. In 1999 Margaret re-buried her son in Milltown cemetery, close to her home in West Belfast. 'It might sound crazy, but I was grateful to the IRA just to be able to bury my son after twenty-one years,' she told me. 'His remains were placed in a lovely coffin and the house was suddenly so full of life as people came to pay their last respects ... I've got no hatred against those who killed Brian anymore. In fact, I'd like to meet the person who took Brian's life. Since I've finally found my peace, I think maybe it's time he found his too.'

BROADER PERSPECTIVE

Repetitive revenge fantasies in the end tend to just increase some-one's torment, often making them feel cruel or corrupt like the person who has hurt them. I've had countless victims and survivors of crime say to me, 'I don't want to hate because I don't want to be like them.' But being able to reframe your story requires placing it within a broader perspective. Often it can take just a single event to shift and enlarge someone's worldview. Rebecca DeMauro's story is a good example of this.

After her twelve-year-old daughter was murdered, Rebecca's ache for retribution became intolerable. Nothing seemed to relieve the pain and when the execution of Andi's killer was called off at the very last minute her world was shattered all over again. It was only after watching on television the trial of an infamous serial killer called Gary Ridgway that her perspective suddenly and fun-damentally shifted. As she was watching edited clips from the victim impact statements and taking comfort from words like 'I hope you rot in hell, you son of a bitch', she saw Ridgway sitting there, his body rigid and his eyes full of loathing. Then Rebecca watched as the father of one of Ridgway's youngest victims came forward. Bob Rule was a Christian and told the court how the murder had challenged the very core of his belief. He then looked at Ridgway and said that because God called on believers to forgive, finally, after a great deal of soul searching, he had found it in his heart to forgive his daughter's killer. As Rebecca watched, she noticed Ridgway's face soften and his lips begin to tremble. Then she saw a single tear run down his cheek. 'At that precise moment I realised that the only way I would be able to go on living was to stop hating,' she said. 'I had to do what Bob Rule had done and let it go, and let Andi rest in peace … I knew that if something didn't change, I would be in the graveyard, dead from a broken heart next to my little daughter.'

MOVING TOWARDS RECONCILIATION/FORGIVENESS

This is the point at which the trauma healing begins, moving from the predictability of the inner circle towards the potentiality of the outer circle. It is also here that restorative justice fits in. The focus of justice for most people is about exchanging suffering for more suffering, but a more healing theory of justice repairs the injury by bringing those harmed by crime and conflict together with those responsible for it. When this is not possible because the person who has hurt you is either absent or unwilling to make amends, or when self-blame or self-harm are the cause of your suffering, the move may be toward an internal reconciliation. I often think of this in terms of doing justice to yourself, in other words not being captured by your own suffering, not being defined by what has hurt you and not being incapacitated by old wounds. By reconciling with someone who has hurt you or by making peace with things you cannot change, a kind of reckoning unfolds. Here it is that forgiveness too can offer the possibility to restore equilibrium or repair the damage done. Forgiving someone does not mean you reconcile with them; it means taking hold of painful emotions and deciding to let go of them.

Rosie Ayliffe was able to find some relief from the pain of losing her daughter by finding forgiveness for the man responsible for Mia's murder. She steeled herself to attend the trial in Australia, explaining, 'I was fearful of this man, Ayad, who had previously been considered too dangerous to appear in court because of the savagery of his attacks ... But I also felt a need to find some degree of understanding of his destructive spree that night.'

While Rosie knew Ayad deserved to be sentenced to life imprisonment, the idea of justice providing some sort of closure for the victims felt completely alien, especially as she knew she would never benefit from the suffering of a man so clearly mentally ill. The act of killing, she reasoned, had been a manifestation of something the perpetrator couldn't control: insanity, possessive fury, a psychotic episode.

'I knew many people were wishing him and his family pain and anguish and even death,' says Rosie. 'I understood their thoughts. But when I read out my victim impact statement I spoke about how although nothing could undo the pain of what had happened, I wished Ayad and his family peace. When I said how Ayad's real-isation of what he had done was worse than anything that could be inflicted on him, he looked up at me for the first time and we stared at each other in silence. I think the fact I refused to vent about hating him made an impact. And I then realised that this was why I had flown halfway around the world – in the hope of achieving that connection. To my mind, it's only through those moments of understanding, when you experience insight into the mind of another being, that change can be initiated.'

From the beginning Rosie never put herself under pressure to forgive, but it was something she wanted to do in honour of her dead daughter. Like Wilma Derksen and Azim Khamisa, and many other parents I've met who have lost children to violence, forgiveness came from the knowledge that to find relief in grief you must move towards love rather than hate. As Rosie says, 'Whether or not people think I am mad to be able to forgive Ayad, I don't care, because it is consistent with Mia's own values since she was a little girl. We both believed that you can only move on in life through love and forgiveness, which was the path she tried so hard to tread herself.'

EPILOGUE

As I came to the end of writing this book, The Forgiveness Project's founding patron, Archbishop Desmond Tutu, died. This was followed just a month later by the death of Buddhist monk and spiritual teacher Thich Nhat Hanh. Both men had been courageous and radical peace activists in their lifetime; both were renowned for being visionary leaders able to speak beyond the boundaries of religion. Both also frequently spoke of the benefits of forgiveness. It felt like the world had lost two moral giants.

Thich Nhat Hanh's life of reflection led him to believe that forgiveness was the key to creating a peaceful, just and sustainable world, and he maintained that 'only when compassion is born in your heart, is it possible to forgive.' He would often reach out to those who felt wounded by their mother or father and in the film *The Power of Forgiveness* recites a meditation for the 'many angry sons and daughters' who cannot make peace with their parents. In a soft, measured voice he is heard instructing a room full of people: 'breathing in I see myself as a five-year-old child; breathing out I hold that five-year-old child with tenderness. Breathing in I see my father as a five-year-old boy; breathing out I smile to my father as a five-year-old boy.' The point he is making is that only when you are able to visualise your cruel father as a fragile and vulnerable five-year-old can you begin to understand and feel compassion for the person he has become.

He would explain that if you are full of anger, you only cause more suffering to yourself as well as to the person you're angry with. The wise, he said, always know to remain still when they are in a place of anger, because 'when you are calm and lucid, you see that the other person is a victim of confusion, of hate and of violence transmitted by society, by parents, by friends, by environment.' At this point anger subsides and leaves room for compassion to stir.

Thich Nhat Hanh's process to soothe the wounded hearts of adult children isn't easy, but it has been adapted and used in multiple settings.

Gayle Kirschenbaum likens her childhood to a war zone. She describes how she was raised in 'enemy territory' because even before she was born her mother assumed she was having a boy and told her two young sons that she would soon be bringing their brother 'Gary' back from the hospital. As she grew older Gayle became the target of her mother's bullying and vindictiveness while knowing that her two brothers were unquestionably favoured. She lived in fear, as almost anything she did or said might set off her mother's rage or trigger the next grudge. As Gayle grew into adulthood, unsurprisingly she began to struggle with issues of trust and abandonment.

But then something happened to shift the trajectory which almost certainly would have resulted in a complete schism between mother and daughter: 'There was a lightbulb moment for me when I played a psychological board game,' says Gayle. 'I threw the dice and when it landed, the facilitator asked me to stand up, close my eyes, and imagine my mother as a little girl. At that time, I knew about some of her childhood hardships, and so I pictured a wounded child full of pain. Then the facilitator asked me to imagine myself as a little girl, which wasn't difficult as I knew all too well my own pain. We were now both little girls who were deeply wounded coming together. That's when I realized I had to

change how I looked at my mother. I had to take her off the ped-
estal of being a mother who should love and adore me, to herself
being a hurt child who didn't know any better.' Gayle went on
to make a documentary film about forgiving her mother, in the
course of which she came to understand much more about why
her mother had treated her the way she had.

Because everything I've learnt about forgiveness has come from
the stories generously shared with me by people who have exca-
vated and experienced powerful healing processes, it feels fitting
to leave the last word of this book to Gayle as she adeptly explains
how she came to forgive her unkind mother and how making the
film *Look At Us Now Mother!* (with her mother's full agreement and
participation) became a pivotal turning point for both of them.[1]

With cameras rolling I looked for answers to why my mom
treated me like she did but as I dug into her past her standard
answer was, 'I don't know. I don't remember.' It was at that
point I knew I needed help from professionals and Mom agreed
to visit a therapist. In the course of this I learned more about
my mother's pain, the untimely death of her baby sister, her
father's suicide attempts and the childhood she never really had.
Invariably, anyone who is abusive to others (unless they suffer
from a serious mental illness) is often a victim of trauma. Hurt
people hurt people. I also came to understand her narcissistic
nature and how it was challenging for her to have a daughter. If
you're female, glamorous and a narcissist, you crave the attention of a man, and your daughter becomes competition for you.

I know many women of my generation who haven't forgiven
their mean and abusive mothers because they never received
an apology. I've never looked for an apology from my mother.
She was incapable of giving one because she was blind to what
she had done. So, I chose to forgive her for my own health and
happiness and to free myself from mental angst and bondage.

Forgiveness is a virtue based on the ability to love when others are not loving you. And then something amazing happened. As soon as I reframed how I looked at my mother, I changed my expectations. I no longer saw my mother as the person who should love, adore and nurture me, but as a child who was in pain herself and who craved love.

As I took my power back and stopped reacting to her criticism, her insults eventually had no impact on me. And as she realised this and saw that I was now actually giving her love, she changed her behaviour towards me and the insults eventually stopped altogether. And so, due to my ability to understand and forgive my mother, we have become close friends today and enjoy each other's company. It's amazing for me to think that the woman I wished would die during my childhood is now my closest friend.

ENDNOTES

Prologue

1 'The edges of human endurance' is a phrase borrowed from Dr Pratāp Rughani, who has long supported the work of The Forgiveness Project. Dr Rughani is an award-winning documentary filmmaker and Professor of Documentary Practices at London College of Communication, who has provided valuable materials into the ethics of creative arts practice and storytelling.

2 Fred Luskin has spent decades researching and teaching the health benefits of forgiveness. See F. Luskin, *Forgive for Good: A Proven Prescription for Health and Happiness* (HarperCollins, 2002).

Chapter 1

1 Julie Nicholson, quoted in Richard Wilson, 'The Futility of Forgiveness', *Prospect* magazine (July 2012).

2 *King Lear*, Act 4, Scene 6.

3 Marco Belpoliti and Robert Gordon (ed.), *The Voice of Memory: Interviews 1961–1987* (New Press, 2001), p. 270.

4 A. Solzhenitsyn, *The Gulag Archipelago 1918–1956* (Harvill Press, 2003), p. 75.

5 One recent study found that having forgiving thoughts makes people feel they have more control over their lives and induces lower physiological stress responses. See C. V. O. Witvliet, T. E. Ludwig and K. L. Vander Laan, 'Granting forgiveness or harboring grudges: Implications for emotion, physiology, and health', *Psychological Science* 121 (2001): 117–123.

6 Desmond Tutu, foreword to catalogue for photographic exhibition, *The F Word: Images of Forgiveness* (The Forgiveness Project, 2004).

7 *Uprising* was shown on BBC One in 2021 in three parts on three consecutive evenings.

8 P. Houghton, *On Death, Dying and Not Dying* (Jessica Kingsley Publishers, 2001), pp 20–21.

9 'Mina Smallman: "I know what Sarah Everard's parents are experiencing"', BBC News, 26 March 2021, https://www.bbc.co.uk/news/av/uk-56450969

10 Reinekke Lengelle, PhD, 'To Forgive is Not a Verb: A reflection and Sawbonna', 28 September 2020, http://writingtheself.ca/2020/09/28/to-forgive-is-not-a-verb-a-reflection-and-sawbonna/

11   http://www.edwardstaubyn.com/Backup/interviews/bookwormpart1.mp3
12   Edward St Aubyn, *Some Hope* (Pan Macmillan, 2012), Chapter 10.

Chapter 2

1   Rebecca Solnit, *Hope in the Dark* (Canongate, 2005), p. 7.
2   Matthew Parris, 'To hell with the foolish idea of forgiveness',
     The Times, 18 July 2015, https://www.thetimes.co.uk/article/
     to-hell-with-the-foolish-idea-of-forgiveness-tj5cq8pv967
3   Colin C. Tipping, *Radical Forgiveness* (Global 13 Publications, 2002), p. 54.
4   joeldiana.com/?page_id=6
5   A research study found that when forgiveness is the result of the influence
     of religious authorities or government and political leaders, it can be
     shallow, limited and unstable. See E. Staub, 'The Origins and Evolution of
     Hate, With Notes on Prevention', in R. J. Sternberg (ed.), *The psychology
     of hate* (pp. 51–66), American Psychological Association, 2005, https://
     doi.org/10.1037/10930-003, and E. Staub, L. A. Pearlman, A. Gubin &
     A. Hagengimana, 'Healing, Reconciliation, Forgiving and the Prevention
     of Violence After Genocide or Mass Killing: An Intervention and Its
     Experimental Evaluation in Rwanda', *Journal of Social and Clinical Psychology*
     243 (2005): 297–334, https://doi.org/10.1521/jscp.24.3.297.65617
6   Richard Wilson, 'The Futility of Forgiveness', *Prospect* magazine (July
     2012).
7   Noted in R. J. O'Shaughnessy, 'Forgiveness', *Philosophy*, 42/162 (1967):
     348; *David Copperfield*, Chapter 42: 'Mischief', http://www.ibiblio.org/
     dickens/html/42066.html
8   C. Barks (trans.), *Rumi: Selected Poems* (Penguin, 2004), p. 36.
9   Lorie Johnson, 'The Deadly Consequences of Unforgiveness', CBN News,
     22 June 2015, https://www1.cbn.com/cbnnews/healthscience/2015/june/
     the-deadly-consequences-of-unforgiveness/
10   Research has shown that having a forgiving attitude is associated with
     several mental health outcomes, including less anxiety, depression and
     other major psychiatric disorders. See Hirsch et al., 2011; Lin et al., 2004;
     Ryan and Kumar, 2005; Toussaint and Cheadle, 2009; Toussaint et al.,
     2008.
        Being forgiving is also associated with fewer physical health symptoms
     and better overall physical health (Lawler et al., 2005; Seawell et al.,
     2014), healthier cardiovascular responses to stress (Lawler et al., 2003), and
     lower rates of cardiovascular disease (Friedberg et al., 2007; Toussaint and
     Cheadle, 2009; Waltman et al., 2009).
        As might be expected, forgiveness is therefore also associated with
     lower rates of mortality (Krause and Hayward, 2013; Toussaint et al.,
     2012).
        The 'Forgive to Live' study found that people high on the scale
     of conditional forgiveness, meaning they will only forgive others on
     conditional terms, died before people who scored low on this measure,
     meaning people able to practise unconditional forgiveness lived up to three
     years longer. (L. L. Toussaint, A. D. Owen & A. Cheadle, 'Forgive to
     Live: Forgiveness, health, and longevity', *Journal of Behavioral Medicine* 35/4,
     (2012): 375–386.)
11   Paul Kix, 'The Downside of Forgiveness', *New York Magazine*, 21 January 2011,
     https://nymag.com/news/intelligencer/70839; James K. Mcnulty, 'Forgiveness

increases the likelihood of subsequent partner transgressions in marriage',
Journal of Family Psychology 24/6, (2010): 787–90, https://www.semanticscholar.
org/paper/Forgiveness-increases-the-likelihood-of-subsequent-Mcnulty/92e8
d742c421309f005e6acb3db6eda77870e72e

12   Christiane Sanderson, 'The Role of Forgiveness After Interpersonal Abuse'
in Stephen Hance (ed.), *Forgiveness in Practice* (Jessica Kingsley Publishers,
2019), p. 140; see also Christiane Sanderson, *Counselling Survivors of Sexual
Abuse* (Jessica Kingsley Publishers, 2008); Christiane Sanderson, *The
Seduction of Children: Empowering Parents and Teachers to Protect Children from
Child Sexual Abuse* (Jessica Kingsley Publishers, 2004); Lenore E. A. Walker
(ed.), *The Battered Woman Syndrome*, 3rd edition (Springer Publishing, 2008).

13   https://www.iicsa.org.uk/key-documents/26895/view/child-protection-
religious-organisations-settings-investigation-report-september-2021-.pdf

14   Christopher C. H. Cook and Wendy Dossett, 'Addiction and Forgiveness',
from Stephen Hance, *Forgiveness in Practice* (Jessica Kingsley Publishers,
2019), p. 230.

15   Derrida's *On Forgiveness* relates to the question of forgiveness regarding the
traumas of history such as the Holocaust and apartheid in South Africa; J.
Derrida, *On Cosmopolitanism and Forgiveness* (Routledge, 2001).

Chapter 3

1   *The Holocaust* was a big-budget, American TV show starring the young
Meryl Streep. It transformed how Germans saw their own history.

2   'Oskar Groening trial: "Book-keeper of Auschwitz" guilty', BBC News, 15
July 2015, https://www.bbc.co.uk/news/av/world-europe-33533009

3   *Poetry Unbound* podcast, https://onbeing.org/programs/
dilruba-ahmed-phase-one/

4   Retitled *The Reawakening* in the US.

5   Primo Levi, *If This Is a Man / The Truce*, tr. Stuart Woolf with an introduction
by Paul Bailey and an afterword by the author (The Orion Press, 1960; Abacus,
1987; *Se questo è un uomo* first published in Italy, 1958), p. 382.

6   Robin Shohet, 'Understanding Revenge: An invitation to let go' in
Stephen Hance (ed.) *Forgiveness in Practice* (Jessica Kingsley Publishers,
2019), p. 123.

7   Chanel Miller, *Know My Name* (Viking, 2020).

8   *The Flipside with Paris Lees*, 'Forgive me, not?', 27 October 2021 https://
www.bbc.co.uk/sounds/play/p0b05w53

9   'Billy Connolly "still loves abusive dad"', BBC News, 5 January 2013,
https://www.bbc.co.uk/news/uk-scotland-20920274

Chapter 4

1   Ben Fuchs, 'Betrayal, Revenge and Forgiveness: A Life Initiation',
Changes – International Journal of Psychology and Psychotherapy, 15/1 (1997),
John Wiley & Sons.

2   Harriet Brown, 'How to Forgive Anyone – and Why Your Health
Depends on It', 27 April 2011, https://www.oprah.com/oprahs-
lifeclass/how-to-forgive-others-health-benefits-of-forgiveness-
fred-luskin/all

3   International Rehabilitation Council for Torture Victims, 'Conversion
Therapy is Torture', 23 April 2020, https://irct.org/media-and-resources/
latest-news/article/1027

4   Jane Graham, 'Jean-Michel Jarre: "My success was so big and violent it was almost abstract", *The Big Issue*, 27 November 2018, https://www.bigissue.com/interviews/jean-michel-jarre-my-success-was-so-big-and-violent-it-was-almost-abstract/

5   David Whyte, *Consolations: The Solace, Nourishment and Underlying Meaning of Everyday Words* (Canongate Books, 2019), p. 52.

6   *Ian Wright: Home Truths*, 6 May 2021 https://www.bbc.co.uk/iplayer/episode/m000vt7g/ian-wright-home-truths

7   A perfect example of this is the friendship between the writer Christopher Isherwood and the artist Don Bachardy. There was a thirty-year difference between them but they remained together from their first meeting in 1953 until Isherwood's death in 1986. Because Bachardy was that much younger, Isherwood accepted that the latter would want other sexual encounters but, as he recorded in his diaries, nothing was more important to him than their relationship, neither his work nor his religion. Simply by sitting still and waiting, he maintained his position in Bachardy's affections. In the end their relationship became fundamentally that of father and son, guru and disciple, as Katherine Bucknell observes in her introduction to their collected letters.

Chapter 5

1   Lis Cashin, *This Is Me: My Journey to Mental Wellbeing* (2020), p. 64; www.lischasin.com

2   Johann Christoph Arnold, *The Lost Art of Forgiving: Stories of Healing from the Cancer of Bitterness* (Plough Publishing House, 1998), p. 114.

3   Stephen Hance (ed.), *Forgiveness in Practice: Uses and Abuses of Self-Forgiveness* (Jessica Kingsley Publishers, 2019), p. 74.

4   'Phase One' from *Bring Now the Angels* by Dilruba Ahmed, © 2020. Reprinted by permission of the University of Pittsburgh Press.

5   J. S. Zechmeister and C. Romero, 'Victim and offender accounts of interpersonal conflict: Autobiographic narratives of forgiveness and unforgiveness', *Journal of Personality and Social Psychology* 82/4 (2002): 675–686, https://doi.org/10.1037/0022-3514.82.4.675

6   J. Blustein, 'On Taking Responsibility for One's Past', *Journal of Applied Philosophy* 17/1 (2000): 1–19.

7   Richard Holloway, *On Forgiveness: How Can We Forgive the Unforgivable?* (Canongate Books, 2002), p. 49.

8   Twitter, @QandA, 23 May 2021, https://twitter.com/qanda/status/1398058400081010688?s=21

Chapter 6

1   Male combat veterans who suffer from PTSD are two to three times more likely to abuse their female partners than veterans not suffering from PTSD. About 33 per cent of combat veterans with PTSD reported having been aggressive with their intimate partner at least once in the previous year. About 91 per cent of combat veterans with PTSD reported being psychologically aggressive with their intimate partner in the previous year. (Figures quoted from DomesticShelters.org, 'The Facts About Abuse in Military Families: A by-the-numbers look at domestic violence among service members', 2 December 2016, https://www.domesticshelters.org/articles/statistics/the-facts-about-abuse-in-military-families)

2   Eckhart Tolle, *The Power of Now* (Hodder & Stoughton, 2001), p. 128.

3   Read more at https://www.drborris.com/politicalforgiveness

4   Research shows forgiveness can be harmful under certain conditions. After
    mass killings, genocide and intractable conflict when members of perpetrator
    and victims' groups continue to live together and the harmdoers do not
    acknowledge their responsibility or express regret, forgiveness may contribute
    to further problems in the relationship between groups. See E. Staub, 'The
    Origins and Evolution of Hate, With Notes on Prevention', in R. J. Sternberg
    (ed.), *The psychology of hate* (pp. 51–66), American Psychological Association,
    2005, https://doi.org/10.1037/10930-003; E. Staub, L. A. Pearlman, A.
    Gubin & A. Hagengimana, 'Healing, Reconciliation, Forgiving and the
    Prevention of Violence After Genocide or Mass Killing: An Intervention and
    Its Experimental Evaluation in Rwanda', *Journal of Social and Clinical Psychology*
    243 (2005): 297–334, https://doi.org/10.1521/jscp.24.3.297.65617

5   Jude Whyte, 'Jude Whyte: Best people of Northern Ireland can hope for is
    to live in parallel universes of barely tolerating each other', *Belfast Telegraph*,
    14 March 2019, https://www.belfasttelegraph.co.uk/opinion/news-analysis/
    jude-whyte-best-people-of-northern-ireland-can-hope-for-is-to-live-in-
    parallel-universes-of-barely-tolerating-each-other-37911450.html

6   https://www.theforgivenessproject.com/stories/brima-koker/

7   P. Gobodo-Madikizela, *A Human Being Died That Night: A South African
    Woman Confronts the Legacy of Apartheid* (Mariner, 2004), p. 117.

Chapter 7

1   Bryan Eneas, 'Sask. First Nation announces discovery of 751
    unmarked graves near former residential school', CBC News,
    24 June 2021, https://www.cbc.ca/news/canada/saskatchewan/
    cowessess-marieval-indian-residential-school-news-1.6078375

2   Parliamentary Debates, Senate, 12 June 2008, 1505 (Mary Simon,
    President, Inuit Tapiriit Kanatami).

3   Research has shown that evidence for a causal relationship between
    intergroup apologies and forgiveness is limited. This is because an apology
    alone is rarely enough to promote forgiveness, and the link between
    apology and forgiveness appears to weaken over time – likely due to
    expectations not being met. See Matthew J. Hornsey and Michael J. A.
    Wohl, 'We are sorry: Intergroup apologies and their tenuous link with
    intergroup forgiveness', *European Review of Social Psychology* 24/1, (2013):
    1–31.

4   https://reformationharvestfire.com/2010/08/a-nation-forgiven-canada/

5   Quoted from an interview McCullough gave to Krista Tippett
    for *On Being* (airdate 2008), https://onbeing.org/programs/
    michael-mccullough-getting-revenge-and-forgiveness/

6   Molly Andrews, 'The Narrative Architecture of Political
    Forgiveness', *Political Psychology* 40/3 (June 2019): 433–447, https://
    repository.uel.ac.uk/download/b478494a756bd78f91c75d0eb89efd
    78d7ee74989adedab7df3ba3316e2b91bb/344924/The%2520Narrative%
    2520Architecture%2520of%2520Political%2520Forgiveness.pdf

7   Marina Hyde, 'Footballers can say it, but for England's politicians, "sorry"
    really is the hardest word', *The Guardian*, 13 July 2021,
    https://www.theguardian.com/commentisfree/2021/jul/13/
    footballers-england-politicians-sorry-euro-2020-players-prime-minister

8   Nancy Berlinger, PhD, 'Resolving Harmful Medical Mistakes:

Is There a Role for Forgiveness?', *American Medical Association Journal of Ethics* 13/9 (September 2011): 647–654, https://journalofethics.ama-assn.org/article/resolving-harmful-medical-mistakes-there-role-forgiveness/2011-09

9   There is an excellent paper that looks at how current investigative responses to medical error compound the harm done, and how restorative approaches have the potential to radically shift the outcomes. Jo Wailling MHR, RN, Allison Kooijman MA, Joanne Hughes, Jane K. O'Hara PhD, 'Humanizing harm: Using a restorative approach to heal and learn from adverse events', *Health Expectations* (2022), https://onlinelibrary.wiley.com/doi/10.1111/hex.13478

10 Gillian Slovo, *Making History: South Africa's Truth and Reconciliation Commission* (OpenDemocracy, 2002).

11 Marc Maron, *WTF* podcast, Episode 1028, 17 June 2019, http://www.wtfpod.com/podcast/episode-1028-eve-ensler?rq=Eve%20Ensler

Chapter 8

1   David Baddiel, *Social Media, Anger and Us*, BBC Two, 13 December 2021.

2   *South African Times*, 27 September 2006.

3   House of Commons Library, 'Hate Crime Statistics', 26 November 2021, https://researchbriefings.files.parliament.uk/documents/CBP-8537/CBP-8537.pdf

4   New Zealand Human Rights Commission, 'COVID-19 fueling discrimination against Tangata Whenua and Chinese communities', 17 February 2021, https://www.hrc.co.nz/news/covid-19-fueling-discrimination-against-tangata-whenua-and-chinese-communities/

5   Asian Australian Alliance, 'Covid-19 Coronavirus Racism Incident Report', https://asianaustralianalliance.net/wp-content/uploads/2020/07/COVID-19-racism-incident-report-preliminary.pdf

6   Refuge, 'A Year of Lockdown', 23 March 2021, https://www.refuge.org.uk/a-year-of-lockdown/

7   'FBI Releases 2020 Hate Crime Statistics', 30 August 2021, https://www.fbi.gov/news/pressrel/press-releases/fbi-releases-2020-hate-crime-statistics

8   Dean Balsamini, 'NYC hate crimes skyrocketed by 139 percent this year: NYPD data', *New York Post*, 3 July 2021, https://nypost.com/2021/07/03/nyc-hate-crimes-skyrocketed-by-139-percent-this-year-nypd/

9   UK Government Home Office, 'Official Statistics: Hate Crime, England and Wales, 2019 to 2020', Updated 28 October 2020, https://www.gov.uk/government/statistics/hate-crime-england-and-wales-2019-to-2020/hate-crime-england-and-wales-2019-to-2020

10 Emma Powys Maurice, 'Counter-terrorism probe launched after trans police officer gets "two million hate comments"', PinkNews, 13 October 2021, https://www.pinknews.co.uk/2021/10/13/counter-terrorism-trans-police-officer-online/

11 'Hate Crimes In Schools Rise By 121% In Just Three Years', LBC, 12 September 2019, https://www.lbc.co.uk/news/hate-crimes-in-schools-rise-racism/; Data from all of the UK's police forces revealed there were 900 hate-related incidents in schools in 2015 but that figure rose to 1,987 in 2018 – an increase of 121 per cent.

12 Guy Lynn, 'Anti-Semitic reports in London hit new high, charity

says', BBC News, 15 June 2021, https://www.bbc.co.uk/news/uk-england-london-57439688

13 Tom Krattenmaker, 'Stopping the rampant hate running through America', USA Today, 2020, https://eu.usatoday.com/story/opinion/2020/11/12/how-end-hate-has-surrounded-politics-and-elections-column/6232592002/

14 'Southampton man arrested over "racist attack" is released', BBC News, 28 February 2021 https://www.bbc.co.uk/news/uk-england-hampshire-56229747

15 Confessions with Giles Fraser podcast, https://podcasts.apple.com/gb/podcast/confessions-with-giles-fraser-unherd/id1445038441?mt=2

16 Michael Hodges, 'Civilisations presenter Mary Beard: "I'm really glad I didn't do TV until I was 50"', Radio Times, 13 April 2018, https://www.radiotimes.com/tv/documentaries/civilisations-bbc-mary-beard/

17 David Baddiel, Social Media, Anger and Us, BBC Two, 13 December 2021.

18 https://threader.app/thread/1417674275046273035

19 https://www.youtube.com/watch?v=kGJGYgoaPyI&list=PLpPQHEkzSCXrSNNLvZbVYhb93B81z7PUT&t=916s

20 https://www.streetgangs.com/tag/calvin-hodges/

Chapter 9

1   Patrick Magee, Where Grieving Begins: Building Bridges After the Brighton Bomb (Pluto Press, 2021), p. 212.

2   Ibid., p. xi.

3   Marian Partington, If You Sit Very Still (Vala Publishing, 2012), pp. 167–69.

4   Margot Van Sluytman, 'Sawbonna: Justice As Lived Experience', Athabasca University, June 2012, https://www.iirp.edu/images/pdf/sawbonna-paper.pdf

5   Glynis Ratcliffe, 'When her father was murdered, this writer turned to poetry', Broadview, 13 October 2021, https://broadview.org/margot-van-sluytman/

6   Forgiving Justice, Swarthmore Lecture, Quaker Home Service (Newell, 2000), p. 44.

7   Professor Lawrence Sherman and Dr Heather Strang, 'Restorative Justice: The evidence', 2007, https://restorativejustice.org.uk/resources/restorative-justice-evidence-%E2%80%93-professor-lawrence-sherman-and-dr-heather-strang

8   From edited extract from Carmen Aguirre, Mexican Hooker #1: And My Other Roles Since the Revolution, Granta, 14 April 2016, https://www.theguardian.com/society/2016/apr/09/carmen-aguirre-why-faced-my-rapist?CMP=Share_iOSApp_Other

9   Kate Graham, '"We forgave man who killed our daughter and even let him move in to our home"', Daily Mirror, 4 August 2021, https://www.mirror.co.uk/news/uk-news/we-forgave-man-who-killed-24689161

10 Justice podcast, Edwina Grosvenor in conversation with James Timpson OBE, Chair of Prison Reform Trust and Chief Executive of Timpson, a successful UK-wide family run business, https://podcasts.apple.com/gb/podcast/justice-with-prison-philanthropist-edwina-grosvenor/id1436859351?i=1000486241154

11 N. Lacey and H. Pickard, 'To Blame or to Forgive? Reconciling Punishment and Forgiveness in Criminal Justice', Europe PMC, 2015, http://europepmc.org/article/MED/26937059

Chapter 10

1   L. Gonzales, *Surviving Survival* (W.W. Norton & Company, 2012)
2   M. Yaconelli, *Messy Spirituality* (Zondervan, 2002), p. 13.
3   For more in-depth reading on every aspect of forgiveness, including within faith traditions, see Stephen Hance, *Forgiveness in Practice* (Jessica Kingsley Publishers, 2019).
4   Matthew 6:14–15, New International Version (NIV).
5   Matthew 18:21–22, New International Version (NIV).
6   'Nun sought justice after torture in Guatemala', *Washington Post*, 20 February 2021, https://www.pressreader.com/usa/the-washington-post/20210220/281526523768704
7   https://www.scribd.com/document/53408350/Speak-Truth-To-Power-Courage-without-Borders-Series-Sister-Dianna-Ortiz-Guatemala-USA-Torture
8   https://www.washingtonpost.com/local/obituaries/dianna-ortiz-nun-who-told-of-brutal-abduction-by-guatemalan-military-dies-at-62/2021/02/19/932ac25a-713a-11eb-85fa-e0ccb3660358_story.html
9   Sarah McClure, 'The Amish Keep to Themselves. And They're Hiding a Horrifying Secret: A year of reporting – an exclusive partnership between Cosmo and Type Investigations – reveals a culture of incest, rape, and abuse', Type Investigations, 14 January 2020, https://www.typeinvestigations.org/investigation/2020/01/14/amish-sexual-abuse-assault/

Chapter 11

1   Andrea J. Miller, Everett L. Worthington and Michael A. Mcdaniel, 'Gender and Forgiveness: A Meta-Analytic Review and Research Agenda', *Journal of Social and Clinical Psychology*, 27/8, (2008): 843–76.
2   Andrew Solomon, 'How the worst moments in our lives make us who we are', youtube.com/watch?v=RiM5a-vaNkg
3   https://broadview.org/margot-van-sluytman/
4   2018 James McTaggart Lecture at the Edinburgh TV Festival
5   An edited extract from Carmen Aguirre, *Mexican Hooker #1: And My Other Roles Since the Revolution*, published by Granta, 14 April 2016, https://www.theguardian.com/society/2016/apr/09/carmen-aguirre-why-faced-my-rapist?CMP=Share_iOSApp_Other
6   https://peacecrane.weebly.com/the-circle-of-reconciliation.html
7   https://www.humiliationstudies.org/documents/BotcharovaTrackTwoDiplomacyChapter.pdf
8   Stephen Levine, *Unattended Sorrow* (Rodale, 2005), p 19.
9   Cited in *The People*, 18 August 2015, 'Stephen Colbert on Learning to Accept the Deaths of His Father and Brothers: 'I Love the Thing That I Most Wish Had Not Happened'', https://people.com/tv/stephen-colbert-plane-crash-killed-his-father-and-brothers-when-he-was-10

Epilogue

1   https://www.gaylekirschenbaum.com/look-at-us-now-mother

ACKNOWLEDGEMENTS

I am profoundly indebted to all those people who have so honestly and generously shared their stories with me over the years and who have unquestionably provided me with the source and inspiration for this book, whether they appear within these pages or not.

A special thank you must go to Rachel Bird, the director of The Forgiveness Project, whose insight and sensitivity has supported me to delve even more deeply into this most elusive of subjects. And to Sandra Barefoot, Marian Partington and Dr Masi Noor who have shared with me their profound knowledge and insight into forgiveness, shame and traumatic loss, and therefore added new layers to my understanding.

I am especially grateful to my brilliant editor, Frances Jessop, who believed in the idea for this book at a time when I mistakenly thought I'd written all I wanted to say about forgiveness. Her skillful editing and endless encouragement made the whole process feel both seamless and enjoyable. Thank you also to Rabbi Jonathan Wittenberg, Stephen Cherry and Manwar Ali for some very helpful fact checking and to Jessica Kingsley, who was the first to realise there was value in bringing these forgiveness stories into print. Also, to Moya Crockett, whose write-up of *The F Word Podcast* drew attention to the charity's work, from which the idea for this book came. I also greatly appreciate Catherine Cardwell for her meticulous reading of early proofs, and Tessa

McWatt for some wise counsel about how best to transform ideas into prose.

A massive thank you also to my dear friend Helen Blodwen Rees, who let me borrow her home in Wales for several weeks so that I could escape London to bury myself in the intense process of writing. And indeed to Ann David who did much the same for me in Devon.

I would like to offer this book in memory of Dame Anita Roddick and Archbishop Desmond Tutu, both of whom were founding patrons of The Forgiveness Project charity and whose belief in the value of the work helped me create the foundation for everything that came next. And a heartfelt thank you to Sue Rae, Jilly Forster and Brian Moody, who similarly played crucial roles in helping The Forgiveness Project get off the ground: without them I would never have been in a position to write a 300-page book about forgiveness eighteen years later! Additional thanks must also go to Katalin Karolyi, Louisa Hext, Judy Ironside, Sophie Levy, Rob Lamond and Simon Marks, who all appeared in my life some years ago with the generous offer to help and contributed enormously to the future of The Forgiveness Project. As indeed did Alistair Little, Eliyes Omar, Martyn Evans, Kate Quigley, Jo Berry, Matthew Davis and Bernd Leygraf. I am also incredibly indebted to the charity's volunteers, patrons and hardworking trustees – past as well as present. Nor will I ever miss an opportunity to offer my sincerest gratitude to those who have supported and funded The Forgiveness Project over the years because they, in effect, have been the lifeblood of the work and thus ensured the charity's survival.

Last but not least, my love and huge appreciation goes to my husband, Dan, my three children, Phoebe, Flora and Reuben, and my sister, Ilinca, and her family, for being there and always supporting me. Also, to my parents, who sadly died a short while before I started writing this book.

Further Reading

Izzeldin Abuelaish, *I Shall Not Hate: A Gaza Doctor's Journey on the Road to Peace and Human Dignity* (Bloomsbury, 2011)

Gwen Adshead and Eileen Horne, *The Devil You Know: Stories of Human Cruelty and Compassion* (Faber & Faber, 2021)

Dilruba Ahmed, *Bring Now The Angels: Poems* (University of Pittsburgh Press, 2020)

Khaled al-Berry, *Life is More Beautiful than Paradise: A Jihadist's Own Story* (Haus Publishing, 2001)

Johann Christoph Arnold, *The Lost Art of Forgiving: Stories of Healing from the Cancer of Bitterness* (Plough Publishing House, 1998)

Rosie Ayliffe, *Far From Home: A True Story of Death, Loss and a Mother's Courage* (Random House Australia, 2021)

Simon Baron-Cohen, *Zero Degrees of Empathy: A New Understanding of Cruelty and Kindness* (Allen Lane, 2011)

Madeleine Black, *Unbroken: One Woman's Journey to Rebuild a Life Shattered by Violence* (John Blake, 2017)

Laura Blumenfeld, *Revenge: A Story of Hope* (Simon & Schuster, 2002)

Camilla Carr and Jonathan James, *The Sky is Always There: Surviving a Kidnap in Chechnya* (Canterbury Press Norwich, 2008)

Lis Cashin, *This Is Me: My Journey to Mental Wellbeing* (That Guy's House, 2020)

Stephanie Cassatly, *Notice of Release: A Daughter's Journey to Forgive her Mother's Killer* (eLectio Publishing, 2017)

Stephen Cherry, *Healing Agony: Reimagining Forgiveness*
    (Continuum, 2012)

Jacques Derrida, *On Cosmopolitanism and Forgiveness* (Routledge, 2001)

Jacob Dunne, *Right from Wrong: My Story of Guilt and Redemption*
    (Harper Collins, 2022)

Thordis Elva and Tom Stranger, *South of Forgiveness* (Scribe, 2017)

Angela Findlay, *In My Grandfather's Shadow: A Story of War, Trauma*
    and the Legacy of Silence (Bantam Press, 2022)

Viktor E. Frankl, *Man's Search For Meaning* (Rider, 2004)

James Gilligan, *Violence: Reflections on our Deadliest Epidemic* (Jessica
    Kingsley, 1999)

Pumla Gobodo-Madikizela, *A Human Being Died That Night:*
    A South African Woman Confronts the Legacy of Apartheid
    (Mariner, 2004)

Charles L. Griswold, *Forgiveness: A Philosophical Exploration*
    (Cambridge University Press, 2007)

Stephen Hance (ed.), *Forgiveness in Practice* (Jessica Kingsley
    Publishers, 2019)

Matt Hawkins and Jennifer Nadel (eds), *How Compassion Can*
    Transform Our Politics, Economy and Society (Routledge, 2022)

Richard Holloway, *Waiting for the Last Bus: Reflections on Life and*
    Death (Canongate, 2017)

————, *On Forgiveness: How Can We Forgive the Unforgivable?*
    (Canongate, 2002)

Azim Khamisa, *From Murder to Forgiveness: A Father's Journey*
    (Balboa Press, 2012)

Sally Kohn, *The Opposite of Hate: A Field Guide to Repairing our*
    Humanity (Algonquin Books of Chapel Hill, 2018)

Anne Lamott, *Hallelujah Anyway: Rediscovering Mercy* (Riverhead
    Books, 2017)

Father Michael Lapsley, SSM, *Redeeming the Past: My Journey from*
    Freedom Fighter to Healer (Orbis Books, 2012)

Primo Levi, *If This is a Man / The Truce,* trans. Stuart Woolf with
    an introduction by Paul Bailey and an afterword by the
    author (The Orion Press, 1960; Abacus, 1987)

Stephen Levine, *Unattended Sorrow: Recovering from Loss and Reviving the Heart* (Rodale, 2005)

Colum McCann, *Apeirogon* (Bloomsbury, 2020)

Michael E. McCullough, *Beyond Revenge: The Evolution of the Forgiveness Instinct* (Jossey-Bass, 2008)

Patrick Magee, *Where Grieving Begins: Building Bridges After the Brighton Bomb* (Pluto Press, 2021)

Tim Newell, *Forgiving Justice: A Quaker Vision for Criminal Justice*, Swarthmore Lecture, Quaker Home Service (Newell, 2000)

Masi Noor and Marina Cantacuzino, *Forgiveness is Really Strange* (Singing Dragon, 2018)

Peter Osborn and Eddy Canfor-Dumas, *The Talking Revolution: How Creative Conversation Can Change the World* (Port Meadow Press, 2018)

Marian Partington, *If You Sit Very Still* (Jessica Kingsley Publishers, 2016)

Edward St Aubyn, *Some Hope* (Picador, 2012)

Kia Sherr, *Forgiveness is a Choice: Teachings About Peace and Love* (Ebury Press, 2022)

Donald Shriver, *An Ethic for Enemies: Forgiveness in Politics* (Oxford University Press, 1995)

Pardeep Singh Kaleka, Arno Michaelis and Robin Gaby Fisher, *The Gift of Our Wounds: A Sikh and a Former Skinhead Find Forgiveness After Hate* (St Martin's Press, 2018)

Rebecca Solnit, *Hope in the Dark: Untold Histories, Wild Possibilities* (Canongate, 2016)

Geoff Thompson, *99 Reasons to Forgive: And Revenge Ain't One* (O-Books 2023)

Eckhart Tolle, *The Power of Now: A Guide to Spiritual Enlightenment* (Hodder & Stoughton, 2001)

Desmond Tutu and Mpho Andrea Tutu, *The Book of Forgiving* (Collins, 2014)

V (formerly Eve Ensler), *The Apology* (Bloomsbury Publishing, 2019)

David Whyte, *Consolations: The Solace, Nourishment and Underlying Meaning of Everyday Words* (Canongate, 2019)

Simon Wiesenthal, *The Sunflower: On the Possibilities and Limits of Forgiveness* (Schocken Books, 1976)

Peter Woolf, *The Damage Done* (Bantam Press, 2009)

Philip Zimbardo, *The Lucifer Effect: How Good People Turn Evil* (Ebury Press, 2007)